# Big Data Management

The big data paradigm presents a number of challenges for university curricula on big data or data science related topics. On the one hand, new research, tools and technologies are currently being developed to harness the increasingly large quantities of data being generated within our society. On the other, big data curricula at universities are still based on the computer science knowledge systems established in the 1960s and 70s. The gap between the theories and applications is becoming larger, as a result of which current education programs cannot meet the industry's demands for big data talents.

This series aims to refresh and complement the theory and knowledge framework for data management and analytics, reflect the latest research and applications in big data, and highlight key computational tools and techniques currently in development. Its goal is to publish a broad range of textbooks, research monographs, and edited volumes that will:

- Present a systematic and comprehensive knowledge structure for big data and data science research and education
- Supply lectures on big data and data science education with timely and practical reference materials to be used in courses
- Provide introductory and advanced instructional and reference material for students and professionals in computational science and big data
- Familiarize researchers with the latest discoveries and resources they need to advance the field
- Offer assistance to interdisciplinary researchers and practitioners seeking to learn more about big data

The scope of the series includes, but is not limited to, titles in the areas of database management, data mining, data analytics, search engines, data integration, NLP, knowledge graphs, information retrieval, social networks, etc. Other relevant topics will also be considered.

Xiaofeng Meng

# Data Privacy and Data Governance

## Concepts and Techniques

机械工业出版社
CHINA MACHINE PRESS

Springer

Xiaofeng Meng
Renmin University of China
Beijing, China

ISSN 2522-0179 ISSN 2522-0187 (electronic)
Big Data Management
ISBN 978-981-95-5786-8 ISBN 978-981-95-5787-5 (eBook)
https://doi.org/10.1007/978-981-95-5787-5

Jointly published with China Machine Press Co., Ltd.
The print edition is not for sale in the mainland of China. Customers from the mainland of China please order the print book from: China Machine Press, Beijing, China.
ISBN of the Co-Publisher's edition: 978-7-111-72818-4

Translation from the Chinese language edition: "数据隐私与数据治理: 概念与技术" by Xiaofeng Meng,


The original submitted manuscript has been translated into English. The translation was done using artificial intelligence. A subsequent revision was performed by the author(s) to further refine the work and to ensure that the translation is appropriate concerning content and scientific correctness. It may, however, read stylistically different from a conventional translation.



This Springer imprint is published by the registered company Springer Nature Singapore Pte Ltd.
The registered company address is: 152 Beach Road, #21-01/04 Gateway East, Singapore 189721, Singapore

# Preface

The year 2021 has just passed, and it can be regarded as the inaugural year for data privacy and data governance. Society as a whole is awakening and exploring its norms and solutions, which is a stark contrast to the social environment when I first started paying attention to this issue back in 2006!

The year 2021 marked a pivotal turning point—widely regarded as the inaugural year for data privacy and data governance in China. A collective societal awakening has begun, as norms and regulatory frameworks for data use are actively being explored and established. This marks a striking contrast to the landscape back in 2006, when I first began paying attention to these issues and public discourse on data privacy was still in its infancy.

Over the past year, various national agencies have taken comprehensive and sustained actions to address data privacy concerns. Key legislative milestones include the Data Security Law of the People's Republic of China, the Personal Information Protection Law of the People's Republic of China, and the Financial Data Security–Data Security Assessment Specifications. These collectively form a multidimensional legal framework that establishes robust protections for information and data security in China, transforming privacy from a legal gray area into a clearly regulated domain.

In the realm of data governance, the 14th Five-Year Plan for the Development of the Digital Economy and the Regulations on the Administration of Algorithmic Recommendation Services for Internet Information Services have introduced targeted mechanisms to address governance challenges associated with data and algorithms. Furthermore, following the State Council's inclusion of data as a factor of production in the Opinions on Building a More Robust Market-Based Allocation System for Production Factors, the 14th Five-Year National Informatization Plan issued by the Office of the Central Cyberspace Affairs Commission explicitly called for "strengthening data governance" as a strategic priority.

In response to national strategic directives, enterprises have also begun actively exploring data privacy solutions. For instance, smartphone manufacturers such as Xiaomi have introduced innovative features like Interception Net and Stealth Mask, integrating privacy protection mechanisms directly into their systems to safeguard user data.

Across society, enthusiasm for data privacy and data governance is at an all-time high. Yet, a critical gap remains between legislative intent and practical implementation. Government regulation is still evolving, with many areas relying heavily on "industry self-discipline," while companies often limit their efforts to baseline "compliance." As a result, there is a widespread and pressing need for a comprehensive resource that systematically explains the concepts, technologies, and practices of data privacy and governance. This book seeks to fill that gap, offering practical strategies for addressing the challenges of a digital economy increasingly driven by data as a key factor of production.

Drawing upon years of research, this book—compiled by the author and their team—provides a systematic exposition of data privacy and data governance from both conceptual and technical perspectives. It is intended as a foundational reference for academics, government agencies, enterprises, and the broader public, serving both as a knowledge framework and as an instructional guide for enhancing data literacy. In today's data-centric era, fostering data literacy is essential—not only to understand data and privacy, but also to equip individuals with the capabilities to navigate and manage them effectively. In fact, data literacy may soon become a core component of scientific literacy. The desire to help build this capacity across society is the very motivation that inspired the writing of this book.

This book provides a comprehensive yet accessible discussion of data privacy and data governance, structured across four main parts:

Part I: Fundamentals
This part introduces the foundational concepts and methodological frameworks of data privacy and governance. It begins with a historical overview of data development to uncover the root causes behind emerging privacy and governance challenges. It further outlines the key elements of privacy, along with frameworks for management, governance systems, and practical governance practices in light of current applications. A central argument is that in the era of data as a production factor and a growing digital economy, privacy protection must evolve from passive measures to active defense, while data governance must transition from full-lifecycle big data management to ecosystem-wide governance in the post–big data era. The part is written in an approachable style, avoiding overly technical language, making it suitable for both professionals seeking a structured understanding and general readers interested in the subject.

Part II: Privacy Protection Techniques
This part delves into privacy protection techniques relevant to data sharing and publication. It covers several mainstream technologies, including centralized differential privacy in cloud platforms, local differential privacy in edge computing, privacy amplification methods to improve data utility, and hybrid approaches that integrate differential privacy with cryptography. The content is technically advanced and intended primarily for specialists and researchers in the field.

Part III: Privacy in Machine Learning
Focusing on machine learning applications, this part examines privacy protection methods in both centralized and federated learning environments. It addresses risks of direct privacy leakage from data breaches, indirect leakage from external attacks, and the use of personalized differential privacy techniques to balance privacy with model utility. Closely aligned with the forefront of machine learning and AI privacy, this part is geared toward professionals and technical audiences.

Part IV: Data Ecosystem and Data Governance
This part explores governance technologies for data markets and ecosystems, rooted in the conceptualization of data as a production factor. It introduces systems for governing data transactions and circulation, as well as approaches to address data monopolies and ensure algorithmic fairness. The core aim is to establish a transparent, end-to-end governance framework capable of preemptive monitoring, real-time protection, and post-incident traceability—ultimately supporting the healthy development of the digital economy. With its broad scope, this part is suitable for professionals, policymakers, and the general public seeking to deepen their understanding of data governance.

In summary, this book addresses the pressing challenges of data privacy and governance in the context of the digital economy. It breaks away from traditional paradigms and proposes three essential conceptual shifts:

1. From a data lifecycle perspective to a data ecosystem perspective.
2. From privacy protection to privacy defense as a form of active management.
3. From accountability and traceability to architectural transparency.

It is our hope that this book will serve as a valuable resource for educational institutions, government agencies, and industry professionals, while also contributing to the advancement of China's digital economy.

The conception of this book began in early 2020. Over the course of a year and a half, the author, together with team members Wang Lexia, Liu Junxu, Fan Zhuoya, Ye Qingqing, Liu Lixin, and Li Zitong, undertook multiple rounds of drafting and revision to bring the manuscript to its present form. Every effort has been made to present the material in a clear, structured, and engaging manner. Should any parts remain unclear or raise questions, we warmly welcome feedback and discussion. We hope this book enables readers to better recognize the pervasive privacy issues in everyday life—and inspires meaningful action.

Beijing, China
August 2025

Xiaofeng Meng

**Competing Interests** The author has no competing interests to declare that are relevant to the content of this manuscript.

# Introduction to This Book

This book is grounded in the Data Security Law of the People's Republic of China and the Personal Information Protection Law of the People's Republic of China, offering a systematic overview of data privacy and data governance from both conceptual and technological perspectives. Part I explores the foundations of data privacy and governance through historical and structural lenses. The subsequent three parts address key challenges in large-scale data collection, machine learning, and privacy-related issues in data governance, presenting the underlying technical principles and summarizing current problems and solutions. Framed within the context of an emerging data ecosystem, the book emphasizes the explanation of relevant technologies and algorithms, complemented by practical case studies and appropriately detailed discussions.

Designed for both technical professionals and general readers with an interest in data issues, this book serves as a valuable resource for developing a foundational understanding of data privacy and governance while fostering data literacy.

# Contents

## Part I Fundamentals

# Part I
# Fundamentals

With the advancement of new infrastructure such as 5G and the Internet of Things, the cost of collecting user data has significantly decreased, leading to the widespread use of such data in machine learning, data analysis, and data mining. However, this surge in data utilization has also brought increasingly prominent ethical concerns, including the leakage and misuse of user data. In April 2020, the Central Committee of the Communist Party of China and the State Council issued the "Opinions on Building a More Perfect Factor Market Allocation System", proposing to accelerate the cultivation of the data factor market. This is the first time that data has been written into the document as a production factor alongside land, capital, labor, and technology. To unlock the full value of data in this new role, it is essential to address the ethical challenges it poses—chief among them, data privacy—and to establish effective data governance mechanisms.

The purpose of this part is intended to help readers develop a foundational understanding of data privacy and data governance. In the first two chapters, we initially sorted out questions such as "What is data privacy", "How is data privacy generated", and "What are the current challenges of data privacy". In exploring the notion of data privacy, we differentiate between privacy and security, and offer detailed explanations of its key characteristics, classifications, and management frameworks. Subsequently, in the third chapter, we focused on the issue of data governance. It begins by tracing the historical development of data governance and examining its general and context-specific features. The chapter then proposes a governance system suited to the evolving data ecosystem and reviews the current state of governance efforts in terms of laws, regulations, and practical implementation.

# Chapter 1
# Introduction

Privacy issues are increasingly coming into the public spotlight, becoming a topic of widespread concern across sectors. For individual users, privacy is closely tied to personal safety. For enterprises, effectively safeguarding data and user privacy is essential for leveraging data as a production factor and driving sustainable business growth.

This chapter aims to trace the origins and evolution of data privacy-examining how privacy concerns first arose, how they gradually expanded into broader data ethics issues, what techniques have emerged to protect privacy, and what major challenges remain today. These discussions lay the groundwork for the more detailed explorations that follow in this book. By understanding the historical trajectory and current landscape of data privacy, it becomes evident that privacy issues are intensifying in tandem with rapid advances in information technique and the expanding scale of data collection. Traditional privacy protection techniques are no longer adequate to address the severity of today's challenges. Therefore, researchers and practitioners must move beyond narrow interpretations of "privacy" and adopt a holistic privacy perspective to develop more comprehensive and effective solutions.

## 1.1 From Social Privacy to Data Privacy

Thc concept of privacy has evolved over approximately 150 years, shaped by two key factors. First, as human civilization has advanced, individuals' awareness of and demand for privacy have grown steadily. Second, the rapid development of information technique has given rise to new tensions between privacy rights and technological change. This section traces the evolution of privacy from the dual perspectives of societal transformation and data development, illustrating how the concept of data privacy emerged through the dynamic interplay between social needs and technological progress.



X. Meng, *Data Privacy and Data Governance*, Big Data Management,
https://doi.org/10.1007/978-981-95-5787-5_1

### 1.1.1 Social Privacy

Based on the distinct characteristics of privacy-related concepts and techniques over time, the development of privacy can be divided into three broad periods, namely the budding period, the formation period, and the development period, corresponding to five stages.

**1. The budding period of privacy is in the era of paper media, corresponding to the media privacy stage.**

In this early stage, privacy concerns primarily revolved around the unauthorized disclosure of personal information through print media, particularly regarding individuals' private lives. These concerns prompted the need for legal and regulatory protection.

During the 19th century, newspapers-then an emerging form of mass media-became the first major technological medium to expose personal privacy to the public. In 1873, amid an economic depression in the United States and under the influence of the rise of "yellow journalism", many sensationalized and privacy-infringing news stories were published. One widely cited incident involved the public disclosure of private details about a home banquet hosted by American lawyer Samuel Warren and his wife, including the unauthorized publication of their daughter's wedding photographs. In response to such intrusions, Warren, together with his colleague Louis Brandeis, published the seminal article "The Right to Privacy" in the Harvard Law Review in 1890 [1]. This article is widely regarded as the formal introduction of the legal concept of the "right to privacy." Although the article initially received limited attention, it laid the foundation for the emergence of privacy as a legal and societal concern. Over the following decades, significant privacy-related legislation emerged, including the United States Privacy Act of 1974 and the European Convention on Human Rights in 1950, which enshrined the right to respect for private and family life.

**2. The formation period of privacy is in the era of computers, corresponding to the computer privacy stage.**

During this stage, privacy concerns centered on structured data stored in centralized corporate databases. The primary threats to privacy arose from unauthorized access, data breaches, and theft targeting corporate information systems. Cryptographic techniques became the predominant means of safeguarding this data.

In the 1960s, as information technique advanced, the widespread adoption of mainframe computers began to reshape traditional notions of privacy. The development of file management and database systems enabled the storage and processing of vast amounts of organizational data. At the same time, the U.S. federal government invested heavily in information technique research, while consumer credit bureaus began to compile financial databases containing sensitive information about millions of individuals. This growing aggregation of personal data-centered around corporations-sparked increasing concern over the risks of data intrusion and leakage, and the consequent threats to individual privacy. In response to these emerging threats, modern cryptographic methods were developed. Key milestones included the establishment of symmetric encryption standards such as the Data Encryption Standard (DES) [2] and the Advanced Encryption Standard (AES) [3], as well as the invention of public-key cryptography [4], which laid the groundwork for secure communications and techniques like encrypted databases.

**3. The development period of privacy is in the era of information technique, including three stages.**

Aligned with major shifts in technological paradigms, this period is categorized into three stages: Internet privacy, big data privacy, and artificial intelligence privacy, corresponding respectively to the Internet era, the Big Data era, and the Artificial Intelligence era.

**(1) Internet Privacy Stage**

In this stage, the focus of privacy protection shifted from corporate data to personal data in the context of data publication, with k-anonymity emerging as the primary protection technique.

During the 1990s, the global Internet began to take shape, and by the early 2000s, its rapid expansion deeply transformed daily life and economic activities. As the number of Internet users surged, so did the volume of personal data generated online. To extract value from this data, data mining and other analytical techniques developed rapidly. While data sharing and openness became essential for technological advancement, the protection of users' personal information grew increasingly critical.

Initially, privacy protection relied on simple anonymization-removing direct identifiers from datasets. However, this approach proved inadequate. In a landmark study in 1997, Professor Latanya Sweeney of Harvard University demonstrated that anonymized health records published by the Massachusetts Insurance Commission could be re-identified by linking them to voter registration data, ultimately exposing the health records of the state's governor. She further showed that 87% of Americans could be uniquely identified by combining just three attributes: gender, birth date, and ZIP code. This discovery profoundly influenced privacy policy and led to the formal proposal of k-anonymity in 1998 [5]. K-anonymity masks individuals by ensuring each record is indistinguishable from at least $k - 1$ others based on quasi-identifiers, thereby significantly reducing the risk of re-identification. Over the following decade, k-anonymity and its variants became foundational tools in data privacy research and practice.

**(2) Big Data Privacy Stage**

In this stage, data consisted primarily of massive volumes of personal information. Privacy concerns shifted to issues of leakage during large-scale data collection, with differential privacy technique becoming the predominant protection framework.

The 2010s witnessed the explosive growth of big data techniques, facilitated by the widespread deployment of cloud computing platforms. During this era, personal data collection became pervasive and continuous. The scale and complexity of this data outstripped the processing capabilities of traditional systems and exposed the limitations of k-anonymity. Although k-anonymity had evolved, it remained vulnerable to background knowledge attacks and significantly compromised data utility due to aggressive perturbation. A notable example occurred in 2006 when Netflix hosted a movie recommendation competition and released a supposedly anonymized dataset of user ratings. While explicit identifiers were removed, researchers from the University of Texas at Austin successfully re-identified users by correlating the Netflix data with publicly available records on Internet Movie Database (IMDb). The incident raised serious privacy concerns and led to legal action, ultimately resulting in the cancellation of the competition.

In the same year, Cynthia Dwork of Microsoft Research introduced the concept of differential privacy [6]. This groundbreaking framework provided a formal, mathematical definition of privacy risk and offered robust guarantees against any background knowledge attacks. By adding calibrated noise to data queries, differential privacy ensured individual-level protection while preserving the statistical utility of datasets. In 2014, Úlfar Erlingsson of Google advanced the field further by proposing the local differential privacy (LDP) framework [7], which shifted the perturbation process to the user side, eliminating reliance on a trusted data curator. LDP has since been adopted by major tech companies such as Google, Apple, and Microsoft, and has drawn significant attention from both academia and industry.

**(3) Artificial Intelligence Stage**

In this stage, the data landscape has shifted toward higher-dimensional, finer-grained, and larger-scale personal and societal data. The main issues in generalized privacy are data privacy issues, algorithm fairness issues, and data transparency issues. Mixed privacy protection technique should be the main research method.

With the proliferation of new infrastructure-such as 5G, the Internet of Things (IoT), and smart urban systems-artificial intelligence and ubiquitous connectivity have become defining trends in modern society. Data is no longer limited to structured personal information. Through mobile devices, wearable technique, urban sensors, and other sources, enormous volumes of heterogeneous, multidimensional personal and societal data are continuously being generated. This complex data environment introduces unprecedented challenges for privacy protection. In this context, data privacy extends beyond the simple prevention of personal information leaks. Increasing attention is being paid to the fairness of machine learning algorithms trained on sensitive data, and to the transparency of how data is collected, used, shared, and circulated [8].

It is worth noting that existing privacy protection techniques-such as cryptographic methods, k-anonymity technique, and differential privacy technique have gradually matured, each with clearly defined strengths and limitations. Cryptographic technique typically offer strong protection but often come with high computational and communication costs. In contrast, k-anonymity technique and differential privacy technique require careful balancing between privacy protection and data utility. Therefore, a major research focus in this stage lies in designing hybrid privacy protection frameworks that integrate multiple techniques-such as combining cryptography with differential privacy technique based on the specific demands of real-world applications.

To summarize, Table 1.1 provides an overview of privacy development across all stages. As the comparison shows, the evolution of privacy has accelerated in tandem with technological advancement. In the past five years, privacy has garnered

**Table 1.1** Stages and characteristics of privacy development

| Period | Stage | Era | Data characteristics | Privacy issues | Protection approaches |
|---|---|---|---|---|---|
| Budding period | Media privacy | Paper media era (1890s–1960s) | Paper information | Media information exposure | Laws and regulations |
| Formation period | Computer privacy | Computer era (1960s–1990s) | Enterprise data | Privacy data attacks and theft | Cryptographic technique |
| Development period | Internet privacy | Internet era (1990s–2010s) | Personal data | Data publication privacy | k-Anonymity technique |
| | Big data privacy | Big data era (2010s–2020s) | Massive personal data | Collected data privacy | Differential privacy technique |
| | Artificial intelligence privacy | Artificial intelligence era (2020s–) | Personal and social data | Privacy, fairness, transparency issues | Hybrid privacy protection technique |

unprecedented attention from both the public and governments. The field has entered a golden age of privacy research. This trend is further confirmed by our analysis of publication volumes on the topic of "privacy" in the China National Knowledge Infrastructure (CNKI), as illustrated in Fig. 1.1.

### *1.1.2 Data Privacy*

From the perspective of social development, it is evident that the concept of privacy has evolved alongside changes in how data is generated and characterized. As data generation methods have transformed and data itself has grown in volume, variety, and granularity, privacy concerns have become increasingly prominent. This section offers a complementary view of privacy evolution through the lens of data development. In earlier stages, privacy was not a primary concern; rather, it gradually emerged as a critical issue as data became more abundant and complex. We divide this evolution into four stages, based on changes in data generation methods and characteristics.

**1. The Era of Early Development of Computers**.

In the 1940s–60s, data was primarily generated manually through natural observation, scientific experiments, and statistical surveys. This data was predominantly numerical and used to support complex scientific computations with the aid of early computers, contributing to advances in disciplines such as the natural sciences and social statistics. During this period, the development of file systems and batch pro-

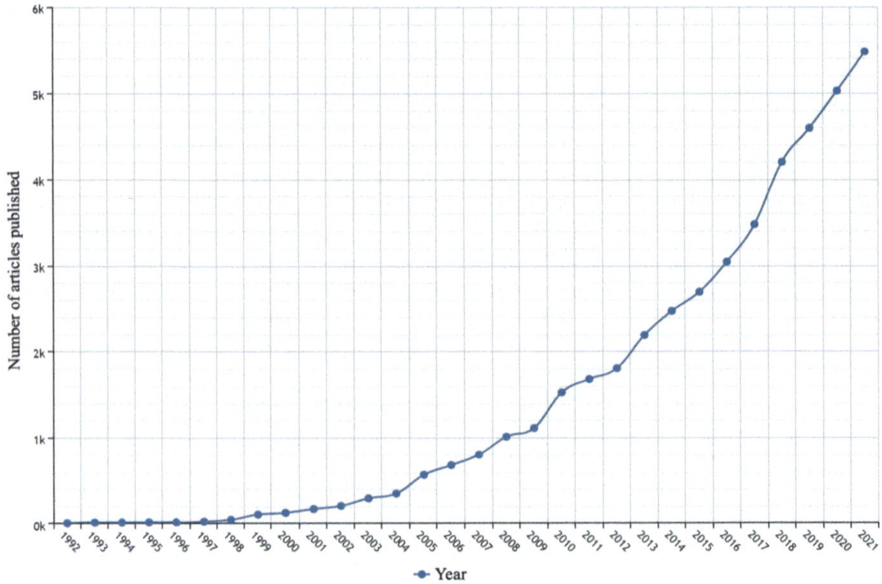


**Fig. 1.1** Change in the number of papers with the theme of "privacy" on CNKI over the years (as of December 31, 2021)

cessing methods enabled basic data management using early storage techniques. The main concerns at this stage were the accuracy, efficiency, and availability of data rather than privacy. Data-related challenges were closely tied to computation and data sharing for scientific or organizational purposes.

**2. The Era of Traditional Databases**.

From the 1960s to the 1990s, data was passively generated during the operation of enterprise systems and other organizational processes. Due to the high cost of data collection, data remained largely enterprise centered. Data during this period was structured, standardized, and relatively limited in volume. Societal understanding of data was still in its "data management" phase, prompting the development of foundational techniques such as relational databases, data warehouses, and data integration systems. The primary concern during this stage was data security, not privacy. Security focused on protecting organizational data from unauthorized access, ensuring data integrity, and maintaining the reliability of system outputs. These concerns were fundamentally distinct from privacy, as they aimed to safeguard corporate assets rather than personal or sensitive individual information.

**3. The Era of Big Data**.

From the 1990s to the present, the cost of data collection has decreased significantly, while the scale and scope of data generation have expanded rapidly. Data is now actively produced in vast quantities by personal mobile devices, wearable techniques, and ubiquitous sensors. This data is highly heterogeneous in structure, increasingly granular, and largely personal in nature. During this period, society has shifted from simply managing data to interpreting and extracting value from it. This shift has fueled the rise of artificial intelligence, machine learning, and data mining-techniques that rely not on symbolic logical reasoning, as in earlier eras, but on pattern recognition and statistical inference from massive datasets. The dominance of data-driven approaches has introduced a range of ethical concerns unique to this era. On one hand, data has become the "fuel" powering algorithmic models, giving rise to issues such as data monopolies and heightened risks to individual privacy. On the other hand, the increasing reliance on opaque, black-box models in algorithmic decision-making has led to widespread concerns about fairness, bias, and explainability. Among these, privacy has become especially salient, evolving into a central concern for governments, organizations, and the general public. It is during this era that data privacy first emerged as a widely recognized and actively debated societal issue.

**4. The Era of 5G and the Internet of Everything**.

As we move toward the era of Industry 4.0, the volume of data is expected to grow exponentially, and the granularity of data that reflects societal behavior will become increasingly refined. Correspondingly, ethical challenges-particularly those related to privacy and fairness-will become more pronounced in data-driven applications. In this context, it is essential to pursue a balanced approach that simultaneously advances both the value and the ethics of data, grounded in the principle of "respecting data." We must neither blindly prioritize the maximization of data value nor categorically reject data utilization out of privacy concerns. Instead, we should acknowledge the distinct nature of privacy issues, consider their interplay with other ethical concerns such as market monopoly and social fairness, and seek solutions from the broader perspective of the data ecosystem.

## 1.2 Big Data Privacy

With the proliferation of IoT devices and the rapid digital transformation across industries, mobile internet service providers are collecting vast amounts of user data-both actively and passively. When combined with big data analytics, this data enables service providers to infer and utilize personal information for commercial purposes such as personalized advertising and behavioral profiling. However, large-scale data collection, storage, and processing also introduce significant privacy and security risks. Notable incidents include the 2018 Google+ API leak, which exposed approximately 50 million user profiles, and the Cambridge Analytica scandal, in which personal data from over 50 million Facebook users was misused for political profiling, sparking widespread public concern. Although the intent behind data collection is often to improve user experience or service quality, the resulting privacy intrusions-such as unsolicited emails, targeted advertisements, and telemarketing-can have substantial negative impacts on individuals' digital autonomy and trust.

Based on the above background, we identify three key privacy challenges in the era of big data:

**1. Large-Scale Data Collection.**
With the widespread deployment of smart devices-such as cameras, smart home systems, and mobile phones-and the continuous expansion of network coverage, massive amounts of personal data are being collected through passive, active, and automated means. This data often contains sensitive information, including medical records, purchase histories, search logs, communication content, and location data. However, users, as the data producers, are often unaware of what data is being collected, who is collecting it, where it is being transmitted, and how it is being used. As a result, individuals lose control over their data, rendering personal privacy breaches increasingly inevitable.
**2. Large-Scale Data Surveillance.**
Extensive data collection has led to pervasive surveillance. Government agencies may gather individuals' medical and communication records, while large technique companies collect shopping, social interaction, and mobility data. Data service providers use such information to construct detailed user profiles for advanced analytics and targeted marketing. In many profiling systems, the number of labels associated with a single user can exceed one hundred. For internet giants like Alibaba and JD.com, these labels can number in the thousands, encompassing not only basic demographic attributes but also physiological, psychological, cultural, and identity dimensions-covering nearly all aspects of a person's social life. While such systems improve efficiency and enable personalized services, they also introduce significant risks to personal privacy and information security.
**3. Large-Scale Data Manipulation.**
The opacity surrounding data collection, processing, circulation, and usage enables data manipulation at scale. Because users lack visibility into and control over their data, service providers can exploit profiling outcomes for commercial gain. Notable examples include the Facebook-Cambridge Analytica scandal, in which users were exposed to targeted, manipulated content, and the commodification of user data by merchants. Although existing legislation prohibits data misuse, inadequate regulatory oversight and the lack of transparency make it difficult to trace and penalize privacy violations resulting from data manipulation.

Traditional privacy protection techniques, which rely primarily on passive defense against attacks, are no longer sufficient. There is an urgent need for more proactive and integrated privacy protection solutions. Privacy protection should be embedded throughout the entire big data processing pipeline. One promising approach is differential privacy, which offers rigorous privacy guarantees without relying on assumptions about an attacker's background knowledge. Even under worst-case scenarios-where the attacker has maximal auxiliary information-differential privacy can still effectively protect individual data. Therefore, the second part of this book focuses on differential privacy, including local differential privacy and hybrid approaches that integrate differential privacy with cryptographic techniques. We present foundational concepts as well as recent advancements in these techniques.

## 1.3 Artificial Intelligence Privacy

The advent of the big data era has significantly accelerated the development of machine learning techniques, bringing artificial intelligence (AI) applications such as facial recognition payment systems, diagnostic assistance tools, and intelligent robots into everyday life. These innovations have transformed production methods and lifestyles, yielding both economic and social benefits. However, they have also introduced new and severe risks to personal privacy, which primarily manifest in the following three aspects: First, data breaches caused by untrustworthy data collectors occur frequently, resulting in substantial economic losses, reputational damage for enterprises, and broader threats to social stability and national security. Second, numerous studies have demonstrated that attackers can infer sensitive information-either about the training data or the model itself-by analyzing the outputs of machine learning systems. Third, the tension between data privacy and data sharing has led to the emergence of "data silos" across the internet landscape. This has given rise to isolated data ecosystems (e.g., the "Alibaba ecosystem" and the "Tencent ecosystem"), and if this trend continues unchecked, it could exacerbate data monopolies and hinder progress in national economic reform.

In addressing privacy concerns in AI, we focus on two technical paradigms: centralized machine learning and distributed federated learning.

**1. Privacy Risks in Traditional Machine Learning**.

To achieve privacy protection AI, legal regulations alone are insufficient; it is also essential that service providers incorporate privacy considerations into the design, training, and deployment phases of machine learning models. The goal is to ensure that personal sensitive data cannot be directly or indirectly accessed by unauthorized entities.

In traditional machine learning, user data is typically collected and stored centrally-on a single server, a cluster, or a cloud platform. This centralized architecture facilitates model training and system deployment, and is thus widely adopted in practice. However, centralizing large volumes of user data significantly increases the risk of data leakage. Once users' data is collected, they usually lose control over how it is used or shared. On the collector's side, data may be exposed either intentionally or inadvertently, leading to direct privacy breaches. Furthermore, attackers may exploit model outputs to infer sensitive attributes of the training data, causing indirect privacy violations.

**2. Privacy Risks in Federated Learning**.

In recent years, Federated Learning (FL) has emerged as a promising paradigm for privacy protection machine learning without requiring centralized data storage. Under this framework, data remains local, and model training occurs directly on distributed devices or institutional nodes. Model updates are transmitted to a central server for aggregation, without exposing raw data, thereby enhancing data privacy.

Federated learning is particularly advantageous in contexts involving sensitive data, such as healthcare records, wearable device data, facial features, and financial information. It also addresses the problem of heterogeneous data across sources, enabling a unified model to be trained on distributed, non-i.i.d. datasets. However, while FL mitigates certain direct privacy risks, it does not eliminate all vulnerabilities. Privacy can still be compromised during both the training and inference stages, especially when model updates or prediction outputs are leaked or analyzed maliciously.

Although most existing privacy attacks on AI models are only effective under specific conditions-such as image classification tasks or relatively simple model architectures-ongoing research is extending these attacks to more complex and generalizable scenarios. Thus, it is critical to adopt a dual approach: strengthening legal frameworks while also embedding privacy protection mechanisms into the technical pipeline of AI development.

In this context, both centralized and federated learning models require effective privacy protection strategies. These strategies typically fall into two main categories: (1) cryptographic approaches, including secure multi-party computation (SMPC) and homomorphic encryption; and (2) perturbation-based approaches, such as differential privacy. These methods will be introduced and explored in detail in Part Three of this book. Moreover, this section also discusses the issue of algorithmic fairness. We examine how fairness concerns arise and how they can be addressed across different stages of AI model development, aiming to support responsible and equitable AI deployment.

## 1.4 Data Governance

As the information economy advances, data-particularly big data-is evolving into a new type of production factor. It is increasingly integrated with traditional factors such as labor, capital, and technique, and plays a pivotal role in creating economic value and enhancing productivity. On April 6, 2020, the Central Committee of the Communist Party of China and the State Council issued the "Opinions on Building a More Complete Market-oriented Mechanism for the Allocation of Production Factors", formally identifying data as a production factor alongside land, labor, capital, and technique, and calling for accelerated development of the data element market.

However, recognizing data as a production factor necessitates addressing the challenges of data governance within the broader data ecosystem. In the context of emerging infrastructure such as 5G and the Internet of Things, data governance extends beyond traditional privacy concerns. It now encompasses complex issues such as data monopolies, fairness in algorithmic decision-making, and data transparency. These issues are not isolated; they interact and reinforce one another. For instance, addressing data monopolies can help prevent large-scale data aggregation, thereby reducing the risk of data mining and privacy breaches. Likewise, privacy protection techniques based on perturbation can limit the extractable value of monopolized datasets, thereby curbing the formation of monopolies. However, overly stringent privacy protections may hinder the detection of unfair decision-making and abuse of data dominance. Thus, achieving a balanced and effective governance framework is imperative. In this regard, we examine four key aspects of data governance: the data element market, data monopolies, data fairness, and data transparency.

**1. Data Element Market**:

In the era of big data, data has become a core strategic resource, profoundly influencing global production, distribution, consumption, and governance. It plays a fundamental role in enhancing national competitiveness. Recognizing data as a factor of production implies that it is essential for enterprise operations and economic planning, much like labor and capital.Data elements primarily originate from internet applications, IoT devices, enterprises, and government agencies. As computing capabilities and AI algorithms advance, the volume and richness of data determine its value. Promoting the open sharing of data resources and improving standards for data circulation and transaction mechanisms are crucial for reforming the market-oriented allocation of data and enabling autonomous, orderly data flow.

**2. Data Monopoly**:

With the accumulation of data, it has become a core resource fueling AI development and a primary competitive asset for technique firms. The disparity in data holdings has led to the emergence of monopolistic data ecosystems and "data lakes" that are siloed and difficult to integrate. According to the "China Privacy Risk Index Analysis Report", led by Professor Meng Xiaofeng, based on data from approximately 30 million mobile app users, 10% of data collectors held 99% of permission data-far exceeding the traditional "80/20 rule." Research from 2018 to 2020 suggests that this imbalance is worsening, posing serious challenges to data equity and fair competition.

**3. Data Fairness**:

Algorithms driven by big data are widely applied in both public and private sectors, including scenarios that affect individuals' fundamental rights and interests. Issues of data fairness, such as "big data-based price discrimination," have drawn increasing attention. In response, the "Personal Information Protection Law of the People's Republic of China", enacted in August 2021, introduced regulatory requirements mandating transparency, fairness, and non-discrimination in automated decision-making involving personal information. Nonetheless, critical questions remain unresolved: How should fairness be defined and measured? How can the sources of algorithmic bias be identified? How should fairness be balanced with model accuracy? These are pressing research challenges.

**4. Data Transparency**:

A root cause of privacy violations, algorithmic unfairness, and data monopolies lies in the lack of transparency in how data generates value. The current data lifecycle-from collection and circulation to usage and decision-making-often occurs in opaque, black-box systems. Users, as the producers of data, typically do not know what data is collected, by whom, how it is processed, or where it is shared. The black-box nature of AI systems exacerbates this issue, making it difficult to detect violations or ensure accountability. Compared to traditional decision-making based on the "data-information-knowledge" hierarchy, modern AI systems rely directly on large volumes of data, and any errors in the data or lack of transparency in the algorithms can lead to untrustworthy outcomes. Data transparency thus serves as a foundational requirement for addressing broader data ethics issues, including privacy, fairness, and monopolistic practices. Enhancing transparency can make data practices more traceable, perceptible, monitorable, and accountable-ultimately restoring trust in the digital ecosystem.

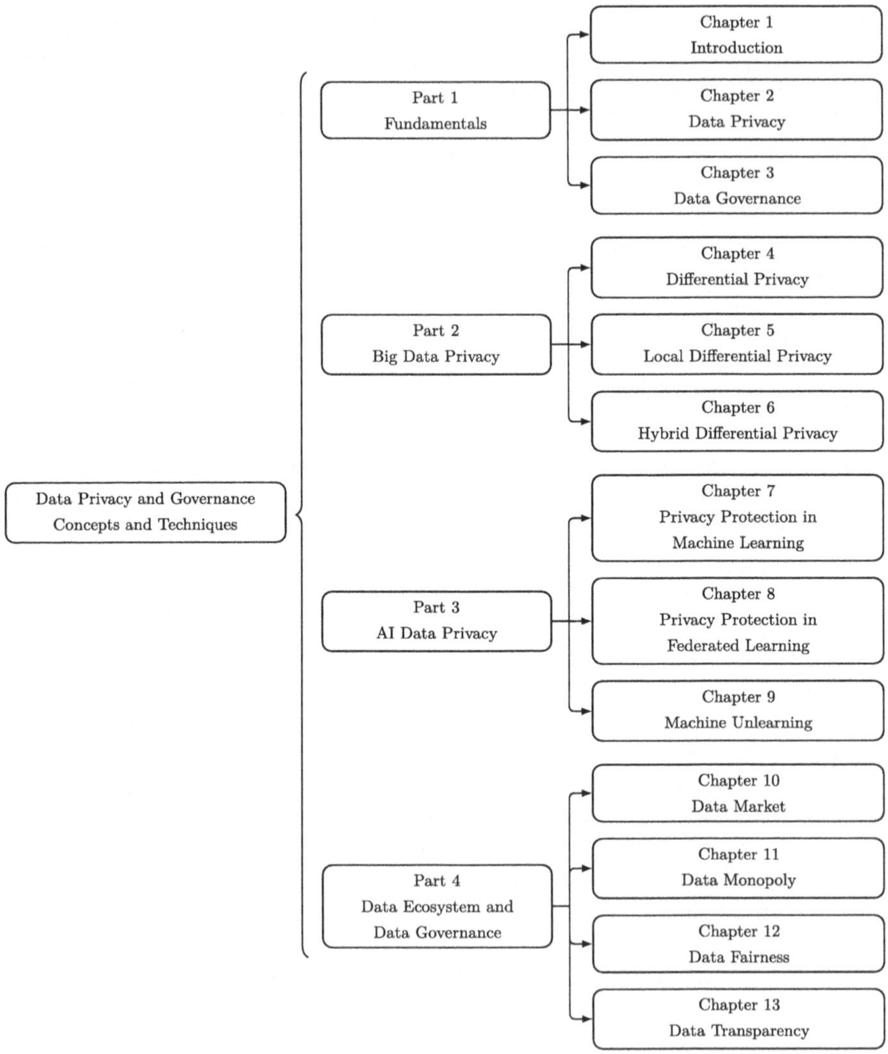


**Fig. 1.2** Organization of this book

## 1.5 Summary

In this chapter, we provided a comprehensive overview of the evolution of privacy concepts, the development of privacy protection techniques, and the key privacy challenges in the current digital landscape. This review aims to help readers understand the historical context and conceptual foundations of privacy, while also offering a clearer and more holistic view of the issues at stake. The subsequent parts of this book are organized around the major privacy challenges identified in this chapter. Each challenge is addressed in a dedicated section comprising three chapters, which introduce the core research problems, representative techniques, and recent advancements in the respective area. The overall structure of the book is illustrated in Fig. 1.2.

## References


1. WARREN S, BRANDEIS L. 1890. The right to privacy[J]. Harvard law review, 4(5):193–220.
2. U.S. DEPARTMENT OF COMMERCE/NATIONAL INSTITUTE OF STANDARDS AND technique. Data encryption standard (DES)[S/OL]. [2021-12-31]. https://csrc.nist.gov/csrc/media/publications/fips/46/3/archive/1999-10-25/documents/fips46-3.pdf
3. DAEMEN J, RIJMEN V. Reijndael: The advanced encryption standard[J]. Dr. Dobb's Journal: Software Tools for the Professional Programmer, 2001, 26(3): 137–139.
4. RIVEST R L, SHAMIR A, ADLEMAN L. A method for obtaining digital signatures and public-key cryptosystems[J]. Communications of the ACM, 1978, 21(2): 120–126.
5. SAMARATI P, SWEENEY L. Protecting privacy when disclosing information: k-anonymity and its enforcement through generalization and suppression[J/OL]. 1998. [2022-02-14]. https://dataprivacylab.org/dataprivacy/projects/kanonymity/paper3.pdf
6. DWORK C, MCSHERRY F, NISSIM K, et al. Calibrating noise to sensitivity in private data analysis[C]//Theory of cryptography conference. Berlin: Springer, 2006: 265–284.
7. ERLINGSSON Ú, PIHUR V, KOROLOVA A. Rappor: Randomized aggregatable privacy protection ordinal response[C]//Proceedings of the 2014 ACM SIGSAC conference on computer and communications security. New York,NY: ACM, 2014: 1054–1067.
8. MENG X, WANG L, LIU J. Data privacy, monopoly and fairness for AI[J]. Big Data Research, 2020, 6(1): 35–46.

# Chapter 2
# Data Privacy

In the era of big data, personal information is continuously digitized, and concerns surrounding personal privacy have become increasingly acute. Within this context, the subject of data privacy refers to individuals or organizational entities, while the object of protection is the personal or group information related to them. This information typically encompasses facts or behaviors that the subject does not wish to disclose. However, due to the distinctive characteristics of big data-such as its large scale, high diversity, and rapid generation-the boundaries of data privacy have become increasingly ambiguous, and its classification has grown more complex.

To address this complexity, this chapter introduces a classification and conceptual framework for understanding data privacy, aiming to provide readers with a foundational understanding of the concept. Drawing on the varying relationships between data owners and data users, we propose a privacy matrix that categorizes data privacy into five distinct types. Each type is discussed in detail, including its definition, real-world scenarios, and applicable protection strategies. Finally, in light of the diverse and evolving risks associated with data use, we propose a hybrid and comprehensive data privacy management framework to guide effective privacy governance.

## 2.1 Introduction

The conflict between data privacy and technological change has been a recurring theme throughout the history of information technology development. In the 19th century, newspapers as a new type of media were the earliest form of information technology to disclose personal privacy, and such privacy breaches were typically protected by law. In the 1960s, the innovation of information technology led to large-scale computers challenging traditional notions of privacy, and cryptographic techniques were commonly used to protect against such privacy threats. In the first



X. Meng, *Data Privacy and Data Governance*, Big Data Management,
https://doi.org/10.1007/978-981-95-5787-5_2

decade of the 21st century, the rapid development of network technology and social media left personal privacy with nowhere to hide, and such privacy breaches were often protected using anonymization and de-identification techniques.

However, in the era of big data, the characteristics of large scale, high velocity, and diversity of big data make it different from small data. The privacy protection methods mentioned above for small data have significant limitations when applied to big data: the fusion of multi-source data brought about by the diversity of big data renders traditional anonymization and de-identification techniques almost ineffective; the real-time analysis enabled by the large scale and high velocity of big data poses a significant bottleneck for traditional encryption and cryptographic techniques. Moreover, large-scale data collection techniques, new storage techniques, and advanced analytical techniques pose even greater challenges for the privacy protection of big data.

Therefore, in the era of big data, safeguarding privacy within data has become critically important. Traditional theories and techniques for privacy protection are no longer sufficient to address the complex challenges posed by big data. As a result, it is essential to re-examine and redefine the approaches to big data privacy preservation.

## 2.2 Definition

Before addressing the challenges of privacy protection in the big data era, it is essential to first understand the concept and core characteristics of data privacy. This section begins by defining data privacy, then introduces its three fundamental characteristics, and finally distinguishes data privacy from the broader concept of information security.

### *2.2.1 What Is Data Privacy*

Data privacy refers to information that individuals, institutions, and other entities do not wish to be known by others, such as personal salaries and medical records. Figure 2.1 illustrates privacy information related to individuals. In specific contexts, the precise definition of data privacy can vary depending on the nature of the data and its owners. For example, a conservative person may regard social relationships as private, while a more open person may be willing to disclose their social connections.

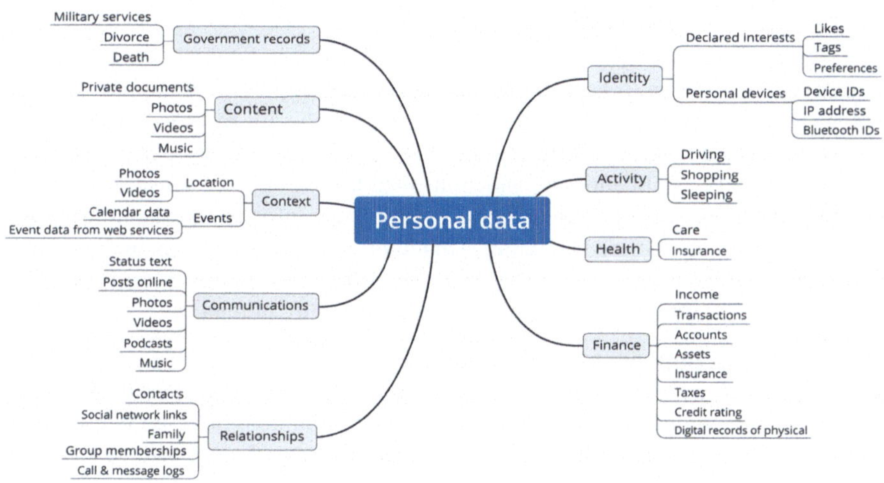


**Fig. 2.1** Privacy information related to individuals

### 2.2.2 *Features*

Based on the definition above, data privacy possesses three fundamental characteristics:

- Subject: The subject of data privacy refers to individuals or organizational groups.
- Object: The object of data privacy pertains to personal or organizational information.
- Content: The content of data privacy includes facts or behaviors that the subject prefers to keep undisclosed.

Furthermore, within the context of big data, due to its distinctive features such as large volume, variety, and high velocity, data privacy boundaries become increasingly difficult to clearly define.

### 2.2.3 *Privacy Versus Security*

In January 2012, during the introduction of the Consumer Privacy Bill of Rights, President Obama emphasized that "Privacy has always been at the heart of our democracy, and it is more needed now than ever before, especially in the era of big data" [1]. Prior research has addressed big data management primarily from the perspective of information security [2]. However, there exist notable distinctions between the concepts of data privacy and information security.

**1. Differences in Definitions**
Data privacy pertains to the protection of information that individuals, organizations, or other entities prefer to keep undisclosed to external parties. Examples include personal behavioral patterns, location data, interests, health records, and financial conditions of organizations, as illustrated in Fig. 2.1. Data privacy emphasizes aspects such as ambiguity, confidentiality, and controlled accessibility of sensitive data.

Information security, in contrast, involves protecting information and information systems against unauthorized activities. Unauthorized operations may include illicit access, disclosure, alteration, destruction, or recording. Information security focuses primarily on the confidentiality, integrity, and availability of data.

**2. Differences in Implementation Techniques**
Information security techniques typically encompass access control mechanisms and cryptographic techniques. Conversely, data privacy techniques involve methods such as anonymization, de-identification, differential privacy, and specialized encryption schemes. Although information security techniques safeguard data at the infrastructure, communication, and access levels, they may not fully prevent privacy breaches. For example, an authorized yet malicious user may misuse Alice's data by integrating it with additional datasets, thereby compromising her privacy. Despite these differences, data privacy and information security share a common objective: ensuring that data is securely accessible and analyzable without compromising individual or organizational privacy.

## 2.3 Classification

Data privacy can be classified from various perspectives. This section begins by describing the essential components of data privacy based on the different entities involved. It then explores two typical categories of data privacy-explicit privacy and implicit privacy-based on their forms of manifestation. Finally, the section outlines five data privacy protection scenarios derived from analyzing data flows among these privacy components.

### 2.3.1 *Privacy Elements*

Considering the roles of different entities involved in managing privacy information, we can categorize the components of data privacy into three distinct groups: users, data collectors, and adversaries.

- **Users**: Users are the subjects whose personal information constitutes the core of data privacy; privacy information originates directly from them.

- **Data Collectors**: Data collectors are third-party entities responsible for gathering and processing substantial amounts of user data. Their objective typically involves analyzing the collected data to infer implicit privacy details about users.
- **Adversaries**: Adversaries are individuals or entities that intentionally attempt to access or compromise users' private information. They may target both users directly and data collectors holding sensitive user information.

Privacy leaks typically arise through interactions and data flows among these three parties. A thorough analysis of these data flows facilitates deeper insights into privacy-related risks and vulnerabilities. Typically, the current possessor of data-referred to as the data owner-includes both users and data collectors. Meanwhile, all entities capable of accessing or using this data-collectively referred to as data users-may include users themselves, data collectors, and adversaries.

### *2.3.2 Explicit Versus Implicit Privacy*

Based on their manifestations, data privacy can be classified into two categories: explicit privacy and implicit privacy.

**1. Basic Definitions**
Let's take a look at their definitions.

**(1) Explicit Privacy**
Explicit privacy refers to sensitive personal information that explicitly exists and is clearly known to the users themselves. Examples include personal identification details such as names, ages, and occupations; location information such as real-time positions, home addresses, and workplaces; and biometric data such as facial characteristics, fingerprints, and DNA sequences. Such information is explicitly recognized by users as sensitive.

**(2) Implicit Privacy**
In contrast, implicit privacy encompasses sensitive information about users that is gathered, processed, and inferred by third parties but might not be explicitly known or recognized by the users. For example, third parties might analyze large volumes of users' location data to deduce their daily travel patterns, utilize purchase histories to determine consumer preferences, or examine financial transactions to predict loan intentions.

In practice, explicit privacy tends to receive more attention from users, as violations of this type of privacy are typically more noticeable. Implicit privacy breaches, however, are harder for users to detect, making them potentially more widespread. Given the expansion of interconnected infrastructure within the Internet of Everything, implicit privacy is becoming increasingly critical and should be a primary focus of contemporary privacy research.

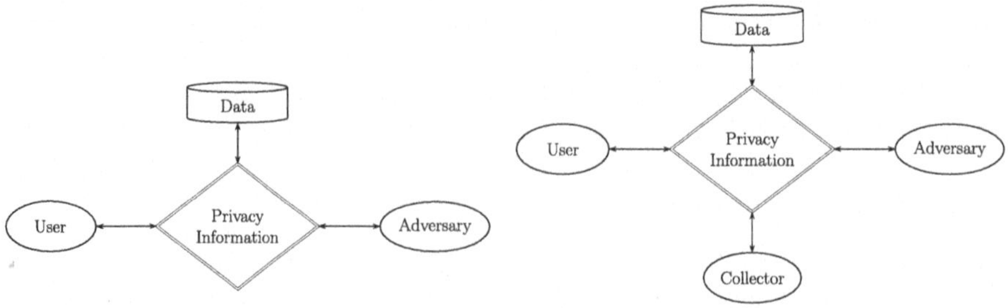


(a) Explicit Privacy (b) Implicit Privacy

**Fig. 2.2** Elements of privacy

**2. Components of Explicit and Implicit Privacy**

Figure 2.2 illustrates the components involved in explicit and implicit privacy. In the context of explicit privacy, the primary components include users and adversaries. Privacy-related information originates directly from user data and is clearly recognized by the users themselves. Privacy breaches occur when adversaries unlawfully access or misuse this information.

Implicit privacy, however, involves an additional critical component: the data collector. Unlike explicit privacy, the sensitive information involved in implicit privacy does not directly originate from raw user data. Instead, it is derived by data collectors through aggregation, analysis, and inference. Users may not be aware of the existence or sensitivity of this inferred information, and breaches occur when adversaries gain unauthorized access to or exploit this derived knowledge.

In addition to the explicit-implicit classification, data privacy can also be categorized by different sources of privacy risks, resulting in three distinct types: surveillance-based privacy, disclosure-based privacy, and discrimination-based privacy.

- **Surveillance-based privacy**: Surveillance refers to unauthorized tracking, monitoring, or collection of sensitive information concerning individuals or groups. For example, websites employing cookies to track user browsing histories or video surveillance systems that monitor personal activities without consent. Protection against this form of privacy violation typically involves accountability mechanisms and legal frameworks.
- **Disclosure-based privacy**: Disclosure involves intentional or accidental release or exposure of data to unauthorized third parties. To mitigate risks associated with this type of privacy breach, protective techniques such as anonymization, differential privacy, encryption, and access control measures are typically employed.
- **Discrimination-based privacy**: Discrimination arises from unintended or hidden biases embedded within big data analytics or automated decision-making processes, resulting in discriminatory outcomes that users typically find difficult to detect or understand. Such biases can inadvertently compromise individual or group privacy. Protection against this type of privacy violation often relies on regulatory oversight and legal intervention.

### 2.3.3 *Use Cases*

Based on the data flows among privacy-related components, data privacy protection scenarios can be categorized into five types, as illustrated in Fig. 2.3: Adversary-User (A-U) Privacy, Data Collector-User (C-U) Privacy, Data Collector-Data Collector Privacy, Adversary-Data Collector Privacy, and User-Data Collector Privacy.

The following subsections provide detailed descriptions of definitions, typical scenarios, and protection mechanisms for each privacy type.

**1. Adversary-User Privacy (A-U Privacy)**

Adversary-User (A-U) privacy refers to sensitive user information directly obtained by adversaries from users themselves. This represents a traditional scenario of privacy leakage.

With advancements in big data, the Internet of Things, and cloud computing, people's everyday activities are becoming increasingly digitalized and meticulously recorded. For example, web browsers record users' internet search histories, GPS sensors embedded in mobile devices continuously track real-time locations, and wearable sensors capture physiological data such as body temperature and perspiration. Such information contains numerous sensitive details; unauthorized access by adversaries directly compromises privacy, revealing personal habits, travel routes, and health conditions.

Since A-U privacy involves explicitly existing sensitive information, it belongs to the category of explicit privacy. Current protective measures primarily focus on technological solutions, such as data encryption and data perturbation methods. Data encryption [3] secures user data by converting plaintext into ciphertext, accessible only through decryption. Encryption relies on algorithms, which transform plaintext into unreadable ciphertext, and keys, which encode and decode data. Encrypting user data thus forms a barrier against unauthorized access.

Privacy protection through data perturbation techniques prevents adversaries from accurately reconstructing original data by altering its content. Common approaches include randomization, anonymization, and differential privacy. Randomization techniques protect sensitive data by introducing randomness into original data or query responses [4]. Anonymization methods, such as $k$-anonymity [5], $l$-diversity [6], and $t$-closeness [7], protect privacy by grouping records to obscure individual distinctions. Differential privacy methods [8], such as Laplace mechanisms [9] and exponential mechanisms [10], add carefully controlled noise to datasets, ensuring minimal privacy impact from single-record changes.

| | | Data Consumer | | |
|---|---|---|---|---|
| | | User | Adversary | Collector |
| Data Owner | User | | P1: Explicit Privacy | P2: Implicit Privacy |
| | Collector | P5: Implicit Privacy | P4: Implicit Privacy | P3: Implicit Privacy |

**Fig. 2.3** Five categories of data privacy preservation scenarios

**2. Data Collector-User Privacy (C-U Privacy)**

Data Collector-User (C-U) privacy refers to sensitive user information collected, stored, and analyzed by third-party data collectors. This scenario is categorized as implicit privacy.

In the digital era, users frequently engage with various smart devices and third-party services that provide substantial convenience. For instance, Alibaba's mobile payment system significantly simplifies transactions, overcoming the cumbersome nature of traditional online banking and credit cards. Social media platforms operated by Tencent and Sina enable real-time interaction, while services like Didi Chuxing and Meituan Dianping address everyday needs through ride-hailing and food delivery.

While users seemingly enjoy these services at no direct cost, they implicitly compensate companies through their data-known as a form of "data payment." Companies collect vast amounts of user-generated data, subsequently employing analytics to discern behavioral patterns. For example, mobile payment records reveal users' financial habits, social networking platforms disclose social relationships, and services such as ride-hailing and food delivery leverage precise geolocation data. Users often remain unaware of the depth and sensitivity of such inferred behavioral patterns.

C-U privacy arises through the interactions between users and data collectors, where users benefit from services while providers utilize collected data for analysis. However, data collection carries inherent privacy risks, as demonstrated by prominent incidents involving platforms such as Facebook and Helsingin Uusyrityskeskus. Currently, protecting C-U privacy mainly relies on social norms and legal frameworks. China's "Information Security Technology-Personal Information Security Specification," implemented on May 1, 2018, stipulates that personal data collection must adhere to legality, minimalism, and authorization principles. Similarly, the European Union's General Data Protection Regulation (GDPR), effective since May 25, 2018, imposes stringent standards on data privacy, including the rights to notification, data portability, and data erasure ("right to be forgotten").

**3. Data Collector-Data Collector Privacy (C-C Privacy)**

Data Collector-Data Collector (C-C) privacy refers to privacy concerns arising from the transfer or circulation of user-sensitive information among third-party data collectors. This category is classified as implicit privacy.

Companies routinely collect large volumes of user data to enhance service quality. However, since companies typically focus on specific domains, the scope of their collected data is often limited accordingly. For instance, Alibaba primarily collects financial transaction data, Tencent focuses on social networking information, and Didi Chuxing concentrates on location and travel trajectory data. To provide comprehensive services, cooperation among companies is inevitable, frequently resulting in data sharing and exchanges. For example, JD.com shares consumer data with subsidiaries such as JD Reading and JD Finance, circulates reading data through cooperation with Jiguang Push, and exchanges user data following the acquisition of 1-Store. Similarly, Alibaba's investment in Didi Chuxing leads to the sharing of location data, cooperation with YTO Express results in logistics data exchange, and its partnership with ZhongAn Insurance facilitates the circulation of user information and credit histories. Such data transactions are also common internationally. For example, data exchanges in the United States typically adopt a business-to-business-to-consumer (B2B2C) hybrid distribution and marketing model, producing prominent data brokerage companies such as Acxiom, CoreLogic, Datalogix, and eBureau.

Due to the significant risks posed by potential leaks involving massive volumes of user data, protecting C-C privacy primarily relies on governmental supervision and legal regulation of data transactions. Relevant regulations include China's "Decision of the Standing Committee of the National People's Congress on Strengthening Network Information Protection" (2012) and the "Data Circulation Industry Self-Discipline Convention" published by the China Academy of Information and Communications Technology (2016). From a technical perspective, blockchain technology offers a promising solution due to its decentralized, transparent nature, facilitating traceability and accountability in data transactions. Blockchain ensures that all data exchanges are transparent and verifiable, making it easier to pinpoint accountability if privacy breaches occur.

**4. Adversary-Data Collector Privacy (A-C Privacy)**
Adversary-Data Collector (A-C) privacy refers to privacy breaches that occur when adversaries attack third-party data collectors who hold substantial volumes of user data. Specifically, this involves adversaries acquiring sensitive user information indirectly from data collectors, thus constituting implicit privacy breaches.

Adversaries typically focus on two primary targets during attacks on data collectors: sensitive user data and analytical models. First, attacks targeting sensitive user data: Because user data from various sources often converges within third-party data collectors, integrating and analyzing such aggregated data can expose deeper layers of implicit user privacy. Many companies possess sophisticated user-profiling systems that incorporate hundreds of user-specific labels, including demographic attributes (gender, age, marital status), location details (frequented areas, residential and workplace addresses), general behavioral insights (shopping habits, income levels, vehicle ownership), travel preferences (application choices, service quality expectations, favored destinations), and financial attributes (mortgages, loans, financial investments, UnionPay transactions). Most of these profiling labels achieve over 95% accuracy. Second, attacks targeting analytical models: Data collectors employ various machine learning models-such as logistic regression, decision trees, support vector machines, and neural networks-to analyze user data and extract valuable insights. Adversarial attacks on these analytical models [11–13] involve querying the models directly to extract sensitive information about users, replicating proprietary models, or constructing comparable models that enable unauthorized access to private information.

Protecting A-C privacy primarily depends on data collectors implementing robust technical safeguards during data storage, analysis, and dissemination. Common technical measures overlap significantly with those for A-U privacy protection (such as encryption, anonymization, and differential privacy), and thus will not be repeated here. Furthermore, practical considerations require balancing data usability against privacy protection since data collectors aim to maximize data value. Consequently, achieving an optimal trade-off between privacy protection and data utility remains crucial for effective A-C privacy management.

**5. User-Data Collector Privacy (U-C Privacy)**
User-Data Collector (U-C) privacy refers to scenarios where users seek access to or control over their personal information held by third-party data collectors.

The widespread adoption of smart devices facilitates extensive user-data collection by third-party organizations. While it may appear as an equitable exchange, with users receiving services in return for their data, the underlying issue remains one of data ownership: users inherently retain ownership rights over their personal data. Thus, companies and enterprises should view stored user data as being entrusted to them, authorized only for specific purposes. Given the prevalence and severity of global data breaches, concerns regarding how user data is managed and utilized have escalated dramatically. Consequently, users increasingly seek transparency about the extent and manner of their data collection. A notable case illustrating this concern occurred in 2011, when a Facebook user from Vienna, Max Schrems, filed a lawsuit against Facebook [14], demanding access to all information Facebook had stored about him, as guaranteed by EU law. After two years of litigation, Schrems successfully acquired all his personal data held by Facebook, amounting to 1,200 pages of PDF documents.

Protecting U-C privacy primarily involves ensuring users' right to access and control their own data, relying heavily on the development and enforcement of legal frameworks. The European Union's General Data Protection Regulation (GDPR) explicitly grants users the right to access their personal data, obligating data collectors to provide clear and effective procedures to fulfill these rights. Furthermore, the GDPR empowers users to object to the use of their personal data, specifically granting the ability to refuse marketing or other data-driven activities conducted by data collectors at any point in time.

## 2.4 Framework

To effectively address big data privacy challenges, it is imperative to develop a comprehensive and integrated framework for data privacy management that responds to diverse privacy risks, accompanied by active exploration of key technological solutions.

The overarching objective of data privacy management is to systematically manage big data privacy by leveraging existing management concepts and methods, similar to approaches used for Web data, Extensible Markup Language (XML) data, and mobile data. Specifically, the management goals encompass the following three aspects.

First, it aims to provide robust technical support for big data applications. Privacy protection is a prerequisite for successful big data utilization; failure to address privacy adequately can significantly hinder practical applications. Thus, it is essential to proactively mitigate privacy risks from malicious disclosures by data collectors, analysts, and end-users of analytical results, and to safeguard privacy across the entire data lifecycle, including data collection, processing, storage, transformation, and destruction.

Second, it seeks effective solutions to unresolved privacy challenges. Numerous sectors currently lack adequate privacy-protection mechanisms. For instance, in medical insurance and healthcare research, there remains the challenge of mining clinical data without inadvertently enabling insurance discrimination, or facilitating personalized genetic medicine without risking medical data misuse. Similarly, in marketing scenarios, there is an ongoing need to ensure consumer data does not become improperly utilized in hiring or insurance-related decisions.

Third, it endeavors to reassure organizations and individuals who wish to publicly share data. For entities interested in publishing their data, ensuring data privacy is essential. Data sharing should be possible without compromising privacy-examples include disclosing location data for research purposes without enabling malicious tracking, or sharing social network information publicly without jeopardizing employment opportunities.

In this section, we propose an Active Privacy Management Framework for Big Data, as depicted in Fig. 2.4.

The framework consists of five primary components: a Privacy Risk Monitoring System, a Privacy Risk Assessment System, an Active Privacy Management System, a Privacy Traceability and Accountability System, and a Legal and Regulatory Support System. Together, these components provide a comprehensive technical foundation for effective management of big data privacy.

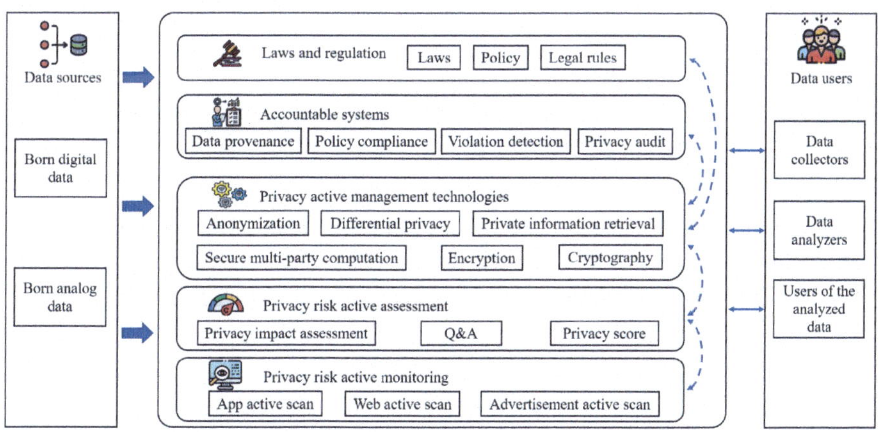


**Fig. 2.4** Active privacy management framework of big data

### 2.4.1 Risk Monitoring

Privacy risk refers to actions involving personal or collective data that may lead to privacy breaches. For instance, malicious attackers embedding unauthorized queries into websites or exploiting social network data to uncover personal relationships are operations that pose privacy risks. The privacy risk monitoring system actively identifies improper or malicious data-processing activities within big data environments. Different operations have varying objectives, such as excessive data collection intended to extract valuable insights; mass email campaigns, free apps, and targeted advertising designed for commercial gain; or identity theft, medical information leaks, hacking, and malware deployment aimed at theft or causing harm. Therefore, privacy risk monitoring serves as the foundational component for proactive privacy management and legal compliance frameworks.

Privacy risk monitoring encompasses two key capabilities:

- **Active detection of external malicious attacks within untrusted application environments.** For example, identifying whether free mobile apps access unauthorized phone data, determining if mobile advertisements track user geolocations without consent, and detecting the use of cookie techniques by web services to monitor users' browsing histories.
- **Proactive communication of privacy risks to higher-level management systems.** Currently, a prevalent technology in privacy risk monitoring involves cost-optimal game-theoretic methods [15].

### 2.4.2 Risk Assessment

Privacy risk assessment follows risk monitoring, providing foundational support and crucial analytical services for big data applications. Privacy risk assessment also has two meanings:

- The ability to actively analyze the privacy risk level at the early stage of a big data application.
- The ability to guide the upper privacy management technology system on how to choose the corresponding technology.

Privacy risk assessment methods include both qualitative and technical approaches. Qualitative assessments can be performed through straightforward question-and-answer (Q&A) evaluations, such as determining whether user data utilized in big data applications directly relates to individual users. If user data does not contain sensitive information, associated privacy risks may be minimal; however, if data is sensitive, assessments must clarify potential leak sources, identify operations that handle user data, and evaluate the trustworthiness of all application-related processes. Technical assessments frequently employ established methodologies such as Privacy

Impact Assessment (PIA) [16] and Expression of Needs and Identification of Security (EBIOS) [18]. PIA leverages threshold-based techniques to determine privacy risks, whereas EBIOS measures privacy risks based on their severity and probability of occurrence.

To further protect sensitive data, privacy risk assessments should be conducted using privacy-preserving techniques that avoid direct contact with raw data. A common approach is secure multi-party computation [17]. Additionally, probabilistic models can evaluate privacy risks at different sensitivity levels. For instance, the Privacy Risk Score (PRS) mechanism [19] automatically assigns numerical scores to relevant operations, thus serving as an effective early-warning indicator.

### *2.4.3 Active Management*

The proactive privacy management system shown in Fig. 2.4 provides crucial technical and managerial support within the broader big data privacy management framework. Its primary functionalities cover four core application requirements:

**1. Support for Diverse Query Requirements**
Queries represent one of the most common interactions in big data environments, typically submitted by data users through interactive interfaces. Proactive privacy management should support various query types, including aggregate queries, top-k queries, workload queries, range count queries, and histogram queries.

**2. Support for Publishing Various Data Types**
Both inherently digital data and analog data converted into digital formats can be represented across different data types, such as relational data, graph data, streaming data, and textual or sequential data. Facilitating the secure and privacy-preserving publication of these datasets in non-interactive environments promotes technological advancements within the industry.

**3. Support for Data Mining and Machine Learning Analyses**
Data analysis is central to big data processing and is essential for extracting actionable insights from large-scale datasets. Common analytical methods include frequent pattern mining (such as top-k itemset mining), linear and logistic regression, support vector machine (SVM) classification, and deep learning models.

**4. Support for Adaptive Selection of Privacy Management Techniques**
Different data types and application scenarios require varying degrees of privacy protection and specific privacy-preserving techniques. Current privacy management techniques include data anonymization, differential privacy, private information retrieval, secure multi-party computation, and encryption methods. The proactive privacy management system must be capable of adaptively selecting suitable privacy-preserving techniques based on the data type and the results of privacy risk assessments. To effectively integrate these privacy management techniques, this paper

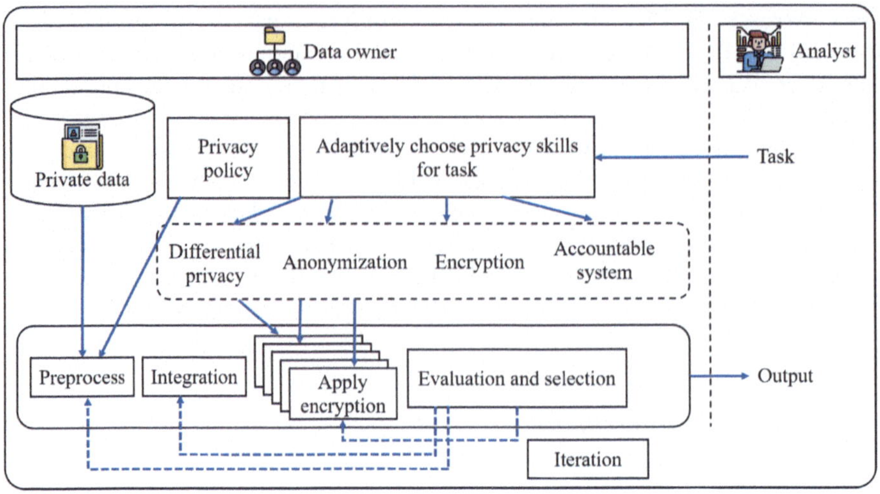


**Fig. 2.5** Proactive privacy protection framework

proposes a proactive privacy-preserving framework, illustrated in Fig. 2.5, designed explicitly for adaptive technology selection in managing big data privacy.

### 2.4.4 *Traceability and Accountability*

Traceability and accountability [20] refer to the mechanisms for holding entities (e.g., project leaders) responsible when their actions violate established policies or regulations. Privacy traceability and accountability act as a crucial link between proactive privacy management and legal and regulatory oversight, serving to reinforce and complement technological privacy controls. Within the broader privacy governance framework, they function similarly to laws and regulations in society-ensuring that violations of operational norms are subject to consequences. While privacy techniques such as anonymization and encryption restrict data access and reduce risks under certain attack models, they are not infallible. When these safeguards fail, privacy traceability and accountability mechanisms are essential for attributing responsibility and enforcing redress.

These mechanisms integrate computer science, social sciences, and legal frameworks to monitor large-scale data operations. Their core functionalities include: (1) identifying and flagging inappropriate operations; (2) detecting policy and regulatory violations using standardized policy languages; and (3) enforcing penalties accordingly. The effective implementation of such systems depends on the integration of supporting techniques, including data traceability, violation detection, and privacy auditing.

### 2.4.5 *Regulations*

Given the complexity and specificity of legal mechanisms in the context of big data privacy, this section offers a brief overview. Legal and regulatory protections serve as external safeguards that complement technical privacy solutions. Relying solely on technical means is insufficient; no technology can replace the deterrent effect and normative force of legal and ethical constraints on privacy violations. Countries such as the United States and members of the European Union have enacted privacy laws to regulate the collection, usage, and dissemination of personal data. In China, the Ministry of Industry and Information Technology issued the Regulations on the Protection of Personal Information of Telecommunications and Internet Users in June 2013. More recently, the Personal Information Protection Law of the People's Republic of China came into effect in November 2021. These laws provide a legal foundation for protecting personal data in the digital era. Accordingly, governments should continue to develop, refine, and enforce comprehensive legal frameworks to ensure robust protection of individual privacy rights.

## 2.5 Privacy Protection Techniques

From the 1960s to the present 60 years, numerous privacy protection techniques have emerged alongside the evolution of data privacy issues. Essentially, these techniques trade data utility or efficiency for privacy. For instance, perturbation based differential privacy sacrifices data availability for privacy assurance, while encryption trades computational or communication costs in data calculation for privacy. Therefore, balancing privacy, efficiency, and utility remains a constant theme in privacy technique research.

From a methodological perspective, privacy protection techniques can be categorized into six types: obfuscation techniques, perturbation techniques, cryptographic techniques, hybrid privacy techniques, distributed computing frameworks, and blockchain-based approaches. In the following sections, we introduce each category in detail, analyze their respective characteristics, and provide comparative evaluations.

### 2.5.1 *Obfuscation*

Obfuscation techniques aim to obscure data attributes by disrupting the one-to-one correspondence between identifying attributes (i.e., attributes or attribute combinations that uniquely represent a data point) and privacy-sensitive attributes. This is achieved through operations such as compression, clustering, partitioning, and generalization, thereby concealing the privacy information of individual data points.

Obfuscation is particularly suitable for data publication scenarios. However, because these techniques often introduce information loss, a key challenge lies in balancing data utility and privacy-specifically, how to minimize distortion and preserve as much meaningful information as possible while ensuring effective privacy protection.

The most representative approach in this category is k-anonymity technique, proposed by Latanya Sweeney and Pierangela Samarati [5]. K-anonymity ensures that each individual's data cannot be distinguished from at least k −1 other individuals in the released dataset. This is typically achieved by forming equivalence classes based on quasi-identifiers, ensuring each group contains at least k records. Methods to enforce k-anonymity technique include suppressing certain attribute values or generalizing them into broader ranges to make the quasi-identifiers of all records in an equivalence class indistinguishable. However, k-anonymity technique is vulnerable to homogeneity attacks [9]. If all records within an equivalence class share the same sensitive attribute value, an adversary with access to background knowledge can infer that sensitive value for a target individual, thus breaching privacy. This limitation has prompted the development of more advanced models such as l-diversity and t-closeness.

To improve this issue and resist homogeneity attacks, l-diversity was introduced by Machanavajjhala Ashwin and colleagues [9]. This model requires that each equivalence class contain at least l distinct values for the sensitive attribute, thereby ensuring a level of semantic diversity and reducing the likelihood that sensitive information can be inferred. However, l-diversity is more complex to implement than k-anonymity and is still vulnerable to skewness attacks. For instance, even if all individuals in an equivalence group have different disease types, if most have a high-probability condition (e.g., cancer) and the global incidence is actually low, adversaries may still infer sensitive information, especially when global attribute distributions are ignored.

To address the shortcomings of l-diversity and to provide stronger protection against skewed distributions, the concept of t-closeness was proposed [10]. T-closeness requires that the distribution of sensitive attributes within each equivalence group be no more than a threshold t away from the overall (global) distribution, thereby maintaining distributional similarity and limiting information gain. At the same time, for dynamic data insertion, modification, and deletion operations, min-variance [11] was proposed. Its main idea is to ensure that the equivalence groups where the records appearing in two consecutive published versions are located have exactly the same set of privacy attributes.

Furthermore, to support dynamic data operations such as insertion, deletion, and modification across multiple data releases, the m-invariance model was developed. It ensures that records retained across consecutive data releases are always grouped in equivalence classes containing the same set of sensitive attribute values, thus preventing privacy breaches caused by changes in grouping over time.

### 2.5.2 Perturbation

Perturbation techniques protects privacy by directly modifying the data, primarily through differential privacy techniques. It is widely used in data publishing and large-scale data collection scenarios. The approach involves adding random noise or probabilistically altering original values to obscure individual level information. While effective in preventing privacy breaches, such modifications can compromise data utility and reduce analytical accuracy. The fundamental challenge lies in balancing the trade-off between privacy protection and data usability.

Differential privacy (DP) was proposed in 2006 by Cynthia Dwork at Microsoft Research [6]. It ensures that the inclusion or exclusion of any single data point does not significantly affect the distribution of the algorithm's output, thereby protecting individual privacy within the results. Specifically, for any two neighboring datasets $D$ and $D'$ that differ by only one record, a randomized algorithm $M$ satisfies differential privacy if, for any subset of possible outputs $S$, the following condition holds: $\Pr(M(D) \in S) \leq e^{\epsilon} \Pr(M(D') \in S) + \delta$, where $\epsilon$ and $\delta$ are privacy parameters that quantify the privacy guarantee.

To design an algorithm that satisfies differential privacy, there are generally two primary approaches for introducing perturbation. The first involves adding noise directly to the computation results, with commonly used techniques including the Laplace mechanism, Gaussian mechanism, and Exponential mechanism (see Chap. 4 for details). The second approach is to perturb the data itself with a certain probability, known as the randomized response mechanism (see Chap. 5 for details).

Differential privacy can be further categorized based on the trust assumptions into central differential privacy (CDP) and local differential privacy (LDP) [21]: Central Differential Privacy assumes a trusted server that collects raw user data, applies noise to aggregate query results, and then releases the sanitized output. While this approach provides higher utility, it relies on the assumption that the central server is secure and trustworthy-an assumption that is often difficult to guarantee in practice. Local Differential Privacy, by contrast, removes the need for a trusted aggregator. Each user perturbs their own data locally before sharing it, ensuring that the raw data is never exposed. Although LDP significantly strengthens the privacy model, it comes at the cost of utility, with estimation accuracy typically degraded by a factor of $O(\sqrt{n})$ compared to CDP, due to the independent noise introduced by each user.

Unlike anonymization-based obfuscation techniques, differential privacy-especially in its local form-is resistant to background knowledge attacks. Even if an attacker has complete information about all users except one, they cannot reliably infer the target's private data.

Differential privacy is now the most widely adopted privacy protection technique in industry. In particular, local differential privacy has been deployed in various real-world data collection and monitoring scenarios. For example, Google uses LDP to gather statistics on users' Chrome browser homepage settings, while Apple applies it to collect data on frequently used emojis and newly typed words on user devices.

### 2.5.3 Cryptography

Unlike obfuscation and perturbation techniques, encryption preserves data utility but introduces additional computational and communication overhead. This is mainly due to the large size of ciphertexts (typically ranging from 128 to 4096 bits) and the substantial cost of performing computations directly on encrypted data. Therefore, the key challenge lies in minimizing these overheads while ensuring robust privacy protection.

Currently, widely used cryptographic techniques primarily include homomorphic encryption and secret sharing. The concept of homomorphic encryption (HE), first proposed by Ron Rivest et al. in 1978 [22], enables certain algebraic operations to be executed directly on ciphertexts. The result remains encrypted and is consistent with performing the operation on the plaintext followed by encryption. Abstractly, denoting encryption by $E(\cdot)$ and the supported operation by $\oplus$, homomorphic encryption satisfies the following properties:

- Additive homomorphic property: $E(a) \oplus E(b) = E(a + b)$
- Multiplicative homomorphic property: $E(a) \oplus E(b) = E(a \times b)$.

Encryption schemes that support only one of these operations are referred to as partially or somewhat homomorphic. For example, RSA and ElGamal support multiplicative homomorphism [12], while Paillier [13] and DGK [14] support additive homomorphism. In contrast, fully homomorphic encryption (FHE) supports both types of operations. However, due to its intensive computation and long encryption/decryption time, FHE is rarely used in practice. Most privacy protection applications instead rely on more efficient partially homomorphic schemes.

Secret sharing supports additive operations on shares and is particularly suitable for distributed computing scenarios. In an $n$-party setup, a data owner divides a value $a$ into $n$ shares $a_i$ and distributes them randomly among participants. No single share reveals information about $a$, but the original value can be recovered by aggregating all shares: $\sum a_i$. A common variant, the $(t, n)$ threshold secret sharing scheme based on polynomial interpolation, allows the original data to be reconstructed from any $t$ out of $n$ shares.

Homomorphic encryption typically incurs high computational overhead, while secret sharing often suffers from high communication overhead. In addition to these, conventional symmetric encryption algorithms such as DES and AES, as well as hash functions like MD5 and SHA-256, also play essential roles in modern cryptographic systems. In practical applications-such as privacy protection queries or secure machine learning-a combination of multiple cryptographic methods is often required to balance efficiency and security.

### 2.5.4 Hybrid Approaches

Obfuscation and perturbation techniques typically compromise data utility, while encryption introduces substantial computational and communication overhead. To harness the respective strengths of both approaches, hybrid privacy techniques have been developed. These techniques integrate perturbation and encryption methods and are generally categorized into two directions based on their integration approach and intended goals: Cryptography for Differential Privacy (C4DP) and Differential Privacy for Cryptography (DP4C) [1].

C4DP enhances differential privacy mechanisms using cryptographic tools. Its goal is to improve both the privacy guarantees and the utility of differential privacy by achieving a better privacy-utility trade-off. C4DP approaches can be broadly divided into two categories: Ciphertext-Based Computation Enhancement: This approach replaces the trusted third party in central differential privacy frameworks with an untrusted entity and performs computations directly on encrypted data. It preserves low computational error while significantly enhancing system-level privacy. Secure Shuffling-Based Enhancement: Applied to local differential privacy settings, this method introduces secure shuffling of user-perturbed data to achieve full anonymity. By combining anonymity with local differential privacy, it improves the accuracy of aggregated results without compromising individual privacy.

DP4C applies differential privacy principles to optimize cryptographic protocols. The focus is on mitigating information leakage caused by metadata, such as the size of intermediate outputs or the frequency of communication, which adversaries may exploit in inference attacks. DP4C introduces calibrated perturbations to these intermediate indicators, thereby reducing the risk of leakage without resorting to excessive padding (e.g., adding large volumes of dummy ciphertexts or messages). This improves both the security and efficiency of cryptographic protocols.

Hybrid privacy techniques aim to strike a balance among data privacy, computational efficiency, and utility. A representative example is the Encode-Shuffle-Analyze (ESA) framework [9], which augments local differential privacy through a secure shuffling mechanism. ESA can be deployed without requiring a trusted third party and has attracted adoption by industry leaders such as Google and Apple. It serves as a successful example of the integration of cryptographic and differential privacy techniques.

### 2.5.5 Distributed Computing Framework

Beyond directly protecting data, another important approach to privacy preservation is the use of *distributed computing frameworks*, including *secure multi-party computation* (SMPC) and *federated learning*. These techniques do not secure data by encryption or perturbation directly; instead, they enable accurate computation in a distributed setting without transferring raw data between parties.

**Secure Multi-Party Computation (SMPC)** [23] allows multiple parties to jointly compute arbitrary functions over their inputs while keeping those inputs private. First introduced by Professor Andrew Yao in 1982 through the "millionaires' problem," SMPC can be classified into *two-party* and *multi-party* protocols based on the number of participants. Representative SMPC protocols include BMR (Beaver, Micali, Rogaway), GMW (Goldreich, Micali, Wigderson), BGW (Ben-Or, Goldwassert, Wigdemon), SPDZ (Smart, Pastro, IDamgård, Zakarias) [24], which rely on cryptographic primitives such as garbled circuits, secret sharing, homomorphic encryption, and oblivious transfer.

Federated Learning enables collaborative model training by keeping data localized on user devices or institutional servers, while only sharing intermediate model parameters with a central coordinator. A notable example is Google's federated learning framework introduced in 2017 [2]. Although federated learning enhances privacy by avoiding centralized data collection, it is still vulnerable to indirect privacy attacks, as the shared model updates may encode sensitive information. To address this, federated learning is often combined with differential privacy or secure aggregation techniques.

While distributed computing frameworks such as SMPC and federated learning provide strong privacy guarantees, they typically incur significant communication overhead. In federated learning, ensuring the privacy of model parameters is especially critical. The key challenge lies in balancing privacy protection with communication efficiency and computational scalability.

### *2.5.6 Blockchain*

Blockchain technique supports privacy protection through mechanisms of traceability and accountability. In contrast to traditional privacy protection techniques-which are often insufficient in the face of large-scale data collection-blockchain's inherent features of transparency, decentralization, and immutability make it naturally suited to enforcing accountability and tracing data usage, especially when other methods fail to provide comprehensive protection [25].

Blockchain originated with Bitcoin. In 2008, Satoshi Nakamoto published the seminal white paper "Bitcoin: A Peer-to-Peer Electronic Cash System", introducing Bitcoin as a digital currency that enables monetary transactions between untrusted parties without relying on a trusted intermediary. Blockchain, the foundational technique of Bitcoin, is a sequential data structure in which data blocks are cryptographically linked. This design guarantees that once data are recorded, they are non-forgeable and tamper-resistant.

A fundamental challenge in blockchain system design is the so-called "impossible triangle," which refers to the trade-offs among three critical properties: decentralization, scalability, and security. These properties cannot be simultaneously optimized, and improving one often comes at the expense of the others.

- Decentralization is the essential principle of blockchain systems. Bitcoin fully implements this with its Proof of Work (PoW) consensus algorithm. However, fully decentralized systems often struggle with scalability and face significant security challenges, such as key theft, smart contract vulnerabilities, and privacy breaches in Bitcoin and Ethereum.
- Scalability is crucial for blockchain applications across various fields. Many studies have proposed methods to balance decentralization and scalability, such as sidechains, cross—chain technique, Proof of Stake (PoS), Delegated Proof of Stake (DPoS), sharding, and the Lightning Network.
- Security is vital for blockchain systems and underpins the application of blockchain technique. It encompasses network, data, node, smart contract, wallet security, and privacy protection.

In summary, advancing general-purpose blockchain systems hinges on achieving an effective balance among decentralization, scalability, and security. This balance remains a key focus of ongoing research and technical innovation.

### 2.5.7 *Technique Comparison*

Among the privacy techniques discussed in this section, obfuscation, perturbation, encryption, hybrid privacy techniques, and distributed computing frameworks are primarily designed to address *privacy protection*, whereas blockchain focuses on *privacy accountability*. In what follows, we compare the major privacy-protection techniques in terms of the trade-offs between data privacy and utility, as well as between privacy and computational efficiency, as illustrated in Figs. 2.6 and 2.7. Note that distributed computing frameworks are excluded from the comparison, as they typically rely on combinations of foundational techniques such as encryption and perturbation.

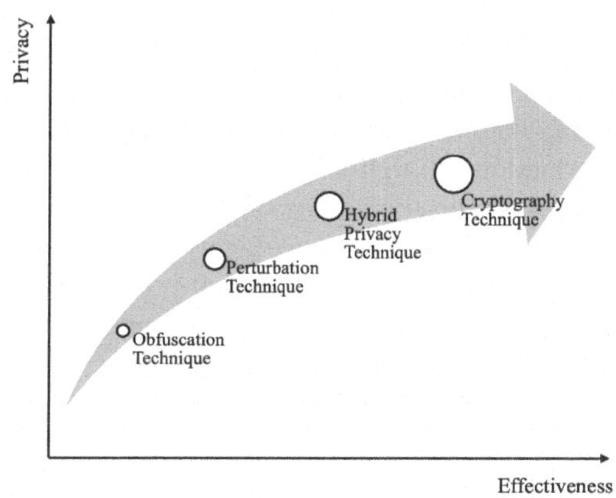


**Fig. 2.6** Comparison of different privacy techniques in terms of privacy and effectiveness

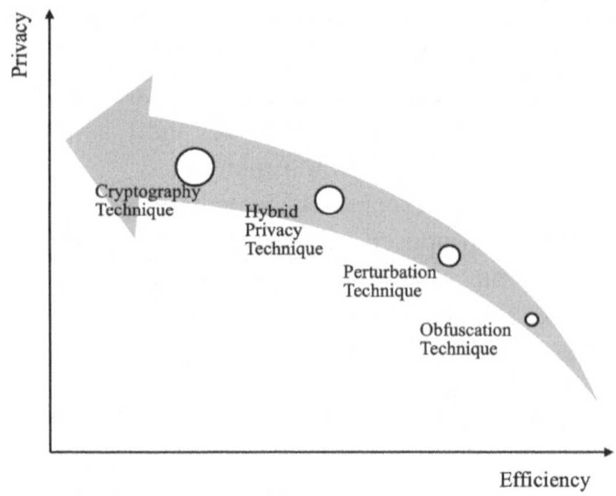


**Fig. 2.7** Comparison of different privacy techniques in terms of privacy and efficiency

By comparison, encryption and obfuscation techniques represent two ends of the spectrum. Encryption provides high levels of privacy and utility but suffers from low efficiency due to computational and communication overhead. In contrast, obfuscation offers high efficiency but generally results in low privacy and utility. Perturbation-based methods and hybrid privacy techniques fall between these two extremes. By combining the strengths of encryption and perturbation, hybrid privacy techniques offer a well-balanced trade-off among privacy, utility, and efficiency. As a result, this book focuses primarily on privacy challenges and solutions based on perturbation-based differential privacy and its hybrid extensions, which are regarded as both practical and theoretically grounded approaches for privacy preservation.

## 2.6 Summary

This chapter began by introducing the concept and characteristics of data privacy and distinguishing it from information security. Traditionally, privacy is intuitively understood as information that individuals, organizations, or other entities prefer to keep undisclosed-information that users are often consciously aware of. However, in the big data context, third-party data collectors can infer deeper layers of sensitive information through large-scale data analysis-information often unknown even to the users themselves. This shift presents significant challenges to traditional notions of privacy. In response, we analyzed the components of data privacy, distinguishing between explicit and implicit privacy. We then described the data lifecycle and proposed five privacy protection scenarios: Adversary-User, Data Collector-User, Data Collector-Data Collector, Adversary-Data Collector, and User-Data Collector. Finally, we introduced a hybrid and comprehensive privacy management framework to enhance the reader's understanding of the multifaceted challenges in data privacy protection.

# References

1. PODESTA J, PRITZKER P, MONIZ E J, et al. Big data: Seizing opportunities, preserving values[R/OL]. (2014-05-01) [2022-08-01]. https://obamawhitehouse.archives.gov/sites/default/files/docs/ 20150204_Big_Data_Seizing_Opportunities_Preserving_Values _Memo.pdf.
2. FENG Dengguo, ZHANG Min, LI Chun. Big data security and privacy protection[J]. Journal of Computer Research and Development, 2014, 37(01): 246–258.
3. GOLDREICH O. Foundations of cryptography: volume 2, basic applications[M]. Cambridge: Cambridge university press, 2004.
4. WARNER S L. Randomized response: A survey technique for eliminating evasive answer bias[J]. Journal of the American Statistical Association, 1965, 60(309): 63–69.
5. SAMARATI P, SWEENEY L. Generalizing data to provide anonymity when disclosing information[C]//Proceedings of the seventeenth ACM SIGACT-SIGMOD-SIGART symposium on Principles of database systems. New York, NY: ACM, 1998: 10–1145.
6. MACHANAVAJJHALA A, KIFER D, GEHRKE J, et al. l-diversity: Privacy beyond k-anonymity[J]. ACM Transactions on Knowledge Discovery from Data (TKDD), 2007, 1(1): 3-es.
7. LI N, LI T, VENKATASUBRAMANIAN S. t-closeness: Privacy beyond k-anonymity and l-diversity[C]//Proceedings of IEEE 23rd International Conference on Data Engineering. Piscataway, NJ: IEEE, 2007: 106-115.
8. DWORK C. Differential privacy[C]//Proceedings of International Colloquium on Automata, Languages, and Programming. Berlin: Springer, 2006: 1–12.
9. DWORK C, MCSHERRY F, NISSIM K, et al. Calibrating noise to sensitivity in private data analysis[C]//Proceedings of Theory of cryptography conference. Berlin: Springer, 2006: 265–284.
10. MCSHERRY F, TALWAR K. Mechanism design via differential privacy[C]//Proceedings of 48th Annual IEEE Symposium on Foundations of Computer Science (FOCS'07). Piscataway, NJ: IEEE, 2007: 94–103.
11. TRAMÈR F, ZHANG FAN, JUELS A, et al. Stealing machine learning models via prediction APIs[C]//Proceedings of the 25th USENIX Security Symp. Berkeley, CA: USENIX Association, 2016: 601–618.
12. GOLDREICH O. Foundations of cryptography: volume 2, basic applications[M]. Cambridge, UK: Cambridge University Press, 2009.
13. PAILLIER P. Public-key cryptosystems based on composite degree residuosity classes[C]//International conference on the theory and applications of cryptographic techniques. Berlin: Springer, 1999: 223–238.
14. DAMGARD I, GEISLER M, KROIGARD M. Homomorphic encryption and secure comparison[J]. International Journal of Applied Cryptography, 2008, 1(1): 22–31.
15. ABBE E A, KHANDANI A E, LO A W. Privacy-preserving methods for sharing financial risk exposures[J]. American Economic Review, 2012, 102(3): 65–70.
16. WRIGHT D, DE HERT P. Privacy impact assessment[M]. Dordrecht: Springer, 2012.
17. CLIFTON C, KANTARCIOGLU M, VAIDYA J, et al. Tools for privacy preserving distributed data mining[J]. ACM Sigkdd Explorations Newsletter, 2002, 4(2): 28–34.
18. ABBASS W, BAINA A, BELLAFKIH M. Using EBIOS for risk management in critical information infrastructure[C]//Proceedings of 5th World Congress on Information and Communication techniques (WICT). Piscataway, NJ: IEEE, 2015: 107–112.
19. LIU K, TERZI E. A framework for computing the privacy scores of users in online social networks[J]. ACM Transactions on Knowledge Discovery from Data (TKDD), 2010, 5(1): 1–30.
20. FEIGENBAUM J, JAGGARD A D, WRIGHT R N. Towards a formal model of accountability[C]//Proceedings of the 2011 New security paradigms workshop. New York, NY: ACM, 2011: 45–56.

21. ERLINGSSON Ú, PIHUR V, KOROLOVA A. Rappor: Randomized aggregatable privacy protection ordinal response[C]//Proceedings of the 2014 ACM SIGSAC conference on computer and communications security. New York, NY: ACM, 2014: 1054–1067.
22. RIVEST R L, SHAMIR A, ADLEMAN L. A method for obtaining digital signatures and public-key cryptosystems[J]. Communications of the ACM, 1978, 21(2): 120–126.
23. YAO A C C. How to generate and exchange secrets[C]//Proceedings of the 27th Annual Symposium on Foundations of Computer Science. Piscataway, NJ: IEEE, 1986: 162–167.
24. DAMGÅRD I, KELLER M, LARRAIA E, et al. Practical covertly secure MPC for dishonest majority–or: breaking the SPDZ limits[C]//European Symposium on Research in Computer Security. Berlin: Springer, 2013: 1–18.
25. MENG X, LIU L. Blockchain-Based Data Transparency: Issues and Challenges[J]. Journal of Computer Research and Development, 2021, 58(2): 237–252.

# Chapter 3
# Data Governance

With the rapid advancement of Internet of Things technologies and the widespread use of mobile devices, the frequency and scale of user data collection have significantly increased, rendering data a fundamental strategic resource for enterprise development. However, in the pursuit of profit maximization, many enterprises tend to exploit data to its fullest extent while overlooking ethical concerns surrounding data collection, usage, and sharing. Today, data ethics issues extend beyond privacy to encompass data monopolies, fairness, and transparency, underscoring the urgent need for comprehensive data governance.

This chapter begins by defining the concept of data governance and explaining how modern data governance differs from traditional forms rooted in government administration, corporate management, and information technology (IT). While sharing certain foundational principles, contemporary data governance also possesses distinct characteristics. It must be understood within the broader context of the current data ecosystem, rather than being confined to the linear view of the data lifecycle. To address this, we propose a four-layer technical architecture for data governance and provide a comparative analysis of governance frameworks adopted by different countries. Drawing upon practical examples, we further illustrate the accelerating momentum of data governance initiatives in China.

## 3.1 Introduction

The term "governance" originates from the Latin word meaning "to steer", and was initially associated with governmental administration, aiming to coordinate the interests of the state and various societal actors. Over time, it was adopted in the business sector as "corporate governance", which focuses on balancing the interests of a company's stakeholders. With the growing abundance of IT infrastructure and digital



X. Meng, *Data Privacy and Data Governance*, Big Data Management,
https://doi.org/10.1007/978-981-95-5787-5_3

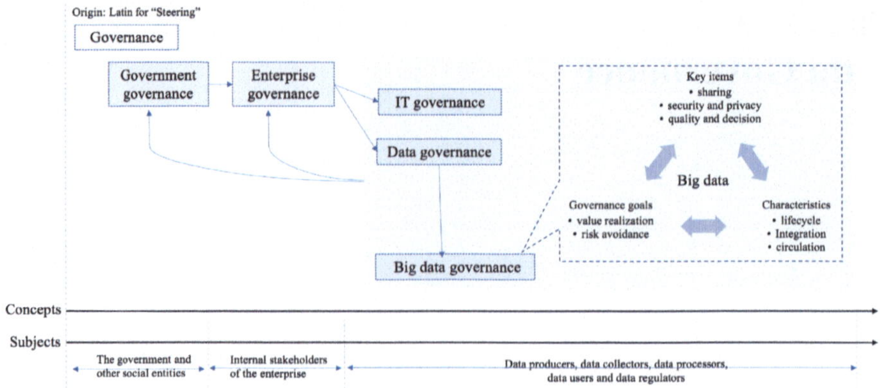


**Fig. 3.1** Development process and involved participants of data governance

resources, the concepts of "IT governance" and subsequently "data governance" emerged.

As data became more fluid, integrated across multiple sources, and influenced by a diverse array of stakeholders, the notion of "big data governance" was introduced. Big data governance emphasizes coordination among various participants throughout the data lifecycle—including data producers, collectors, users, processors, and regulators. Its core objective is to unlock the value of big data while managing its risks and ensuring that the rights, responsibilities, and interests of all stakeholders are respected.

The evolution of data governance and the roles of key stakeholders involved are illustrated in Fig. 3.1 [1].

The application characteristics of big data applications and the goals of data governance shape the core priorities of modern data governance. Currently, its key focus areas and associated challenges are concentrated in the following three domains:

**1. Ensuring High-Quality Decision-Making Data**

Unlocking the value of big data requires the integration of heterogeneous data from multiple sources. However, the diversity of data origins and the involvement of multiple stakeholders across the data lifecycle often result in problems such as questionable data authenticity, potential tampering, and inconsistencies in data standards and formats. These issues can compromise data quality and, consequently, undermine data-driven decision-making. Therefore, data governance must ensure end-to-end traceability throughout the big data lifecycle to safeguard data reliability and utility.

**2. Regulating the Use of Personal and Privacy-Sensitive Data**

The fluidity of big data flows means that data producers often lack visibility and control over the acquisition and dissemination of their data. Users are typically unaware of what data is collected, by whom, for what purpose, and how it is ultimately used. Furthermore, large-scale data aggregation may lead to monopolistic practices that distort market competition, erode consumer welfare, hinder innovation, and heighten the risk of privacy breaches. Yet, data regulators often lack the tools and mechanisms to effectively evaluate and monitor these risks. Additionally, the fusion of multi-source data can further exacerbate privacy vulnerabilities. Hence, robust data governance is required to assess and regulate the use of personal and sensitive data.

**3. Enabling Secure and Responsible Data Sharing**
Data sharing is essential for realizing the full potential of big data and mitigating data monopolies, but it must be balanced with privacy protection. On one hand, personal privacy must be safeguarded during inter-organizational data exchange. On the other hand, due to legal and operational constraints, data analysis often needs to be conducted across distributed datasets—using techniques such as federated learning or secure multi-party computation—without directly transferring raw data. Given the lack of complete trust among stakeholders, governance mechanisms must also ensure verifiability and accountability in data-sharing processes. As such, data governance must facilitate secure, privacy-preserving data sharing while balancing the interests of data producers, users, and other involved parties.

Overall, modern data governance extends beyond privacy to encompass broader ethical considerations such as data monopolies, fairness, and transparency. In the sections that follow, this chapter will explore data governance through the lenses of the data lifecycle and the broader data ecosystem, analyze key regulatory frameworks, and illustrate the state of data governance in China and beyond through representative case studies.

## 3.2 Famework

In discussions surrounding data governance, perspectives from society, academia, and industry have traditionally centered on the data lifecycle, addressing privacy and security challenges at each stage. We refer to this as the cyclical perspective. However, given the structural evolution of the digital society—where data fuels algorithms, which in turn power platforms and generate systemic effects—it becomes necessary to adopt a broader and more integrated ecological perspective. Unlike the narrow focus of the lifecycle view, the ecological perspective encompasses the full spectrum of interactions within the data ecosystem. Building a healthy and well-ordered ecosystem requires attention to four core dimensions: privacy, fairness, anti-monopoly, and transparency. Grounded in the concept of a social data infrastructure, we propose a four-layer framework for data governance [2]:

**1. Data Layer: Centered on Privacy Protection**
In today's digital environment, data privacy and security concerns largely stem from large-scale data collection, surveillance, and manipulation—practices that often result in serious infringements on personal privacy. Contemporary big data privacy problems are characterized by the "BCD" model: • Beyond Users: Data collectors pursue objectives that override the interests of users. Data is used not only to enhance services but also to generate profit through data commodification. • Cheap Services:

Users are provided with free or low-cost services in exchange for high-value personal data, often without full awareness of the trade-off. • Deceptive Means: Permissions far beyond what is needed for service delivery are obtained through misleading or non-transparent consent mechanisms.

These challenges underscore the importance of designing privacy-centric governance mechanisms at the foundational data layer.

**2. Algorithm Layer: Centered on Fairness**
Algorithms are the driving force behind artificial intelligence, yet fairness issues persist throughout their lifecycle—from proposal and training to deployment. The Governance Principles for the New Generation of Artificial Intelligence explicitly include "fairness and justice" as foundational values, emphasizing the protection of stakeholder rights and the promotion of equal opportunities. To realize these principles, continuous improvements in technical design and management practices are required to mitigate biases and discrimination embedded in data collection, algorithm development, system implementation, and application.

**3. Application Layer: Centered on Anti-Monopoly Measures**
Data has become a strategic asset and a key driver of technological innovation. However, the uneven distribution of data resources has led to monopolistic behavior among technology companies. Large-scale data collectors accumulate vast amounts of user information, creating "data lakes" and significantly impeding data interoperability across firms. Based on an empirical analysis of 30 million user records and 300,000 app datasets, it was observed that 10% of data collectors obtain 99% of all permissioned data—a data monopoly far exceeding the traditional Pareto distribution. Longitudinal studies over three consecutive years confirm that this monopolistic pattern is not improving, but rather intensifying. Addressing such concentration is essential to ensure equitable access to data and foster healthy market competition.

**4. Ecosystem Layer: Centered on Transparency**
The root of many ethical challenges—such as privacy violations, algorithmic bias, and monopolistic control—lies in the opacity of data processes. From a systems perspective, establishing data transparency as the foundation of the data ecosystem is critical. Transparency can be understood both narrowly and broadly. In the narrow sense, it refers to the traceability and auditability of data throughout its lifecycle. In the broader sense, it includes algorithmic transparency, which requires that algorithmic processes be interpretable and explainable.For instance: Prior to data collection, users should be informed of how their data will be used. After collection, third parties must assess the credibility and provenance of data sources. During decision-making, stakeholders must ensure that algorithmic decisions are transparent and accountable. In an era where privacy breaches are increasingly common and traditional protections are insufficient, data transparency serves as a systemic safeguard. It plays a central role in reconciling privacy, efficiency, and fairness in the age of artificial intelligence.

## 3.3 Comparative Studies

In response to growing concerns over data privacy and governance, international organizations and national authorities have introduced a range of laws, regulations, and policy frameworks addressing data-related issues from multiple dimensions. This section first compares the legal and regulatory landscapes of China, the United States, and the European Union, and then provides an overview of China's recently enacted "Data Security Law" and "Personal Information Protection Law".

### *3.3.1 EU: Comprehensive Regulation*

The European Union adopts a comprehensive legislative model, establishing uniform legal norms across member states to regulate data collection, processing, use, and sharing by both public and private actors. Notable regulations include:

- General Data Protection Regulation (GDPR) (effective May 25, 2018) [3]: This landmark regulation establishes strong user rights such as data access and the right to be forgotten, aiming to safeguard personal privacy and prevent data misuse. It is widely regarded as the most stringent data protection framework to date.
- European Data Strategy (released February 19, 2020) [4]: Aims to build a unified data governance architecture, enhance data infrastructure investment, strengthen individual rights and data literacy, and foster a public data space to drive the EU data economy.
- Data Governance Act (Proposal) (published November 25, 2020) [5]: Seeks to facilitate intra-EU data sharing, reinforce citizens' and enterprises' control and trust in data use, and support economic and social development.
- Digital Services Act (Proposal) (published December 15, 2020) [6]: Focuses on protecting fundamental rights in the digital space, creating accountability mechanisms for online services, and fostering innovation and competition within the EU single market.

### *3.3.2 US: Sector-Specific Model*

The United States adopts a sector-specific legislative approach, supplemented by industry self-regulation. Rather than a unified federal framework, privacy protections are distributed across various statutes, regulatory bodies, and court decisions, each targeting specific sectors or types of data. This fragmented model emphasizes individual privacy rights and supports industry-specific compliance mechanisms. Key developments include: California Privacy Rights Act (CPRA) (enacted November 3, 2020) [7]: A significant expansion of the California Consumer Privacy Act

(CCPA), the CPRA created the California Privacy Protection Agency and strengthened enforcement capabilities for consumer privacy rights in California, a leading state in U.S. data regulation.

### 3.3.3 *China: Toward Integration*

China has placed increasing emphasis on data governance, especially in the context of rapid digital development, global economic shifts, and the country's broader push toward a rule-of-law society. While earlier legal protections for personal data were limited and fragmented, recent years have seen the introduction of comprehensive laws aimed at establishing a robust and unified governance framework. Key milestones include:

- **Cybersecurity Law of the People's Republic of China** (effective June 1, 2017) [8]: Aims to protect cyberspace sovereignty, ensure national security, safeguard citizens' rights, and promote the healthy development of informatization.
- **Measures for the Administration of Data Security (Draft for Comments)** (released May 28, 2019) [9]: Explores regulatory approaches to data collection, processing, utilization, and supervision.
- **Opinions on Improving Market-Oriented Allocation of Production Factors** (April 2020): Issued by the Central Committee of the Communist Party and the State Council, this document officially recognizes data as a new production factor alongside land, labor, capital, and technology, and calls for the development of a data element market.
- **Data Security Law of the People's Republic of China** (passed June 10, 2021; effective September 1, 2021) [10]: A foundational piece of legislation that establishes a national-level data security governance framework, promoting secure, lawful, and regulated data circulation and use.
- **Personal Information Protection Law of the People's Republic of China** (promulgated August 20, 2021; effective November 1, 2021) [11]: China's first comprehensive personal data protection law, providing clear rules for the collection, processing, and cross-border transfer of personal information, and establishing individual data rights and compliance obligations for data handlers.

By comparing data governance policies across countries, we can observe distinct regulatory approaches. The European Union adopts a unified and comprehensive legislative framework, characterized by stringent data protection laws. While this approach ensures strong individual privacy protections, it may, to some extent, slow down the pace of big data industry development. In contrast, the United States follows a sector-specific model, combining fragmented legislation with industry self-regulation. China adopts a hybrid approach, integrating elements of both models and tailoring its regulatory system through a combination of national and local legislation in alignment with its socio-political and economic context.

Notably, the "Cybersecurity Law of the People's Republic of China", the "Data Security Law", and the "Personal Information Protection Law" together constitute the cornerstone of China's information and data security legal framework and serve as fundamental pillars of its data governance system. Among them, the "Data Security Law" and the "Personal Information Protection Law", both enacted in 2021, are regarded as foundational statutes in the field of data governance, drawing significant attention from legal and technological communities. While both laws address issues related to data circulation and security, they emphasize different dimensions of governance.

The "Data Security Law" focuses on data security at the macro (societal and national) level, prioritizing the security and orderly flow of data. It broadly defines "data" as any recorded information in electronic or non-electronic form, thereby distinguishing it from the narrower concept of "information." The law regulates the entire data lifecycle—including collection, storage, management, processing, application, and circulation—through a legal lens. It establishes legal standards for data use and transactions, institutionalizes data security protocols, delineates the responsibilities of relevant stakeholders, and encourages cross-border data cooperation while maintaining security oversight. However, translating key legislative concepts such as privacy protection, data ownership, data transaction mechanisms, and anti-monopoly measures into enforceable practice remains a challenge that demands continued theoretical and practical exploration.

The "Personal Information Protection Law", on the other hand, addresses data protection at the micro (individual) level and serves as the foundational institutional framework for personal information security. It clearly defines key concepts, including personal information, sensitive personal information, personal information processors, automated decision-making, de-identification, and anonymization. Notably, the law extends its jurisdiction beyond China's borders by adopting both territorial and extraterritorial principles. It also establishes four fundamental principles governing the processing of personal information:

- **Legality, Legitimacy, Necessity, and Good Faith**: Personal information must be processed lawfully, reasonably, with a clear necessity, and in good faith. It prohibits deceptive, fraudulent, or coercive practices, such as unauthorized data collection or discriminatory pricing based on personal profiles.
- **Purpose Specification and Data Minimization**: Data processing must have a specific and legitimate purpose, be directly related to the stated objective, and minimize the impact on individual rights. The scope of collection must be limited to what is necessary for achieving the processing purpose, thereby preventing excessive data collection.
- **Openness and Transparency**: Processing activities must be conducted in an open and transparent manner. Data processors are required to publicly disclose processing rules and clearly communicate the purpose, methods, and scope of data processing to users.
- **Data Accuracy and Security Assurance**: Data processors must ensure the accuracy and integrity of the personal information they handle to prevent harm caused

by erroneous data. They are also responsible for adopting security measures to protect data from unauthorized access, leakage, or misuse.

Based on these core principles, the law introduces comprehensive provisions on personal information processing, imposes constraints on cross-border data transfers, and clearly defines the rights of data subjects and the responsibilities of data processors.

## 3.4 Practices

To translate legal and theoretical frameworks into practical outcomes, countries around the world are actively exploring implementation models for data governance. These efforts aim to move beyond policy documents and academic discourse, embedding data governance mechanisms into real-world infrastructure and institutional practices. Representative exploratory initiatives include the following:

- **Secure Multi-Party Computation Deployment**: In June 2018, the research achievements of Professors Yao Qizhi and Xu Wei in secure multi-party computation were commercialized through the establishment of Huakong Qingjiao Information Technology (Beijing) Co., Ltd. (Huakong Qingjiao). The company completed a 500 million RMB Series B funding round in October 2021 and has since developed a full-suite, product-level privacy-preserving computation solution. This solution is expected to play a significant role in facilitating the secure integration and circulation of multi-party data.
- **Proposal for Data Broker Clearinghouses**: In January 2019, Apple CEO Tim Cook published an article in Time magazine, advocating for the U.S. Federal Trade Commission to establish data broker clearinghouses. These would enable users to track, access, and delete their personal information, thus enhancing individual control and transparency over data usage.
- **Development of Data Trading Markets**: Following the release of the national "Action Outline for Promoting the Development of Big Data" in 2015, various data trading platforms have been established across China. These include state-operated exchanges handling bulk data transactions and privately-owned platforms operating through API-based models. Such platforms aim to regulate data trading, usage, and distribution while supporting traceability and compliance. For instance, the "Shanghai Data Regulation (Draft)" was open for public consultation from September 30 to October 20, 2021, and a state-mandated data exchange is planned in Pudong New Area as a pilot platform for data asset trading.
- **Construction of Data Trust Infrastructure**: In February 2020, the European Union launched a €7 million data trust initiative to build a data pool composed of both personal and non-personal data within the EU. This initiative aims to support responsible data reuse by governments and businesses while protecting individual rights. Similarly, on August 29, 2021, China launched its "Data Asset

Trust Cooperation Plan" in Beijing. Inspired by financial trust models, the initiative seeks to rebalance the asymmetric relationship between data subjects and data controllers and to promote a mutually beneficial framework for data circulation and privacy protection.

- **Introduction of Market-Based Data Pricing Mechanisms**: At the "2021 Third Bund Financial Summit" held on October 22, 2021, Professor Huang Qifan proposed that data benefits are co-produced by data generators and data processors, and that both parties should share in the revenue. Drawing inspiration from the Bayh-Dole Act, he suggested that Internet platforms should return 20% to 30% of data transaction proceeds to data producers, thus leveraging market mechanisms to achieve a more equitable allocation of data-generated value.

These initiatives reflect, on one hand, the pressing need across sectors to develop effective data governance mechanisms and, on the other, the growing momentum in transforming theoretical frameworks into institutional practice. Although China began its data governance journey later than the EU, it has made rapid progress and is now considered a global leader in implementing innovative governance models.

## 3.5 Summary

As China advances the implementation of its national big data strategy and accelerates the construction of a Digital China, data governance has emerged as a critical area of national and corporate development. The ongoing expansion of data sharing across sectors has raised the bar for privacy protection, regulatory oversight, and data utilization practices. In response, China has issued a series of regulatory frameworks and actively explored implementation paths through practical initiatives.

However, significant challenges remain. Ensuring fair, secure, and efficient data governance continues to demand coordinated efforts across disciplines, industries, and regulatory bodies. In the concluding chapters of this book, we will delve deeper into key governance issues—including the development of the data element market, data fairness, monopolistic practices, and data transparency—while proposing forward-looking strategies to guide future development.

## References


1. MENG X, LIU L. Blockchain and Data Governance (in Chinese)[J]. China Science Foundation, 2020, 34(01):12–17.
2. MENG X. Computational Social Science in the Wave of Artificial Intelligence[J]. People's Forum.Academic Frontier, 2019(20): 32–39.
3. Voigt P, Von dem Bussche A. The eu general data protection regulation (GDPR)[J]. A Practical Guide, 1st Ed., Cham: Springer International Publishing, 2017, 10(3152676): 10–5555.

4. Chinese Academy of Sciences Network Information Work Network. European Commission releases "European Data Strategy" report [EB/OL]. (2020-02-19)[2021-12-31]. http://www.ecas.cas.cn/xxkw/kbcd/201115_128157/ml/xxhzlyzc/202003/t20200306_4554759.html
5. CCPIT Research Department. The European Union passes the "Data Governance Act" [EB/OL]. (2021-12-08)[2022-01-07]. https://www.ccpit.org/a/20211208/20211208vqyf.html
6. WTO Express. ITIF believes that the European "Digital Market Act" is a preventive antitrust measure [EB/OL]. (2021-06-01)[2022-01-07]. http://chinawto.mofcom.gov.cn/article/br/bs/202106/20210603067038.shtml
7. Security Insider. Full Chinese translation of the "California Privacy Rights Act (CPRA)" [S/OL]. [2021-02-22]. https://www.secrss.com/articles/29390
8. Xinhua News Agency. "Cybersecurity Law of the People's Republic of China" [S/OL]. [2016-11-07]. http://www.cac.gov.cn/2016-11/07/c_1119867116.html
9. China Network Information Network. Notice of the National Internet Information Office on the "Data Security Management Measures (Draft for Comment)" open for comments [EB/OL]. (2021-11-14)[2022-01-07]. http://www.gov.cn/hudong/2019-05/28/content_5395524.htm
10. People's Congress of China. "Data Security Law of the People's Republic of China" [S/OL]. [2021-06-10]. http://www.npc.gov.cn/npc/c30834/202106/7c9af12f51334a73b56d7938f99a788a.html
11. People's Congress of China. "Personal Information Protection Law of the People's Republic of China" [S/OL]. [2021-8-20]. http://www.npc.gov.cn/npc/c30834/202108/a8c4e3672c74491a80b53a172bb753fe.shtml

# Part II
# Big Data Privacy

In the era of big data, user data faces three primary challenges: large-scale data collection, large-scale data surveillance, and large-scale data manipulation. Large-scale data collection involves the extensive acquisition of massive amounts of user data through ubiquitous devices in daily life, such as cameras, mobile phones, and wearable technology, using active, passive, and automatic methods. Large-scale data surveillance refers to the process of data collectors creating detailed user profiles by continuously collecting data, which is often used for purposes like targeted marketing, thus engaging in large-scale surveillance. Large-scale data manipulation goes beyond the aforementioned practices by associating and altering data to provide legitimate services, but it can also lead to illegal activities such as data abuse and trafficking. These three challenges are prevalent in modern life and present a significant threat to individual privacy.

To address the aforementioned challenges, the most feasible approach today is to leverage differential privacy technology to proactively protect data at its source. This part presents differential privacy as a key technology for ensuring privacy in the era of big data. Initially, it introduces the fundamentals of differential privacy and explores its typical applications in data publishing and analysis. Next, the paper discusses local differential privacy, which eliminates the reliance on a trusted third party, as compared to the basic differential privacy model. In this approach, users locally perturb their data before submission. Finally, the paper highlights the integration of differential privacy with cryptographic computation, aiming to combine the high efficiency of differential privacy with the usability of cryptographic techniques, thereby striking a balance between data privacy, availability, and computational cost.

# Chapter 4
# Differential Privacy

Differential privacy is a privacy framework introduced by Dwork et al., grounded in rigorous mathematical theory. Initially developed to address privacy concerns during data release in statistical databases, differential privacy ensures that the probability distribution of an algorithm's output remains nearly unchanged when a single record is added, removed, or modified in the dataset. This mechanism prevents attackers from inferring sensitive information about individual records by observing the output variations. In terms of implementation, the algorithm achieves differential privacy by adding noise that meets the definition of differential privacy to the data being released.

This chapter begins by presenting the fundamentals of differential privacy, including its formal definition, core properties, commonly used perturbation mechanisms, and representative application scenarios. It then explores data release and analysis techniques within the framework of differential privacy and concludes with an overview of recent developments in the field.

## 4.1 Introduction

Differential privacy, as the name implies, is designed to protect against differential attacks. Before formally defining the concept, let's consider a simple example to illustrate it. Suppose there is a database in Bob's class that records students' grade evaluations. Three students are rated as "excellent," and the rest are rated as "good." The database only allows aggregate queries-specifically, how many students are rated as "excellent." Bob first queries the database and finds that three students are rated "excellent." He then excludes himself from the query and sees that the result remains three. From this, he can infer that his own grade is not "excellent".



X. Meng, *Data Privacy and Data Governance*, Big Data Management,
https://doi.org/10.1007/978-981-95-5787-5_4

In this case, Bob, acting as an attacker, gains access to individual-level information from a query that was intended to reveal only group-level statistics. This type of inference is known as a differential attack. In contrast, the goal of differential privacy is to ensure that an attacker's knowledge remains nearly the same, regardless of whether any single individual's data is included in the dataset.

In the example above, how can we achieve differential privacy? The answer lies in adding noise. Originally, Bob's two query results are deterministic values-both equal to 3. However, with differential privacy, noise is added to the output, turning these fixed numbers into random variables governed by probability distributions.

When Bob is excluded from the dataset, the result might be 2, 3, or 4. Similarly, if Bob is included, the result could also be 2, 3, or 4. In other words, the output is no longer a fixed value. More importantly, the probabilities of obtaining each possible output are nearly the same regardless of whether Bob is included in the dataset. As a result, it becomes statistically indistinguishable whether the query was made on a dataset with or without Bob, preventing the attacker from learning anything specific about his presence.

This simple example demonstrates the core idea of differential privacy: Adding carefully calibrated noise to query results so that the inclusion or exclusion of any individual has a negligible impact on the output. In the next section, we present the formal definition of differential privacy.

### *4.1.1 Basic Definition*

Differential privacy was first introduced by Dwork et al. in 2006. It is a privacy-preserving technique designed for data release, ensuring that an attacker cannot determine whether a particular individual's data is included in the dataset based on the published results. The core approach to achieving differential privacy is to add carefully calibrated random noise, so that the output remains statistically similar whether or not any single individual is present in the dataset. Moreover, differential privacy provides a quantifiable way to measure the extent of privacy leakage.

Before formally defining differential privacy, it is necessary to first define the notion of distance between two databases.

**Definition 1** The distance between databases. The $L_1$ norm of a database $x$ is denoted as $||x||_1$. The definition of $||x||_1$ is as follows:

$$||x||_1 = \sum_{i=1}^{|x|} ||x||_i$$

The $L_1$ distance between two databases $x$ and $y$ is defined as $\|x - y\|_1$. If we interpret $\|x\|_1$ as the size of database $x$-that is, the total number of records it contains-then $\|x - y\|_1$ represents the number of differing records between the two databases. This value serves as a measure of the *distance* between $x$ and $y$.

With the definition of distance between databases in place, we can now formally define differential privacy. Intuitively, it ensures that a randomized algorithm produces similar output distributions when applied to similar input databases—typically differing by only one record.

**Definition 2** Differential Privacy. For a randomized algorithm $\mathcal{M}$ with a value range of $Range(\mathcal{M})$, if for any subset $\mathcal{S}$ of $Range(\mathcal{M})$ and any pair of adjacent databases $x$ and $y$ in the domain of $\mathcal{M}$ ($||x - y||_1 \leq 1$), we have

$$\Pr[\mathcal{M}(x) \in \mathcal{S}] \leq \exp(\varepsilon)\Pr[\mathcal{M}(y) \in \mathcal{S}] + \delta$$

then we say that the algorithm $\mathcal{M}$ satisfies $(\varepsilon, \delta)$-differential privacy. When $\delta = 0$, we say that the algorithm $\mathcal{M}$ satisfies $\varepsilon$-differential privacy.

It can be seen that the smaller the value of $\varepsilon$, the more similar the output distributions produced by a differential privacy algorithm when applied to a pair of adjacent databases. This makes it more difficult for an attacker to distinguish between the two databases, thereby offering a higher level of privacy protection. Conversely, a larger $\varepsilon$ implies less similarity between the distributions, resulting in a weaker privacy guarantee. In general, $\varepsilon$ is referred to as the *privacy budget*.

The concept of differential privacy can also be illustrated using Fig. 4.1. In this figure, $f(\cdot)$ represents a standard database query function that returns a deterministic result. After being processed by a randomized mechanism $\mathcal{M}$ , the output is no longer a fixed value but is drawn from a probability distribution. The parameter $\varepsilon$ controls the similarity between the output distributions on a pair of adjacent databases.

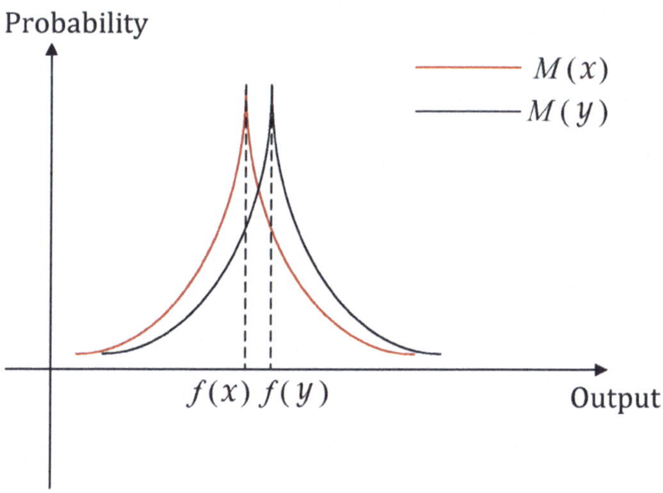


**Fig. 4.1** Output probability of differential privacy algorithms in neighborhood datasets

When $\varepsilon$ is very small, the outputs on adjacent inputs are nearly indistinguishable, making it difficult for an attacker to infer whether a particular individual's data is included-thus enhancing privacy protection.

When evaluating whether a randomized algorithm satisfies differential privacy, we often refer to the ratio form of its definition:

$$\frac{\Pr[\mathcal{M}(x) \in \mathcal{S}]}{\Pr[\mathcal{M}(y) \in \mathcal{S}]}$$

This expression is used to compare the probabilities that the mechanism $\mathcal{M}$ produces outputs in the set $\mathcal{S}$ when applied to two adjacent databases $x$ and $y$.

### 4.1.2 Basic Properties

Differential privacy has four important properties: sequential composition, parallel composition [1], post-processing invariance, and quasi-convexity [2].

**Theorem 1** (Sequential Compositionality) *Suppose there are k randomized algorithms, where the i-th algorithm satisfies $\varepsilon_i$-differential privacy. When these algorithms are applied sequentially to the same database, the overall process satisfies $\left(\sum_{i=1}^{k} \varepsilon_i\right)$-differential privacy.*

According to this property, when several randomized algorithms are applied sequentially to a dataset, their privacy budgets combine additively. Intuitively, the more randomized algorithms applied, the greater the distance between the noisy dataset and the original dataset.

The proof of this property is as follows:

Let $r$ represent a result sequence composed of the outputs $r_i$ from individual randomized algorithms $M_i$. We define the corresponding randomized algorithm for the output result $r$ as $M_i^r$. The probability that the sequence $M_i^r(x)$ outputs the result $r$ is:

$$\Pr[M(x) = r] = \prod_i \Pr\left[M_i^r(x) = r_i\right]$$

Since each randomized algorithm $M_i^r$ satisfies the definition of differential privacy, we have

$$\prod_i \Pr\left[M_i^r(x) = r_i\right] \leq \prod_i \Pr\left[M_i^r(y) = r_i\right] \times \prod_i \exp\left(\varepsilon_i \times |x \oplus y|\right)$$

According to the definition of differential privacy, it follows that the combined algorithm composed of the $M_i$ satisfies $\left(\sum_{i=1}^{k} \varepsilon_i\right)$-differential privacy.

**Theorem 2** (Parallel Compositionality) *Suppose a database x is partitioned into k disjoint subsets, denoted as* $x_1, x_2, x_3, \ldots, x_k$. *There are k randomized algorithms* $M_1, M_2, M_3, \ldots, M_k$*, each operating on a different subset and having respective privacy budgets* $\varepsilon_1, \varepsilon_2, \varepsilon_3, \ldots, \varepsilon_k$. *Then, the combined outputs* $M_1(x_1), M_2(x_2), M_3(x_3), \ldots, M_k(x_k)$ *satisfy* $\max_{i \in \{1,2,\ldots,k\}} \varepsilon_i$*-differential privacy.*

According to this property, when queries are applied to disjoint subsets of a database and each subset is processed by a different differentially private algorithm, the overall privacy guarantee depends only on the maximum privacy budget among the algorithms, rather than their sum.

The proof of this property is as follows:

For databases $A$ and $B$, let $A_i = A \cap D_i$ and $B_i = B \cap D_i$, where $D_i$ denotes the domain of the $i$-th disjoint subset. Similarly, let $r$ be a result sequence composed of the outputs $r_i$ from individual randomized algorithms $M_i$. We denote the composed randomized mechanism for generating result $r$ as $M_i^r$. The probability that the sequence $M_i^r(A_i)$ outputs $r$ is given by:

$$\Pr[M(x) = r] = \prod_i \Pr\left[M_i^r(A_i) = r_i\right]$$

Since each randomized algorithm $M_i^r$ satisfies the definition of differential privacy, we have

$$\begin{aligned} &\prod_i \Pr\left[M_i^r(A_i) = r_i\right] \\ &\leq \prod_i \Pr\left[M_i^r(B_i) = r_i\right] \times \prod_i \exp\left(\epsilon \times |A_i \oplus B_i|\right) \\ &\leq \prod_i \Pr\left[M_i^r(B_i) = r_i\right] \times \exp(\epsilon \times |A \oplus B|) \end{aligned}$$

This shows that the parallel composition of these randomized algorithms satisfies differential privacy with a privacy budget equal to the maximum among all individual budgets.

**Theorem 3** (Post-processing Invariance) *Suppose there is a privacy-preserving algorithm A that satisfies a certain privacy requirement, and a randomized algorithm M whose input space is the output space of A, and whose randomness is independent of the data and randomness in A. Then* $M^* = M(A(\cdot))$ *is also a privacy-preserving algorithm that satisfies the privacy requirement.*

According to this property, as long as the post-processing algorithm does not directly use sensitive information, the data before post-processing can maintain its privacy. That is, if an algorithm satisfies $\varepsilon$-differential privacy, then any further processing on the results of this algorithm will not weaken the level of privacy protection.

The proof of this property is as follows:

For adjacent databases $x$ and $y$, let $R$ be the output space of the privacy-preserving algorithm $\mathcal{A}$, and $R'$ be the output space of the randomized algorithm $M$. For $S \subseteq R'$, let $T = \{r \in R : M(r) \in S\}$. Then,

$$\begin{aligned}
\Pr[M(\mathcal{A}(x)) \in S] &= \Pr[\mathcal{A}(x) \in T] \\
&\leq \exp(\epsilon)\Pr[\mathcal{A}(y) \in T] \\
&= \exp(\epsilon)\Pr[M(\mathcal{A}(y)) \in S]
\end{aligned}$$

From the above equation, it can be seen that $M^* = M(\mathcal{A}(.))$ satisfies differential privacy.

**Theorem 4** (Convexity) *Suppose $M_1$ and $M_2$ both satisfy $\varepsilon$-differential privacy. Then, for any $p \in [0, 1]$, let $M_p$ be a randomized algorithm that outputs the result of $M_1$ with probability $p$ and the result of $M_2$ with probability $1 - p$. In this case, $M_p$ also satisfies $\varepsilon$-differential privacy.*

According to this property, if two randomized algorithms offer the same level of privacy protection (i.e., they have the same privacy budget, $\varepsilon$), and if these algorithms are independent of the dataset, then we can freely choose either algorithm for data protection without affecting the privacy guarantee.

### *4.1.3 Commonly Used Perturbation Mechanisms*

When differential privacy is employed for privacy protection, the data to be processed can be categorized into two main types: continuous data and discrete data. Continuous data typically consists of numerical values within a continuous range, such as the height of a tree or the width of a house. Discrete data, on the other hand, consists of distinct, countable values, such as the seven colors of the rainbow or the five fingers on a human hand.

The core idea of differential privacy is to add noise to the data to obscure any individual contribution, ensuring that an adversary cannot deduce whether a particular individual's data was part of the dataset. The type of noise added depends on the nature of the data. For continuous data, the **Laplace mechanism** is commonly used to add noise, as it is well-suited for numerical values and provides a simple way to introduce randomness. For discrete data, the **exponential mechanism** is often employed, which is designed for categorical data and works by probabilistically selecting outputs based on their utility scores.

In the following sections, we will explain these two perturbation mechanisms in more detail, highlighting how they operate and why they are suitable for their respective data types.

**1. Laplace Mechanism**

Before introducing the **Laplace mechanism**, it is important to first understand the concept of **sensitivity**. Differential privacy protects user privacy by adding perturbation (or noise) to the data. However, the amount of perturbation must be carefully chosen. If the perturbation is too large, it will degrade the usability of the data and reduce its utility. On the other hand, if the perturbation is too small, it may not sufficiently protect user privacy, leaving users vulnerable to potential attacks.

Clearly, the magnitude of the perturbation plays a crucial role in ensuring a balance between privacy protection and data utility. The parameter that controls the size of the perturbation is known as **sensitivity**. Sensitivity quantifies how much a single data point can change the output of a query. The higher the sensitivity, the larger the perturbation required to maintain privacy. By controlling sensitivity, differential privacy ensures that the noise added to the data is appropriate for the desired level of privacy protection while maintaining the usefulness of the data.

**Definition 3** (*Function Sensitivity*) For a query function $f(\cdot)$ that operates on a pair of adjacent datasets $x$ and $x'$, the maximum change in the returned result is the function sensitivity of the query function.

$$\text{Sensitivity}(f) = \max_{x,x'} ||f(x) - f(x')||_1$$

Here, $||f(x) - f(x')||_1$ refers to the Manhattan distance between the query results of $f$ on $x$ and $x'$. It is important to note that the function sensitivity is determined solely by the query function itself and is independent of the dataset being queried.

With the definition of function sensitivity in place, we can now introduce the Laplace mechanism. For queries on continuous data, the Laplace mechanism adds noise drawn from the Laplace distribution $\text{Lap}\left(0, \frac{\text{Sensitivity}(f)}{\varepsilon}\right)$ to the query result in order to achieve differential privacy. In this expression, $\text{Sensitivity}(f)$ refers to the sensitivity of the query function, and $\varepsilon$ is the privacy budget, which controls the amount of noise added and thus the level of privacy protection.

**Definition 4** (*Laplace Mechanism*) Let $x$ represent the database being queried, $M(x)$ represent the final query result, $f(x)$ represent the original query function's returned result, and let $Y$ represent the noise that follows a Laplace distribution, i.e., $Y \sim \text{Lap}\left(0, \frac{\text{Sensitivity}(f)}{\varepsilon}\right)$. The Laplace mechanism can be expressed as:

$$M(x) = f(x) + Y$$

This mechanism ensures that $M(x)$ satisfies $\varepsilon$-differential privacy.

According to this definition, it can be observed that the smaller the privacy budget and the larger the perturbation, the lower the result usability and the higher the level of privacy protection.

Now, we will prove that the Laplace mechanism satisfies $\varepsilon$-differential privacy.

Assume $x$ and $y$ are two adjacent datasets, i.e., $||x - y||_1 \leq 1$, and $f$ represents the result of the original query function without noise. Let $M(x)$ represent the final result of the query function, $p_x$ be the probability density function (pdf) of $M(x)$, and $p_y$ be the pdf of $M(y)$. For any point $z$ in the range of $f$, we have:

$$\begin{aligned}\frac{p_x(z)}{p_y(z)} &= \prod_{i=1}^{k}\left(\frac{\exp\left(-\frac{\varepsilon|f(x)_i - z_i|}{\Delta f}\right)}{\exp\left(-\frac{\varepsilon|f(y)_i - z_i|}{\Delta f}\right)}\right)\\ &= \prod_{i=1}^{k}\exp\left(\frac{\varepsilon\left(|f(y)_i - z_i| - |f(x)_i - z_i|\right)}{\Delta f}\right)\\ &\leq \prod_{i=1}^{k}\exp\left(\frac{\varepsilon\,|f(x)_i - f(y)_i|}{\Delta f}\right)\\ &= \exp\left(\frac{\varepsilon\cdot\|f(x) - f(y)\|_1}{\Delta f}\right)\\ &\leq \exp(\varepsilon)\end{aligned} \tag{4.1}$$

The first inequality in the above equation follows from the triangle inequality. The last inequality is derived from the definition of function sensitivity along with the assumption that $||x - y||_1 \leq 1$. Similarly, it can be shown that $\frac{p_x(z)}{p_y(z)} \geq \exp(-\varepsilon)$. Therefore, the Laplace mechanism satisfies $\varepsilon$-differential privacy, completing the proof.

**2. Exponential Mechanism**

The Laplace mechanism adds noise to numerical results to achieve differential privacy. For discrete data, we use the **exponential mechanism**. The exponential mechanism selects elements from a discrete set of candidates according to a probability distribution derived from a utility function.

Suppose the set of all possible outputs is $\mathcal{R} = \{r_1, r_2, \ldots, r_n\}$, and let $x$ be the input dataset. The utility function $u : \mathcal{X} \times \mathcal{R} \to \mathbb{R}$ assigns a real-valued score to each possible output $r \in \mathcal{R}$ given input $x$. The higher the score $u(x, r)$, the more likely $r$ will be chosen by the mechanism.

The sensitivity of the utility function $u$ is defined as:

$$\Delta u = \max_{\substack{r\in\mathcal{R}\\ x\sim x'}} |u(x, r) - u(x', r)|$$

where $x \sim x'$ denotes a pair of adjacent datasets.

**Definition 5** (*Exponential Mechanism*) Given a utility function $u : \mathcal{X} \times \mathcal{R} \rightarrow \mathbb{R}$, a privacy budget $\varepsilon$, and sensitivity $\Delta u$, the exponential mechanism $\mathcal{M}_E$ selects an output $r \in \mathcal{R}$ with probability proportional to

$$\mathcal{M}_E(x, u, \mathcal{R}) \propto \exp\left(\frac{\varepsilon \cdot u(x, r)}{2\Delta u}\right).$$

Then $\mathcal{M}_E$ satisfies $\varepsilon$-differential privacy.

It should be noted that the expression $\exp\left(\frac{\varepsilon u(x,r)}{2\Delta u}\right)$ does not directly represent a probability value. To obtain the actual probability of outputting a specific result $r \in \mathcal{R}$, normalization over the entire output space $\mathcal{R}$ is required. Specifically, the probability that the exponential mechanism outputs $r$ on input $x$ is given by:

$$P_x(r) = \frac{\exp\left(\frac{\varepsilon u(x,r)}{2\Delta u}\right)}{\sum_{r' \in \mathcal{R}} \exp\left(\frac{\varepsilon u(x,r')}{2\Delta u}\right)}.$$

We now prove that the exponential mechanism satisfies $\varepsilon$-differential privacy.

Assume that $x$ and $y$ are two adjacent datasets, i.e., $||x - y||_1 \leq 1$. Let $P_x(r)$ and $P_y(r)$ be the probabilities that the mechanism outputs $r$ when applied to datasets $x$ and $y$, respectively. Then we have:

$$\begin{aligned}
\frac{\Pr[\mathcal{M}_E(x, u, \mathcal{R}) = r]}{\Pr[\mathcal{M}_E(y, u, \mathcal{R}) = r]} &= \frac{\left(\frac{\exp\left(\frac{\varepsilon u(x,r)}{2\Delta u}\right)}{\sum_{r' \in \mathcal{R}} \exp\left(\frac{\varepsilon u(x,r')}{2\Delta u}\right)}\right)}{\left(\frac{\exp\left(\frac{\varepsilon u(y,r)}{2\Delta u}\right)}{\sum_{r' \in \mathcal{R}} \exp\left(\frac{\varepsilon u(y,r')}{2\Delta u}\right)}\right)} \\
&= \left(\frac{\exp\left(\frac{\varepsilon u(x,r)}{2\Delta u}\right)}{\exp\left(\frac{\varepsilon u(y,r)}{2\Delta u}\right)}\right) \cdot \left(\frac{\sum_{r' \in \mathcal{R}} \exp\left(\frac{\varepsilon u(y,r')}{2\Delta u}\right)}{\sum_{r' \in \mathcal{R}} \exp\left(\frac{\varepsilon u(x,r')}{2\Delta u}\right)}\right) \\
&= \exp\left(\frac{\varepsilon\left(u\left(x, r'\right) - u\left(y, r'\right)\right)}{2\Delta u}\right) \\
&\quad \cdot \left(\frac{\sum_{r' \in \mathcal{R}} \exp\left(\frac{\varepsilon u(y,r')}{2\Delta u}\right)}{\sum_{r' \in \mathcal{R}} \exp\left(\frac{\varepsilon u(x,r')}{2\Delta u}\right)}\right) \\
&\leq \exp\left(\frac{\varepsilon}{2}\right) \cdot \exp\left(\frac{\varepsilon}{2}\right) \cdot \left(\frac{\sum_{r' \in \mathcal{R}} \exp\left(\frac{\varepsilon u(x,r')}{2\Delta u}\right)}{\sum_{r' \in \mathcal{R}} \exp\left(\frac{\varepsilon u(x,r')}{2\Delta u}\right)}\right) \\
&= \exp(\varepsilon).
\end{aligned}$$

Symmetrically, we have

$$\frac{\Pr\left[\mathcal{M}_E(x, u, \mathcal{R}) = r\right]}{\Pr\left[\mathcal{M}_E(y, u, \mathcal{R}) = r\right]} \geq \exp(-\varepsilon)$$

The proof is complete.

### *4.1.4 Applications*

The previous sections introduced the concept of differential privacy and its core mechanisms. In this subsection, we illustrate how differential privacy is applied in real-world scenarios by examining Microsoft's use of the technology.

Microsoft has applied differential privacy to protect geographic location data. They developed a system called **PrivTree**, which leverages differential privacy to obscure individual users' location information within a geographic database. PrivTree uses mathematical techniques to "blur" specific location details, ensuring individual privacy while preserving the overall utility and statistical accuracy of the dataset.

The process by which **PrivTree** "blurs" users' geographic location data consists of two main steps: **map partitioning** and **location perturbation**. In the first step, the map is divided into sub-regions based on the density of location data. In the second step, each sub-region undergoes perturbation to protect individual privacy. This perturbation may involve randomly removing, adding, or swapping individuals' locations within a region, based on statistical rules, thereby preserving privacy while maintaining overall data utility.

Given the original location data and a set of parameters-such as the scale of Laplace noise and the threshold for whether a region should be partitioned-PrivTree executes a differential privacy algorithm and produces a privacy-preserving version of the data. This approach is versatile and can be applied to a wide range of location-based datasets.

Differential privacy is a privacy-preserving technique grounded in strong theoretical foundations. It addresses many challenges that traditional cryptographic methods were either ill-suited for or unable to solve. Moreover, it has a wide range of applications in everyday life. The following sections of this chapter will illustrate how differential privacy is applied in both data release and data analysis.

## 4.2 Privacy Protection Data Publishing

Based on the principles of differential privacy, data publishing methods can generally be categorized into two types, depending on the sequence of noise addition and data processing: **(1) Perturbation-First Methods**: These methods begin by adding noise to the original data or its statistical information. Afterward, optimization techniques such as quadratic programming or convex optimization are applied to the noisy data. The final published output is the result of this optimization. Although these methods often require a larger privacy budget, they offer strong privacy guarantees, potentially at the expense of data utility. **(2) Preprocessing-First Methods**: In contrast, these methods first perform data transformation or compression, and then apply noise to the processed data. By reducing the dimensionality or complexity of the data before perturbation, these methods can achieve higher query accuracy and better utility. However, the initial preprocessing step may result in some loss of original information [3].

Currently, differential privacy-based data publishing is mainly divided into two categories: **histogram-based methods** and **partition-based methods**. These approaches will be discussed in detail in the following sections.

### *4.2.1 Histogram Publication*

Histograms are accurate graphical tools used to represent the distribution of numerical data (see Fig. 4.2). They are typically visualized as a series of vertical bars or line segments, where the height of each bar reflects the frequency or proportion of data within a specific range. The horizontal axis usually denotes data categories or attribute values, while the vertical axis indicates frequency or count. In constructing a histogram, a dataset is partitioned into several non-overlapping intervals or "buckets" based on a specific attribute. Each bucket is associated with a count or other statistical summary representing the number of records that fall within that interval.

Histogram data publishing under differential privacy can be classified into two approaches, depending on whether perturbation or preprocessing is applied first.

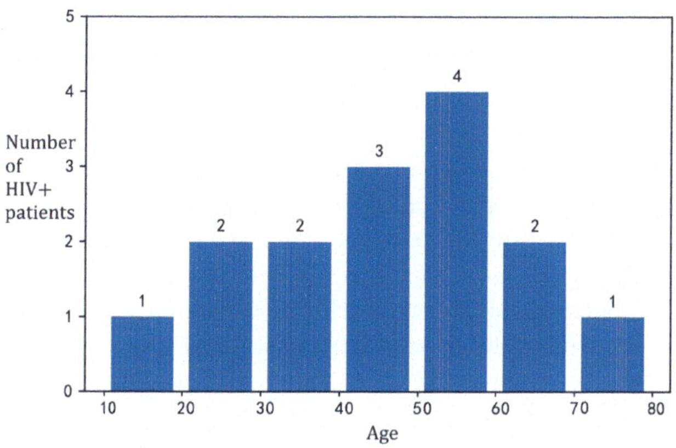


**Fig. 4.2** Histogram release without noise

**Perturbation-first histogram publishing** directly adds noise to the statistical count of each bucket, thereby perturbing the raw data output. In this method, the *function sensitivity* $\delta f$ is generally 1, as modifying a single record typically affects only one bucket's count.

Since histogram buckets are mutually independent, a change in one data record influences at most $\delta f$ buckets. When the privacy budget is $\varepsilon$, the Laplace mechanism adds noise sampled from Lap $\left(\frac{\delta f}{\varepsilon}\right)$, or more specifically, Lap $\left(\frac{1}{\varepsilon}\right)$, to each bucket.

This section introduces four representative perturbation-first histogram publishing methods: the basic Laplace mechanism [4], **Boost1** [5], **NoiseFirst** [6], and **DPCube** [7].

The data release method based on Laplace noise [4] is a representative early approach for perturbation-first histogram publication. This method uses the Laplace mechanism to solve the problem of publishing equal-width histograms that satisfy differential privacy. Suppose the original histogram has $n$ equal-width bins, i.e., $H = \{H_1, H_2, \ldots, H_n\}$, and $\tilde{H}$ is the histogram after applying the Laplace mechanism. The method is expressed as:

$$\tilde{H} = \{\tilde{H}_1, \tilde{H}_2, \ldots, \tilde{H}_n\}, \quad \tilde{H}_i = H_i + \text{Lap}\left(\frac{1}{\varepsilon}\right)$$

To discuss the drawbacks of this method, we first introduce the concept of long-range queries. Long-range queries contrast with unit-length queries. A unit-length query refers to querying the size of just one bin in the histogram, while a long-range query refers to a query that spans multiple adjacent bins.

The disadvantage of the Laplace noise-based data release method is that, when faced with long-range queries, the noise from multiple adjacent bins accumulates in a single query, resulting in a significantly larger error in the query result.

From the previous discussion on the variance introduced by Laplace noise, we know that the noise variance in $\tilde{H}$ is $\frac{2n}{\varepsilon^2}$, which means that a large $n$ leads to a significant increase in the error caused by noise. This, in turn, reduces the usability of $\tilde{H}$.

To address the issue of noise accumulation, one effective strategy is to improve the accuracy of published equal-width histograms through post-processing techniques. The second perturbation-first histogram publishing method introduced here, **Boost1**, is built on this principle.

Boost1 employs least squares optimization along with consistency constraints to infer the true histogram from the noisy version $\tilde{H}$. Let $H^*$ denote the optimized histogram. Boost1 aims to solve the objective function min $\|H^* - \tilde{H}\|_2$, seeking a solution that best approximates the original histogram under a set of linear constraints.

This optimization problem is equivalent to a linear regression task, where the unknowns are the true counts of the unit intervals. Each observed query result in $\tilde{H}$ is modeled as a fixed linear combination of these unknowns plus additive noise. Thus, finding $H^*$ is equivalent to estimating the true counts using a least squares approach.

Although standard linear algebra techniques can be used to compute the least squares solution, in this context, an intuitive closed-form solution can be derived to enhance computational efficiency and interpretability.

For a given query, let $\tilde{h}$ denote the actual histogram range that responds to the query. This is a subset of the full noisy histogram $\tilde{H}$, composed of a series of hierarchical intervals. These intervals are organized into a tree structure $T$, where each node $v \in T$ corresponds to an interval. Each node has $k$ child nodes, representing $k$ equal-sized subintervals of its parent interval.

The root of the tree corresponds to the full interval $[x_1, x_n]$, which is recursively partitioned into subintervals. At the leaf level, each node corresponds to a unit-length interval $[x_1], [x_2], \ldots, [x_n]$, covering the entire domain.

For clarity, we define the height $l$ of the tree as the number of nodes along the path from a leaf to the root (including both endpoints), rather than the number of edges. Under this definition, the tree height is $l = \log_k n + 1$.

To represent the tree as a sequence of query intervals, the child intervals of each node are ordered according to a breadth-first traversal of the tree. For a node $v \in T$, we use $\tilde{h}[v]$ to denote the histogram interval associated with node $v$.

We begin by defining an initial, potentially inconsistent estimate for each node $v \in T$. To obtain a consistent estimate, we introduce $z[v]$, which represents the adjusted value corresponding to the final consistent histogram estimate $h^*[v]$. The value $z[v]$ is computed recursively from the leaf nodes up to the root.

Let $l$ denote the height level of node $v$, and let $\text{succ}(v)$ represent the set of immediate child nodes of $v$. Then, the consistent estimate $z[v]$ is defined as follows:

$$z[v] = \begin{cases} h^*[v], & \text{if node } v \text{ is a leaf node,} \\ \frac{k^l - k^{l-1}}{k^l - 1} h^*[v] + \frac{k^{l-1} - 1}{k^l - 1} \sum_{u \in \text{succ}(v)} z[u], & \text{otherwise.} \end{cases} \quad (4.2)$$

Intuitively, $z[v]$ represents a weighted average of two estimates for the count of $v$, where the weights are inversely proportional to the variances of the individual estimates.

The consistent estimate for $\tilde{h}[v]$ is recursively computed starting from the root node and progressing towards the leaf nodes. At the root node, $h^*[r]$ is simply set to $z[r]$. As we move down the tree, if for some node $u$, $h^*[u] \neq \sum_{w \in \text{succ}(u)} z[w]$, then we evenly distribute the discrepancy $h^*[u] - \sum_{w \in \text{succ}(u)} z[w]$ among the child nodes to correct the values of each descendant. The following theorem demonstrates that this approach yields the minimal $L_2$ solution.

**Theorem 5** *Given the noised sequence $\tilde{h} = \tilde{H}(I)$, the following recursive relationship provides the unique minimal $L_2$ solution $h^*$. Let $u$ denote the parent node of $v$:*

$$h^* = \begin{cases} z[v], & \text{if } v \text{ is the root node} \\ z[v] + \frac{1}{k}\left(h^*[u] - \sum_{w \in \text{succ}(u)} z[w]\right), & o.w. \end{cases} \quad (4.3)$$

This theorem demonstrates that the overhead of computing $H^*$ is minimal, as it requires only two linear scans of the tree: a bottom-up scan to compute the intermediate values $z$, and then a top-down scan to compute the final solution $h^*$ from $z$.

Since $H^*$ is consistent, range queries can be efficiently computed by simply summing the counts of the unit intervals. In addition to being consistent, $H^*$ also provides higher accuracy. The asymptotic error of this method is $O\left(\frac{\log^3 n}{\varepsilon^2}\right)$, which is smaller than the asymptotic error bound $O\left(\frac{n}{\varepsilon^2}\right)$ of the LP method. This suggests that Boost1 achieves both lower error and higher accuracy. The objective function $\min \|H^* - \tilde{H}\|_2$ indicates that Boost1 does not initially reduce the noise in each bucket, but instead optimizes based on the noisy data $\tilde{H}$.

It is important to note that this method is specifically designed for the publication of one-dimensional non-attribute histograms and is only applicable to range queries of unit length.

The third perturbation-first histogram publishing method is NoiseFirst [6], which is based on the V-optimal histogram technique. The V-optimal histogram utilizes dynamic programming to merge adjacent buckets, minimizing the reconstruction error, which is typically measured using the Sum of Squared Errors (SSE) or squared error. NoiseFirst enhances the histogram generated by Linear Programming (LP) and publishes the V-optimal histogram. This process requires reconstructing $\tilde{H}$, which introduces both reconstruction error and noise error. Consequently, the objective function is composed of these two components:

$$\min E\left(\mathrm{SSE}(\tilde{H}, H^*) + \frac{2n - 4k}{\varepsilon^2}\right)$$

NoiseFirst supports longer-range counting queries, with an asymptotic error bound of $O\left(n - \frac{k}{\varepsilon^2}\right)$, which is smaller than the error bound of Linear Programming (LP). However, this method is limited to the publication of one-dimensional V-optimal histograms. Additionally, when determining the number of buckets $k$ for $\tilde{H}$, $k$ is typically set manually to $n/10$. This choice of $k$ does not effectively balance the noise error and reconstruction error.

The fourth perturbation-first histogram publishing method is **DPCube**, which segments the original dataset into cells and adds Laplace noise to each cell during counting. It then optimizes the cells using a kd-tree structure to generate a multi-dimensional V-optimal histogram. This method can handle multidimensional histograms but tends to have unstable query accuracy and relatively large errors in the published data.

To summarize the four perturbation-first histogram publishing methods discussed above: for one-dimensional histograms, **Boost1** and **NoiseFirst** offer higher accuracy than LP and DPCube. However, these two methods are limited to one-dimensional histograms and exhibit poor scalability. While **DPCube** supports multidimensional histograms, it tends to have higher error rates and less accuracy, indicating that more work is needed for the publication of multidimensional histograms.

Next, we will introduce **preprocessing-first histogram publishing methods**. In this approach, the structure of the histogram is reorganized before adding noise to the count results of each bucket. Noise is then introduced to the reorganized histogram structure. This approach not only improves the accuracy of results for long-range queries but also helps to reduce the error introduced by the added noise. The typical ways of reorganizing the original histogram include: (1) re-partitioning histogram buckets through clustering, represented by **P-HPartition** [8]; (2) reorganizing the histogram based on a hierarchical tree structure, represented by **Boost2** [5]; and (3) compressing the histogram using Fourier transforms, represented by the **Fourier Perturbation Algorithm** [9]. We will elaborate on these three representative methods.

The first method, **P-HPartition** [8], utilizes adaptive hierarchical clustering for histogram publishing to determine the optimal number of merged buckets. This method combines a greedy bisection strategy, which splits the original $n$ buckets from top to bottom, with each bisection point determined by the exponential mechanism. Let $k$ be the number of buckets after the final split, then the $k$ buckets correspond to $k$ clusters: $C_k = \{C_1^k, C_2^k, \ldots, C_k^k\}$. The error in P-HPartition consists of two parts: **noise error** and **reconstruction error**. The noise error is given by $\frac{k}{\varepsilon}$, and the reconstruction error, denoted as $\mathrm{ComErr}_{C_k}$, is defined as follows::

$$\mathrm{ComErr}_{C_k} = \sum_{i=1}^{n} \sum_{H_j \in C_i^k} \left| H_j - \overline{C_i^k} \right|, 1 \le j \le n$$

$$\overline{C_i^k} = \sum_{H_j \in C_i^k} \frac{H_j}{\left|C_i^k\right|}$$

In this case, $\overline{C_i^k}$ represents the average of the cluster $C_i^k$.

The overall error of P-HPartition is:

$$\mathrm{Error}(C_k) = \frac{k}{\varepsilon} + \mathrm{ComErr}_{C_k}$$

The second method, named Boost2 [5], reorganizes the histogram based on an $m$-ary tree, where $m$ is the fan-out of the tree. With $n$ being the number of histogram buckets, in Boost2, the height of the $m$-ary tree $1 + \log_m n$ determines the sensitivity of the reorganized histogram. To achieve the goal of privacy protection, Boost2 adds Laplace noise of magnitude $\mathrm{Lap}\left(1 + \log_m \frac{n}{\varepsilon}\right)$ to the data represented by each node in the tree. Additionally, Boost2 employs a post-processing count that combines least squares and query semantic consistency to constrain the noisy counts in the $m$-ary tree, making the response to range count queries more accurate.

The third method, known as the Fourier Perturbation Algorithm (FPA) [9], publishes histograms using lossy compression based on the Discrete Fourier Transform (DFT). For a histogram $H = \{H_1, \ldots, H_n\}$, the method first applies the DFT to $H$, resulting in the transformed histogram $F(H)$. It then selects $k$ coefficients from

$F(H)$, denoted as $F(H)^k$. Laplace noise is added to these $k$ coefficients, resulting in the noisy coefficients $\tilde{F(H)}^k$. Finally, $n-k$ zeros are appended to $\tilde{F(H)}^k$, and the inverse DFT is applied to obtain the final processed data $\tilde{H}$. The error of FPA consists of noise error $\left(\frac{2k^2}{\varepsilon^2}\right)$ and reconstruction error $\left(\sum_{i=k+1}^{n}|F_i|^2\right)$. The choice of $k$ is crucial in FPA; a larger $k$ increases noise error, while a smaller $k$ increases reconstruction error.

Compared to the three methods above, Boost2, based on hierarchical tree transformation, is only applicable to one-dimensional equal-width histograms, and its actual accuracy depends on the number of buckets. P-HPartition, based on clustering transformation, is also limited to one-dimensional histograms, with its accuracy depending on the effectiveness of mean clustering. The accuracy of FPA, based on Fourier transformation, primarily depends on the choice of $k$. In practical scenarios, the selection of the appropriate method should be based on the specific requirements and context.

### *4.2.2 Partition-Based Publication*

Partition-based publishing methods that satisfy differential privacy are typically preprocessing-first. These methods involve designing an index for data partitioning and releasing privacy-sensitive data based on the structure of this index. Common index structures include grid-based and tree-based structures, so partition-based publishing can be classified into partitions based on tree structures and partitions based on grid structures. When considering partitioning, it is important to determine whether the partitioning is based on the underlying data. If partitioning is done on the underlying data, it is referred to as data-dependent partitioning, as the partition structure itself may inadvertently leak some data information. If the partitioning is done on the query space, it is referred to as data-independent partitioning, where the partitioning does not directly depend on the underlying data. In the following sections, we will discuss partitioning methods based on tree structures and grid structures, considering both data-dependent and data-independent approaches.

**1. Tree-Based Partitioning**

**In tree-based partitioning, the representative work for data-independent partitioning is Quad-Post** [10]. This method uses a complete quadtree to partition the two-dimensional geometric query space in a top-down fashion. During the partitioning process, all leaf-to-root paths in the complete quadtree have the same length, and all intermediate nodes maintain the same fan-out. Since the structure of the quadtree itself does not reveal any privacy-sensitive information about the underlying data, Laplace noise is added only to the count values in the leaf nodes for query counting. To enhance the accuracy of the published results, Quad-Post optimizes from two perspectives: it carefully allocates the privacy budget $\varepsilon$ and aims to maximize query accuracy.

When allocating the privacy budget, Quad-Post employs two counting methods for budget distribution: geometric distribution and uniform distribution. By leveraging the sequential and parallel composition properties of differential privacy, Quad-Post allocates the privacy budget along leaf-to-root paths using sequential composition, ensuring that the total privacy budget across each path sums to $\varepsilon$. At the same time, nodes at each level are independent of one another, allowing for the use of parallel composition for budget allocation.

When maximizing query accuracy, Quad-Post uses unbiased least squares estimation to post-process the noisy query responses.

While responding to queries, Quad-Post encounters both noise error and uniform assumption error. Its strength lies in the efficient allocation of the privacy budget, which minimizes noise error. However, its limitat1ion is that it is applicable only to two-dimensional data and suffers from a relatively large uniform assumption error.

**In tree-based partitioning, the representative work for data-independent partitioning is kd-standard** [10].

As its name implies, **kd-standard** uses a **kd-tree** to partition the original data space. A key step in building the kd-tree is determining the median to define the splitting line during partitioning. If this median is computed without differential privacy, it risks revealing sensitive information. To ensure privacy, **kd-standard** employs both the **noisy mean mechanism** and the **exponential mechanism** to determine the median. Among these, the **exponential mechanism** introduces less noise, making it the more accurate option. The detailed procedure is as follows:

Let $C = \{x_1, x_2, \ldots, x_n\}$ be a dataset sorted in ascending order over the interval $[a, b]$, and let $x_{\text{mid}}$ denote the true median of $C$. For any value $x \in [a, b]$, let $\text{rank}(x)$ represent the rank of $x$ within $C$. Let $A$ be the selection algorithm. The probability that $x$ is selected by $A$ is given by:

$$\Pr(A(C) = x) \propto \exp\left(-\frac{\varepsilon}{2}\left|\text{rank}(x) - \text{rank}\,(x_{mid})\right|\right) \tag{4.4}$$

According to the above formula, the value closest to $x_{\text{mid}}$ is most likely to be selected by the exponential mechanism, thereby preserving the privacy of the true median $x_{\text{mid}}$.

In **kd-standard**, the privacy budget is also divided into two parts: one for determining the median and the other for adding noise to the data counts in the partitioned space.

Compared with the previously introduced **Quad-Post**, both methods are theoretically capable of publishing the corresponding index structures. However, they share a common limitation: the stopping condition for top-down partitioning significantly affects the partitioning quality. If the partition granularity is too fine, excessive noise will be introduced; conversely, if the granularity is too coarse, the accuracy of range counting queries will deteriorate.

**2. Grid-based Partitioning**

In grid-based partitioning, the granularity of the grid plays a critical role in balancing noise error and uniformity assumption error. In the following, we introduce two representative grid-based partitioning methods: **UG** (Uniform Grid) and **AG** (Adaptive Grid).

UG [11] uniformly partitions two-dimensional spatial data into $n \times n$ equal-width grid cells and adds Laplace noise to each cell based on the chosen granularity $n$. For a query rectangle $Q$, let $N$ denote the total number of data records, $r$ the ratio of the area of $Q$ to the total grid area $n \times n$, and $c_0$ a constant. The error in responding to $Q$ consists of two components:

$$\text{Error}(Q) = \frac{\sqrt{2r}n}{\varepsilon} + \frac{\sqrt{r}N}{nc_0}$$

The noise error is given by $\frac{\sqrt{2r}\,n}{\varepsilon}$, while the uniformity assumption error is $\frac{\sqrt{r}\,N}{nc_0}$. To better balance these two types of errors, UG sets the partition granularity to $n = \sqrt{\frac{N\varepsilon}{C}}$, where $C = \sqrt{2}\,c_0$.

Although UG reasonably sets the partition granularity, it does not take into account the sparsity of the data distribution. If the data in a grid cell is too sparse, the noise error tends to increase; on the other hand, if the data is too dense, the partitioning may be insufficiently refined, leading to a high uniformity assumption error.

To address this, we introduce the second method, AG [11], which proposes an adaptive partitioning strategy to mitigate the problem of overly sparse or overly dense grid cells. It first performs a coarse-grained partitioning of $n_1 \times n_1$ cells using a privacy budget of $\alpha\varepsilon$ $(0 < \alpha < 1)$, and then refines each coarse grid cell into $n_2 \times n_2$ fine-grained grids using the remaining budget $(1 - \alpha)\varepsilon$.

For a query rectangle $Q$, let $NC$ denote the noise count from the grid cells intersected in the first-level partitioning. Then, the query error consists of the following components:

$$\text{Error}(Q) = \frac{\sqrt{2}}{(1-\alpha)\varepsilon} \cdot \sqrt{\frac{(m_2)^2}{4}} + \frac{NC}{m_2 c_0}$$

The query error in AG also consists of noise error and uniformity assumption error. To balance the overall query error for a given rectangle $Q$, the AG method typically sets

$$n_2 = \sqrt{\frac{NC(1-\alpha)\varepsilon}{\sqrt{2}c_0/2}}.$$

Compared with UG and AG, both methods support range queries and aim to balance noise and uniformity assumption errors. However, UG does not account for data distribution density during partitioning, whereas AG lacks a heuristic strategy when balancing errors. In practice, the accuracy of both methods is highly dependent on the choice of partition granularity.

# 4.3 Privacy Protection in Data Analysis

## *4.3.1 Classification Analysis*

Classification is a fundamental task in data analysis, which involves determining the category to which input data belongs. Classification tasks can be binary or multi-class. Unlike regression problems, where the output is a continuous value, classification problems yield a discrete value that specifies the category of the input. Classification is widely applied in real-world scenarios, such as facial recognition and spam email detection. A commonly used method in classification is the Decision Tree, where the internal nodes represent decisions based on specific attributes, and the leaf nodes represent the final categories.

In this section, we will introduce three decision tree implementations based on differential privacy: SuLQ-based ID3, DiffP-C4.5, and DiffGen.

These methods operate similarly to ID3, where the goal is to select the best splitting attribute and recursively construct the decision tree based on information gain. Given a dataset $D$ with $k$ classes $C_k$, and an attribute $A$ with $n$ distinct values, the dataset $D$ can be divided into $n$ subsets $\{D_1, D_2, \ldots, D_n\}$ according to the values of $A$. Let $D_{ik}$ denote the subset of $D_i$ that belongs to class $C_k$. The information gain for attribute $A$ in dataset $D$, denoted as $\text{InformationGain}(D, A)$, can be expressed as

$$\text{InformationGain}(D, A) = E(D) - E(D \mid A)$$

In the above equation, $E(D)$ represents the empirical entropy of $D$, which is given by:

$$E(D) = -\sum_{k=1}^{K} \frac{|C_k|}{|D|} \log_2 \frac{|C_k|}{|D|}$$

where $K$ is the number of classes, and $C_k$ is the subset of $D$ that belongs to class $C_k$.

Meanwhile, $E(D \mid A)$ represents the conditional empirical entropy of dataset $D$ given attribute $A$, and is calculated as:

$$E(D \mid A) = -\sum_{i=1}^{n} \frac{|D_i|}{|D|} \sum_{k=1}^{K} \frac{|D_{ik}|}{|D_i|} \log_2 \frac{|D_{ik}|}{|D_i|}$$

where $D_i$ is the subset of $D$ formed by partitioning based on the values of attribute $A$, and $D_{ik}$ is the subset of $D_i$ that belongs to class $C_k$.

The first method, SuLQ-based ID3 [12], is based on an interactive framework. It adds Laplace noise to various counts in the computation process of $E(D)$ and $E(D \mid A)$, such as $|D|$, $|D_i|$, $|C_k|$, etc., and then calculates $E(D \mid A)$. When the dataset has a large number of attributes, this method needs to divide the privacy budget $\varepsilon$ into several parts to separately calculate the conditional empirical entropy of different attributes for $D$, thus accumulating a large amount of noise and wasting the privacy budget.

The second method, DiffP-C4.5 [13], uses the exponential mechanism when selecting the splitting attribute. In the exponential mechanism, the information gain is used as the scoring function for attribute $A$, and its value is used to measure the probability of being selected. This method does not split the privacy budget but instead uses the entire budget to select the best splitting attribute. However, the downside is that this method is applicable to decision trees built on interactive query interfaces and is only suitable for a small number of analytical queries. As the number of queries increases, the classification accuracy will decrease.

The third method, DiffGen [14], combines the exponential mechanism and information gain to determine the attribute to split. Unlike the previous methods, it uses a classification tree to partition all records in the dataset into leaf nodes in a top-down manner, rather than using an interactive approach. Laplace noise is then added to the count of records in each leaf node. Its analysis accuracy is higher than the first two methods. However, when the number of classification attributes is very large, since DiffGen builds a classification tree for each classification attribute, it must maintain a large number of classification trees, which leads to a decrease in the efficiency of the exponential mechanism's selection method and may exhaust the privacy budget.

In summary, how to classify datasets with a large number of classification attributes and how to consider the allocation of privacy budgets when building decision trees are still questions worth exploring for future researchers.

### *4.3.2 Frequent Pattern Mining*

Frequent pattern mining is a common task in data analysis. Frequent patterns are those that appear frequently in a dataset, such as itemsets, subsequences, or substructures. Frequent pattern mining aims to identify these recurring patterns. In frequent pattern mining, a potential privacy issue is that the mined frequent patterns themselves may leak some user information. Frequent pattern mining based on differential privacy primarily aims to protect the frequency of patterns from being disclosed. Here, we will introduce two methods for frequent pattern mining based on differential privacy.

The first method is called TF (Top-K Frequent Pattern Discovery) [15]. This method can be implemented in two steps: First, select $k$ patterns from all frequent itemsets with a length greater than or equal to $l$; second, add Laplace noise to the frequencies of these $k$ patterns.

Assume $D$ is a transaction database containing $n$ transactions, and $|I|$ is the size of the itemset. The privacy budget $\varepsilon$ is evenly divided into two parts. The second step of TF is easier to implement than the first step, as it only requires adding $\text{Lap}(2k/n\varepsilon)$ noise to the frequency of each frequent pattern. In the first step, $k$ patterns need to be selected from the candidate set $C$, where the size of the candidate set is $|C| \approx |I|^l$. The candidate set is usually large, and enumerating to select $k$ frequent patterns would incur a significant computational cost. TF uses the exponential mechanism and truncated frequency to select $k$ patterns from the candidate set. For any pattern $r$, its truncated frequency is

$$f'(r) = \max\left(f(r), f_k - \gamma\right),$$

where $\gamma$ is a tuning parameter, and $f_k$ is the frequency of the $k$-th most frequent pattern in the candidate set. It can be seen that in each selection, TF selects a frequent pattern from $C$ with probability

$$\Pr(r) \propto \exp\left(\frac{\varepsilon n f'(r)}{4k}\right).$$

The second method is named PrivBasis [16]. This method combines the $\theta$-basis and mapping techniques to mine top-$k$ frequent patterns. The method can be summarized in three steps. First, identify all frequent items $F$ in the dataset $D$ with a frequency no less than $\theta$, effectively mapping the dataset $D$ to the set $F$. Second, construct all $\theta$-frequent item pairs $R$ based on $F$, and build the $\theta$-basis set based on sets $F$ and $R$. Third, establish the candidate set $C$ containing all $\theta$-frequent itemsets, and add noise to the frequencies of all itemsets in the candidate set.

The key step of PrivBasis is the construction of the $\theta$-basis set. During the construction process, PrivBasis employs the concept of maximal cliques. Using $F$ as nodes and $R$ as edges, generate the graph $Graph(F, R)$, and then identify all maximal cliques in this graph, with each maximal clique serving as a $\theta$-basis.

Comparing the two methods, TF performs poorly when the value of $k$ or $l$ is large. In contrast, PrivBasis offers better performance and efficiency. However, PrivBasis struggles to balance pattern utility and privacy protection. It may distort the original top-$k$ pattern characteristics, leading to significant deviations in the perturbed pattern frequencies. Additionally, neither TF nor PrivBasis considers the length of the records themselves, indicating room for improvement.

### *4.3.3 Regression Analysis*

Regression analysis is a mathematical method rooted in the principles of statistical theory. It involves processing large volumes of statistical data to determine the correlation between a dependent variable and several independent variables. The goal is to construct a regression equation or functional model with good fitting properties, enabling the prediction of future trends in the dependent variable. Among the commonly used techniques, linear regression and logistic regression are the most prevalent. Linear regression models the relationship between one or more independent variables and a continuous dependent variable using a least squares approach, resulting in a linear regression equation. Logistic regression, on the other hand, is used for binary classification by estimating the probability of an event's occurrence.

The formal representation of the regression analysis problem is as follows: The training dataset $D = \{d_1, d_2, \ldots, d_n\}$ consists of $n$ tuples, each with $p + 1$ attributes: $X_1, X_2, \ldots, X_p, Y$, where $\boldsymbol{x}_i \in \mathbb{R}^p$ and $y_i \in \{0, 1\}$ (for logistic regression) or $y_i \in [-1, 1]$ (for linear regression). Each data point $d_i = (\boldsymbol{x}_i, y_i)$, where $\boldsymbol{x}_i = (x_{i1}, x_{i2}, \ldots, x_{ip})$ is a feature vector. Let $\rho(\boldsymbol{x}_i)$ denote the prediction function parameterized by a weight vector $\boldsymbol{w}^*$. For linear regression, the prediction function is defined as:

$$\rho(x_i) = \boldsymbol{x}_i^{\mathrm{T}} \boldsymbol{w}^*$$

The prediction function for logistic regression is

$$\rho\left(y_i = 1 \mid \boldsymbol{x}_i\right) = \exp\left(\boldsymbol{x}_i^{\mathrm{T}} \boldsymbol{w}^*\right) / \left(1 + \exp\left(\boldsymbol{x}_i^{\mathrm{T}} \boldsymbol{w}^*\right)\right)$$

Once the weight vector is obtained, it can be used to make predictions for new data tuples. Let $f(d_i, \boldsymbol{w})$ denote the objective (or loss) function for a training instance $d_i$ and weight vector $\boldsymbol{w}$. Then, the optimal weight vector $\boldsymbol{w}^*$ is given by:

$$\boldsymbol{w}^* = \arg\min_{w} \sum_{i=1}^{n} f\left(d_i, w\right)$$

For linear regression, the objective function is

$$f\left(d_i, w\right) = \left(y_i - \boldsymbol{x}_i^{\mathrm{T}} w\right)^2$$

The objective function for logistic regression is

$$f\left(d_i, w\right) = \log\left(1 + \exp\left(\boldsymbol{x}_i^T w\right)\right) - y_i \boldsymbol{x}_i^T w$$

Regression analysis problems can typically be reduced to the optimization of objective functions as described above. However, directly publishing the weight vector $\boldsymbol{w}^*$ may lead to the leakage of sensitive information embedded in both the prediction function and the training dataset. To mitigate this risk, differential privacy techniques can be employed.

We now introduce three regression analysis methods that incorporate differential privacy.

The first method is called LPLog [17], which applies the Laplace mechanism to logistic regression in order to protect the learned weight vector $\boldsymbol{w}^*$. After solving the optimization problem to obtain the weight vector, Laplace noise is added directly to $\boldsymbol{w}^*$, and the resulting noisy vector is then used to construct the prediction function $\rho(x_i)$. However, due to the strong correlation between inputs and outputs in regression tasks, the sensitivity of the weight vector is relatively high. As a result, the magnitude of the added noise can be substantial, leading to a noticeable drop in prediction accuracy.

The second method is called ObjectivePerb [18], which primarily involves directly perturbing the objective function. In this method, noise is added to the mean of the objective function computed over the $n$ tuples in the dataset $D$. The modified objective function is represented as:

$$\bar{f}_D(\boldsymbol{w}) = \frac{1}{n}\sum_{i=1}^{n} f(d_i, \boldsymbol{w}) + \frac{1}{n}\boldsymbol{b}^{\mathrm{T}}\boldsymbol{w}$$

where $\boldsymbol{b}$ is a vector of Laplace noise. The weight vector is then computed by minimizing the perturbed objective function, along with a regularization term to control the norm of $\boldsymbol{w}$:

$$\boldsymbol{w}^* = \arg\min\left(\bar{f}_D(\boldsymbol{w}) + \frac{1}{2}\Delta\|\boldsymbol{w}\|^2\right)$$

Here, $\Delta$ is a constant. It is important to note that in ObjectivePerb, the magnitude of the noise added is determined by the sensitivity of the weight vector $\boldsymbol{w}^*$ rather than the sensitivity of the objective function $f_D(\boldsymbol{w})$. As a result, the cost of calculating sensitivity is also high in this method. Furthermore, this approach is not highly generalizable and is only applicable to objective functions with strong constraints and convex properties, making it unsuitable for standard logistic regression.

The third method is called the **FM (Functional Mechanism)** [19], which can be applied to both linear regression and logistic regression. Let $f_D(\boldsymbol{w}) = \sum f(t_i, \boldsymbol{w})$. In the FM mechanism, noise is first added to $f_D(\boldsymbol{w})$ to obtain the perturbed objective function $\bar{f}_D(\boldsymbol{w})$. Then, the weight vector is determined by solving:

$$\boldsymbol{w}^* = \arg\min\left(\bar{f}_D(\boldsymbol{w}) + \frac{1}{2}\Delta\|\boldsymbol{w}\|^2\right).$$

In the FM mechanism, noise is added not based on the sensitivity of $\boldsymbol{w}^*$, but based on the objective function $f_D(\boldsymbol{w})$. Suppose $\boldsymbol{w} = (w_1, w_2, \ldots, w_p)$ is a weight vector, then the objective function $f_D(\boldsymbol{w})$ is first expressed in polynomial form:

$$f_D(\boldsymbol{w}) = \sum_{d_i \in D} f(d_i, w) = \sum_{j=1}^{J}\sum_{\phi\in\Phi_j}\sum_{d_i\in D}\lambda_{\phi_i}\phi(\boldsymbol{w})$$

where $\lambda_{\phi_i} \in \mathbb{R}$ is the coefficient of $\phi(\boldsymbol{w})$, $\Phi_j$ represents the set of all products of $w_1, w_2, \ldots, w_p$, and $\phi(\boldsymbol{w}) \in \Phi_j$.

Similarly, given an adjacent dataset $D'$ of $D$, the objective function on $D'$ can also be expressed in polynomial form, and then the sensitivity of $f_D(\boldsymbol{w})$ can be determined:

$$\|f_D(w) - f_{D'}(w)\|_1 \leq 2\max_t \sum_{j=1}^{J}\sum_{\phi\in\Phi_j}\|\lambda_{\phi_t}\|_1$$

The FM mechanism adds Laplace noise to each coefficient $\lambda_{\phi_i}$ of the polynomial based on the sensitivity of $f_D(\boldsymbol{w})$ and the privacy budget $\varepsilon$, thereby obtaining the perturbed objective function and weight vector, bypassing the direct calculation of the sensitivity of the weight vector. The objective function of linear regression is a polynomial, which aligns with the FM mechanism. The objective function of logistic regression cannot be expressed as a polynomial. To address this, the FM mechanism proposes an approximate polynomial representation based on the standard logistic regression objective function:

$$\hat{f}_D(\boldsymbol{w}) = \sum_{i=1}^{\pi} \sum_{k=0}^{2} \frac{f^{(k)(0)}}{k!} \left(\boldsymbol{x}_i^{\mathrm{T}} \boldsymbol{w}\right)^k - \left(\sum_{i=1}^{n} y_i \boldsymbol{x}_i^{\mathrm{T}}\right) w$$

The sensitivity of $\hat{f}_D(\boldsymbol{w})$ can be calculated based on the above equation, and the weight vector can be derived accordingly.

To summarize, three regression analysis methods based on differential privacy have been introduced. The first method has low regression accuracy and large noise error. The second method is only applicable to objective functions that meet certain conditions. Although the third method has higher efficiency and performance, it currently only applies to objective functions with linear representations and has certain limitations.

## 4.4 Summary

This chapter first introduces the foundational concepts of differential privacy, including its formal definition, commonly used properties such as sequential composition, parallel composition, and post-processing invariance, as well as widely used perturbation mechanisms like the Laplace and exponential mechanisms. Next, the chapter explores data release and data analysis methods under differential privacy, providing examples of fundamental techniques and summarizing recent progress in the field. In the context of data release , the focus is on histogram-based and partition-based approaches. For data analysis, key topics include classification, frequent pattern mining, and regression analysis. Despite significant advancements, differential privacy still faces several challenges, such as supporting data release in dynamic environments and enabling privacy protection in distributed settings. As a leading approach to privacy preservation, differential privacy continues to offer substantial opportunities for further research and development.

# References

1. MCSHERRY F. Privacy integrated queries: an extensible platform for privacy-preserving data analysis[C]//Proceedings of the 2009 ACM SIGMOD International Conference on Management of Data, June 29-July 2, 2009. New York: ACM, 2009:19–30.
2. KIFER D, LIN B. Towards an axiomatization of statistical privacy and utility[C]//Proceedings of the 29th ACM SIGMOD International Conference on Management of Data / Principles of Database Systems, June 6-11, 2010. New York: ACM, 2010:147–158.
3. Xiaojian Zhang, Xiaofeng Meng. Differential Privacy in Data Publication an Analysis[J]. Chinese Journal of Computers, 2014, 37(4):927–949.
4. DWORK C, MCSHERRY F, NISSIM K, et al. Calibrating noise to sensitivity in private data analysis[C]//Proceedings of the Third conference on Theory of Cryptography, March 4–7, 2006. Berlin: Springer, 2006:265–284.
5. HAY M, VIBHOR R, GEROME M, et al. Boosting the accuracy of differentially private histograms through consistency[J]. Proceedings of the VLDB Endowment, 2010, 3(1):1021–1032.
6. XU J, ZHANG Z, XIAO X, YANG Y, et al. Differentially private histogram publication[C]//Proceedings of the 2012 IEEE 28th International Conference on Data Engineering, April 1–5, 2012. New Jersey: IEEE, 2012:32–43.
7. XIAO Y, XIONG L, FAN L, et al. 2012. DPCube: DPCube: Differentially private histogram release through multidimensional partitioning[C]//Proceedings of the 2012 IEEE 28th International Conference on Data Engineering, April 1–5, 2012. New Jersey: IEEE, 2012:1305–1308.
8. ACS G, CASTELLUCCIA C, CHEN R. Differentially private histogram publishing through lossy compression[C]// Proceedings of the 2012 IEEE 12th International Conference on Data Mining, December 10–12, 2012. New Jersey: IEEE, 2012:1–10.
9. RASTOGI V, NATH S. Differentially private aggregation of distributed time-series with transformation and encryption[C]//Proceedings of the 2010 ACM SIGMOD International Conference on Management of Data, June 6–10, 2010. New York: ACM, 2010:735–746.
10. CORMODE G, PROCOPIUC M, SHEN E, et al. Differentially private spatial decompositions[C]//Proceedings of the 28th International Conference on Data Engineering, April 1–5, 2012. New Jersey: IEEE, 2012:20–31.
11. QARDAJI W, YANG W, LI N. Differentially private data release for data mining[C]//Proceedings of the 2013 IEEE 29th International Conference on Data Engineering, April 8–12, 2013. New Jersey: IEEE, 2013:757–768.
12. BLUM A, DWORK C, MCSHERRY F, NISSIM K. Practical privacy: The SulQ framework[C]//Proceedings of the 24th ACM SIGMOD International Conference on Management of Data / Principles of Database Systems, June 14–16, 2005. New York: ACM, 2005:128–138.
13. ARIK F, ASSAF S. Data mining with differential privacy[C]//Proceedings of the 16th ACM SIGKDD International Conference on Knowledge Discovery and Data Mining, July 25–28, 2010. New York: ACM, 2010:493–502.
14. NOMAN M, CHEN R, BENJAMIN F, et al. Differentially private data release for data mining[C]//Proceedings of the 17th ACM SIGKDD International Conference on Knowledge Discovery and Data Mining, August 21–24, 2011. New York: ACM, 2011:493–501.
15. RAGHAV B, SRIVATSAN L. Discovering frequent patterns in sensitive data[C]//Proceedings of the 16th ACM SIGKDD International Conference on Knowledge Discovery and Data Mining, July 24–28, 2010. New York: ACM, 2010:503–512.
16. LI N, WAHBEH H, SU D, et al. PrivBasis: Frequent Itemset Mining with Differential Privacy[J]. Proceedings of the VLDB Endowment, 2012, 5(11):1340–1351.

17. SMITH A. Privacy-preserving statistical estimation with optimal convergence rates[C]//Proceedings of the 43rd Annual ACM Symposium on Theory of Computing, June 6–8, 2011. New York: ACM, 2011:813–822.
18. KAMALIKA C, CLAIRE M. Privacy-preserving logistic regression[J/OL]. Advances in Neural Information Processing Systems, 2008, 21[2022-01-30]. https://papers.nips.cc/paper/2008/file/8065d07da4a77621450aa84 fee5656d9-Paper.pdf.
19. ZHANG J, ZHANG Z, XIAO X, et al. Functional Mechanism: Regression Analysis under Differential Privacy[J]. Proceedings of the VLDB Endowment, 2012, 5(11):1364–1375.

# Chapter 5
# Local Differential Privacy

Traditional differential privacy techniques typically centralize the original dataset in a data center and then release statistics that satisfy differential privacy. This approach is referred to as *centralized differential privacy*. It relies on the assumption of a trusted third-party data collector-that is, the data collector is assumed not to misuse or leak users' sensitive information. However, in real-world scenarios, such trust is often difficult to guarantee. To address this issue, *local differential privacy* (LDP) has emerged. LDP redefines privacy guarantees at the user level and shifts the data perturbation process to the user's local device, ensuring that the data received by the data collector already satisfies differential privacy. Because of its minimal trust assumptions and strong practical applicability, LDP has been widely adopted by companies such as Google, Apple, and Microsoft.

This chapter first introduces the fundamentals of local differential privacy, including its definition, key properties (with a focus on its similarities and differences compared to centralized differential privacy), and a widely used perturbation mechanism-the randomized response. Next, it explores data analysis tasks in both simple and complex datasets under the LDP framework. For simple datasets, the focus is on frequency and mean estimation, which form the basis of many LDP techniques. For complex datasets, the discussion covers key-value data, graph data, and time-series data. The chapter concludes with a summary and directions for future research.

## 5.1 Introduction

With the rapid development of big data collection and analysis technologies, privacy protection in big data has become an increasingly critical concern. In response, a variety of privacy-preserving techniques have been proposed, including data encryption, anonymization, and differential privacy. However, each of these methods faces specific limitations when applied in large-scale data environments. For instance,



X. Meng, *Data Privacy and Data Governance*, Big Data Management,
https://doi.org/10.1007/978-981-95-5787-5_5

anonymization techniques rely heavily on assumptions about an attacker's background knowledge and provide protection only under certain adversarial models. Data encryption methods, while secure, often involve high computational and communication overhead, limiting their practicality in real-world applications. Although centralized differential privacy offers strong and mathematically rigorous privacy guarantees, it assumes the presence of a fully trusted data collector-a condition that is often difficult to satisfy in practice.

Given these limitations, *Local Differential Privacy (LDP)* [1] has emerged as a solution in scenarios involving untrusted third-party data collectors. LDP inherits the quantifiable privacy guarantees of centralized differential privacy while enhancing protection for individual sensitive data. Specifically, it moves the data privatization process to the user's end, enabling users to locally perturb their data before sharing, thus ensuring privacy without relying on a trusted aggregator.

This section presents an overview of the core principles and architecture of local differential privacy. It begins by formally defining LDP, then compares it with traditional centralized differential privacy to highlight its fundamental properties. Furthermore, it introduces commonly used perturbation mechanisms under the LDP model and concludes by summarizing six major application scenarios where LDP has demonstrated strong utility and adoption.

### 5.1.1 Definition

The local differential privacy (LDP) protection model fully considers the potential risks of data collectors stealing or leaking user privacy during the data collection process. In this model, each user first privatizes their data locally and then sends the processed data to the data collector. The data collector performs statistical analysis on the collected data to derive meaningful insights. This process ensures that individual privacy is preserved, even during analysis. The formal definition of local differential privacy is as follows.

**Definition 6** ($\varepsilon$-*Local differential privacy*) Given $n$ users, each corresponding to one record, a privacy algorithm $\mathcal{A}$ with domain Dom($\mathcal{A}$) and range Ran($\mathcal{A}$), satisfies $\varepsilon$-local differential privacy if, for any two records $t$ and $t'$ ($t, t' \in \text{Dom}(\mathcal{A})$), and for any possible output $t^* \subseteq \text{Ran}(\mathcal{A})$, the following inequality holds:

$$Pr[\mathcal{A}(t) = t^*] \leq e^{\varepsilon} \times Pr[\mathcal{A}(t') = t^*] \tag{5.1}$$

From Definition 6, it can be seen that local differential privacy ensures that the algorithm $\mathcal{A}$ satisfies $\epsilon$-local differential privacy by constraining the similarity between the output results of any two records. In other words, given a specific output of the privacy algorithm $\mathcal{A}$, it is difficult for the data collector to infer which record was the original input.

In contrast, centralized differential privacy defines the privacy of algorithm $\mathcal{A}$ based on neighboring datasets, and thus relies on a trustworthy third-party data collector. However, local differential privacy enables each user to independently process their own data, shifting the privatization process from the data collector's side to the user's side. This effectively removes the dependency on a trusted third party.

While Definition 6 provides a theoretical guarantee that an algorithm satisfies $\epsilon$-local differential privacy, practical implementation of this guarantee requires the use of a perturbation mechanism.

### *5.1.2 Fundamental Properties*

Local Differential Privacy (LDP) is built upon the foundation of centralized differential privacy, inheriting its composability properties while extending them. LDP employs perturbation mechanisms, such as randomized response, to guard against privacy breaches that may result from untrustworthy third-party data collectors. Below, we compare the two technologies by analyzing their similarities, differences, and application scenarios.

**1. Composition Properties**

Local differential privacy effectively inherits both the sequential and parallel composition properties from centralized differential privacy. Sequential composition allows the privacy budget $\varepsilon$ to be distributed across multiple steps of an algorithm, while parallel composition ensures that privacy is maintained when differential privacy algorithms are applied to disjoint subsets of the data.

In terms of definition, centralized differential privacy is based on neighboring datasets, whereas LDP is defined at the granularity of individual records within those

**2. Untrusted Third Parties**

In centralized differential privacy, a key assumption is the existence of a trustworthy third-party data collector. Each user submits their raw data record to this collector, trusting that the collector will not leak or misuse sensitive personal information. The data collector then applies a differential privacy algorithm to process query requests from data analysts.

In contrast, local differential privacy assumes the third-party data collector is untrustworthy. As a result, the data privatization process is shifted from the data collector's end to the user's end. Each user perturbs their data locally using a privacy-preserving algorithm before sending it to the data collector. The collector, in turn, responds to queries from data analysts based on this already-perturbed data.

The architectural differences between centralized and local differential privacy frameworks are illustrated in Fig. 5.1.

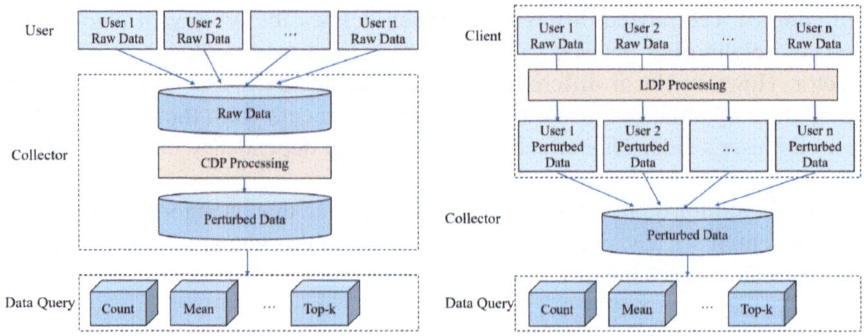


(a) Centralized Differential Privacy Processing Framework

(b) Local Differential Privacy Processing Framework

**Fig. 5.1** Centralized and local differential privacy data processing frameworks

**3. Data Perturbation Mechanism**

In centralized differential privacy, to ensure that a designed algorithm satisfies $\varepsilon$-differential privacy, a noise injection mechanism is required. Two commonly used mechanisms are the Laplace mechanism [2] and the exponential mechanism [3]. The Laplace mechanism is suitable for queries on continuous data, while the exponential mechanism is used for queries on discrete data. Both mechanisms rely on the global sensitivity of the query function [2], which is defined on neighboring datasets that differ by at most one record. This setup ensures that attackers cannot accurately infer individual data records from the released statistical results, thus effectively protecting individual privacy.

In local differential privacy, each user perturbs their data locally before sending it to the data collector, and no user has access to others' data. Currently, randomized response is the primary technique used to achieve $\varepsilon$-local differential privacy. Additionally, local perturbation mechanisms can also adopt techniques from centralized differential privacy to meet the privacy requirements in a local setting.

## *5.1.3 Common Perturbation Mechanisms*

Currently, the Randomized Response (RR) technique [4] is the mainstream perturbation mechanism used for local differential privacy protection. Additionally, the Laplace mechanism [2], commonly applied in traditional centralized differential privacy, is also applicable in some local scenarios. This section primarily focuses on the Randomized Response technique.

Warner proposed the use of Randomized Response (RR) for privacy protection in 1965 [4]. The core idea is to introduce uncertainty into individuals' responses to sensitive questions, thereby protecting the original data. The method generally involves two key steps: perturbation and correction.

To concretely introduce the Randomized Response technique, let's first consider a specific problem scenario. Suppose there are $n$ users, and the true proportion of AIDS patients among them is $\pi$, which we do not know. To estimate this proportion, we ask a sensitive question: "Are you an AIDS patient?" Each user responds with either "yes" or "no", but due to privacy concerns, they do not directly answer the true answer. Instead, they use a biased coin to determine their response, where the probability of heads is $p$ and the probability of tails is $1 - p$. If the coin lands heads, they answer truthfully; if tails, they answer the opposite.

**Perturbation**: Using the above perturbation method, we can statistically estimate the number of AIDS patients. Suppose the statistical result shows that $n_1$ users answered "yes," then $n - n_1$ users answered "no." Clearly, according to the above statistics, the proportions of users answering "yes" and "no" are:

$$Pr[X_i = \text{"Yes"}] = \pi p + (1 - \pi)(1 - p) \tag{5.2}$$

$$Pr[X_i = \text{"No"}] = (1 - \pi)p + \pi(1 - p) \tag{5.3}$$

Obviously, the above statistical proportions are not unbiased estimates of the true proportions, so it is necessary to correct the statistical results.

**Correction**: Construct the following likelihood function:

$$L = [\pi p + (1 - \pi)(1 - p)]^{n_1}[(1 - \pi)p + \pi(1 - p)]^{n-n_1} \tag{5.4}$$

The maximum likelihood estimate $\hat{\pi}$ of $\pi$ can be obtained:

$$\hat{\pi} = \frac{p - 1}{2p - 1} + \frac{n_1}{(2p - 1)n} \tag{5.5}$$

The following expectation of $\hat{\pi}$ ensures that $\hat{\pi}$ is an unbiased estimator of the true distribution $\pi$:

$$E(\hat{\pi}) = \frac{1}{2p - 1}\left[p - 1 + \frac{1}{n}\sum_{i=1}^{n} X_i\right] = \frac{1}{2p - 1}[p - 1 + \pi p + (1 - \pi)(1 - p)] = \pi \tag{5.6}$$

Thus, the corrected estimate $N$ of the number of AIDS patients can be obtained:

$$N = \hat{\pi} \times n = \frac{p - 1}{2p - 1}n + \frac{n_1}{2p - 1} \tag{5.7}$$

To ensure that it satisfies $\varepsilon$-local differential privacy, according to the definition, the privacy budget $\varepsilon$ is set as

$$\varepsilon = \ln\frac{p}{1 - p} \tag{5.8}$$

## 5.1.4 Application

Local differential privacy protection technology [7] is currently a strong privacy protection technology with a wide range of application scenarios and has been practically deployed in large IT companies. Local differential privacy technology inherits from centralized differential privacy technology while extending new features, endowing the technology with two major characteristics: (1) Fully considering the background knowledge of any attacker and quantifying the degree of privacy protection; (2) Localizing the perturbation of data to defend against privacy attacks from untrustworthy third-party data collectors. Based on the above two characteristics, research on local differential privacy technology has garnered significant attention in both academia and industry.

**1. Frequent Item Statistics**
Frequent item statistics, as the name suggests, refers to identifying the most frequent items within a set of candidate items. When the candidate set is relatively small, we can directly estimate the frequency of each item using existing frequency statistics methods and then identify the frequent items. However, when the candidate set is large (for example, $2^{128}$ combinations), directly calculating the frequency of each item becomes computationally expensive. Under local differential privacy, in addition to computational cost, communication cost must also be considered, while striving for better error bounds.

**2. Frequent Itemset Mining**
In this scenario, each user has an itemset of varying lengths. For instance, Apple Inc. may wish to tally the emojis typed by all users, with each user inputting a subset of the emoji collection. Under local differential privacy, frequent itemset mining is challenging primarily because simply encoding and perturbing each user's data leads to very low usability, as the number of itemset combinations grows exponentially with the number of items. Moreover, directly employing frequent item statistics methods is not feasible, as these methods generally only yield globally frequent items and are impractical for identifying frequent items within non-frequent itemsets.

**3. Contingency Table Data Publishing**
Contingency tables are frequency tables that list observed data classified by attributes, and count queries are one of the most common types of queries, with each frequency in the contingency table corresponding to a count query under specific conditions. As a commonly used data analysis tool, the publication of contingency table data is a prerequisite for conducting certain specific data analyses. Under local differential privacy, the challenge of publishing contingency table data mainly lies in the high-dimensional combinations of the contingency table requiring significant data perturbation to satisfy $\varepsilon$-local differential privacy.

**4. Graph Data Analysis**
Graph data analysis is an important means of knowledge discovery. Since graph data also contains a wealth of personal sensitive information, such as the nodes and

edges in social networks representing individual users and their social relationships respectively, it is necessary to apply certain privacy protection during the process of graph data analysis.

**5. Spatiotemporal Data Queries**
Location-based services have become an indispensable part of daily life. To avoid privacy leakage, the collection of spatiotemporal data needs to consider privacy protection. Under centralized differential privacy, many research works have conducted in-depth exploration of this issue. Under local differential privacy, the problem was first proposed by Chen et al. [5], and they considered providing different privacy guarantees for each user, that is, setting different privacy budgets according to the individual privacy protection needs of each user. With the continuous development of indoor positioning technology, the collection of indoor location data has also attracted attention. Kim et al. [6] proposed to add local differential privacy protection in indoor positioning systems to support the estimation of crowd density at specific indoor locations.

**6. Data Mining and Machine Learning Task Analysis**
Under centralized differential privacy, numerous research works have conducted in-depth exploration of privacy-preserving data mining and machine learning. However, research works based on local differential privacy are relatively limited. The research challenges under local differential privacy mainly include two aspects: First, data mining tasks and machine learning models are generally data-driven and require interactive queries based on the dataset. Under local differential privacy, noise accumulation will occur, thereby reducing data usability. Moreover, by abandoning the trusted data center, local differential privacy introduces more data perturbation and noise compared to centralized differential privacy, making it a stricter privacy model.

## 5.2 Privacy Protection for Simple Datasets

This section provides an overview of the two basic queries supported by local differential privacy protection: frequency statistics for discrete data and mean statistics for continuous data.

### *5.2.1 Frequency Estimation*

For discrete data, the application scenario of frequency statistics queries is as follows: $n$ users possess a sensitive attribute of discrete type. The value of user $u_i$ $(1 \leq i \leq n)$ for this attribute is $x_j \in \chi$ $(1 \leq j \leq k)$, where $|\chi| = k$ represents the number of candidate values for this attribute. The data collector needs to count the frequency of each value $x_j$ $(1 \leq j \leq k)$ of this sensitive attribute, denoted as $f_j$.

Frequency statistics is a core issue in local differential privacy research and serves as the foundation for many research problems. Since the Randomized Response (RR) technique can only perturb binary data, a more generalized gradient representation form, $k$-RR, has been proposed to address this limitation. The formal definition of $k$-RR is as follows:

$$\Pr\left[M(v) = v'\right] = \begin{cases} \frac{e^{\varepsilon}}{k-1+e^{\varepsilon}}, & \text{if } v = v' \\ \frac{1}{k-1+e^{\varepsilon}}, & \text{if } v \neq v' \end{cases}$$

Here, $v$ and $v'$ represent the original data and the perturbed data, respectively. For variables containing $k(k \geq 2)$ candidate values, a direct response can be given. Specifically, the true result is responded to with a probability of $\frac{e^{\varepsilon}}{k-1+e^{\varepsilon}}$, and any one of the remaining $k-1$ results is responded to with a probability of $\frac{1}{k-1+e^{\varepsilon}}$, thereby satisfying $\varepsilon$-local differential privacy. When $k = 2$, $k$-RR degenerates into the general Randomized Response (RR), hence $k$-RR is a more generalized definition form. The main drawback of the $k$-RR method is that its estimation error always increases with the number of candidate values $k$, making it unsuitable for scenarios where $k$ is very large.

The Randomized Aggregatable Privacy-Preserving Ordinal Response (RAPPOR) method [8] is a well-known technique for frequency statistics, particularly when dealing with string-valued variables. The method uses the following process: It first introduces a hash function and applies Bloom Filter technology [9] to represent each distinct string as a binary vector $B = \{0, 1\}^h$ of length $h$, while also recording the mapping relationship matrix between the string and the vector. The randomized response technique is then used to perturb each bit of the vector $B$. Once the user has perturbed their data, they send the resulting vector to the third-party data collector. The data collector counts the number of occurrences of 1 in each bit position, corrects the count based on the perturbation, and combines the mapping matrix to finalize the frequency statistics for each string. The Lasso regression method [10] is used for this correction. (1) The transmission cost between users and the data collector is relatively high, as each user is required to transmit a vector of length $h$ to the data collector. (2) The data collector must pre-collect a list of candidate strings in order to perform frequency counting, which can be a significant overhead in some applications.

To address the first limitation of the RAPPOR method, which is the high communication cost, Bassily et al. proposed the SHist method. In SHist, each user encodes their string and then randomly selects one bit from it. After perturbing this bit using the randomized response technique, the user sends the result to the data collector. This approach significantly reduces the communication cost compared to transmitting the entire vector.

Regarding the second limitation of RAPPOR, which is the need for a pre-collected list of candidate strings, Kairouz et al. introduced the O-RAPPOR method. O-RAPPOR is designed for scenarios where the values of the variables are unknown.

It builds upon the encoding and decoding methods of RAPPOR to address the issue of unknown variable values.

Additionally, based on the $k$-RR method, Kairouz et al. [12] also proposed the O-RR method for scenarios where the values of the variables are unknown.

The above methods all consider the scenario where the perturbed output is a single value, that is, for any given input variable, the data perturbation process results in only one output value, which we call one-to-one perturbation. Considering the one-to-many scenario, such as fuzzy matching of strings, where the output result for a specified input is a set, the above methods are no longer applicable. Based on this, the $k$-Subset method has been proposed [13]. The $k$-Subset method generalizes the definition of the perturbed output from $k$-RR. The $k$-Subset method expands the output to a set form, which is a one-to-many perturbation approach. Compared to the one-to-one perturbation of $k$-RR, $k$-Subset effectively reduces the matching error between inputs and outputs during the perturbation process, thereby improving the accuracy of data publication.

In summary, the above introduces frequency statistics methods under local differential privacy. Table 5.1 provides a comparative analysis of the main advantages and disadvantages, communication cost, asymptotic error bounds, and computational overhead of the aforementioned methods. The communication cost refers to the expense of data transmission from each user to the data collector, which we approximate as being proportional to the amount of data. In the asymptotic error bounds, $n$ denotes the total number of users, $k$ denotes the number of attribute candidate values, $h$ represents the length of the Bloom Filter string, and $c$ represents the size of the output set in the $k$-Subset method. The computational overhead refers to the computational cost incurred by the data collector when aggregating user data, categorized into three levels: high, medium, and low.

### 5.2.2 Mean Estimation

For continuous data, the mean statistics query scenario is as follows: $n$ users each have a continuous sensitive attribute, with the value of user $u_i$ (where $1 \le i \le n$) for this attribute denoted as $v_i$. The data collector's task is to compute the mean of all values $v_i$ for these $n$ users, which is represented as $m = \frac{1}{n}\sum_{i=1}^{n} v_i$.

Under local differential privacy, the core idea behind mean statistics is to introduce positive or negative noise to individual values. By aggregating a large number of perturbed results, the noise can be effectively neutralized, ensuring that the statistical results meet certain usability thresholds. Two primary perturbation mechanisms are used for mean statistics in local differential privacy: the Laplace mechanism [2] and the randomized response mechanism [4]. The Laplace mechanism adds noise following a Laplace distribution to the values, ensuring the results satisfy $\varepsilon$-local differential privacy. In contrast, the randomized response mechanism first discretizes the continuous data and then applies the randomized response technique to perturb the data, also ensuring that the perturbed results satisfy $\varepsilon$-local differential privacy.

**Table 5.1** Comparison and analysis of frequency statistics methods under local differential privacy

| Method name | Advantages | Disadvantages | Communication cost | Asymptotic error bound | Computational overhead | Known candidate values |
|---|---|---|---|---|---|---|
| RAPPOR | Low publication error, high data usability | Requires consideration of Bloom Filter parameter settings | $O(h)$ | $O\left(\frac{k}{\varepsilon\sqrt{n}}\right)$ | High; additional regression computation | Yes |
| SHist | Sampling technique reduces communication cost | Query accuracy is unstable, computational cost is positively related to the number of users | $O(1)$ | $O\left(\frac{\sqrt{k\log k}}{\varepsilon\sqrt{n}}\right)$ | High; additional encoding and string matching | Yes |
| $k$-RR | No encoding and decoding process, simplifies data perturbation | Low data usability with low privacy budget | $O(1)$ | $O\left(\frac{\sqrt{k^3}}{\varepsilon\sqrt{n}}\right)$ | Low; only involves frequency statistics | Yes |
| O-RAPPOR | Hashing technique hides attribute candidate value list | Requires consideration of Bloom Filter parameter settings | $O(h)$ | $O\left(\frac{k}{\varepsilon\sqrt{n}}\right)$ | High; additional regression computation | No |
| O-RR | Hashing technique hides attribute candidate value list | Low data usability with low privacy budget | $O(1)$ | $O\left(\frac{\sqrt{k^3}}{\varepsilon\sqrt{n}}\right)$ | Low; only involves frequency statistics | No |
| $k$-Subset | Suitable for contingency table and other statistical queries | Additional error from single value frequency statistics | $O(1)$ | $O\left(\frac{k}{\varepsilon\sqrt{n}}\right)$ | Medium; needs to calculate element frequencies based on set frequencies | Yes |

The mean estimation method based on randomized response under local differential privacy was first proposed by Duchi et al. [14], and is commonly referred to as **MeanEst**. The core idea is to transform each $i$th tuple $t_i \in [-1, 1]^d$ in a $d$-dimensional dataset of $n$ tuples into a binary-valued tuple $t_i^* \in \{-B, B\}^d$, according to a specific probability distribution combined with randomized response, while ensuring that the final result is an unbiased estimator.

The scaling parameter $B$ depends solely on the privacy budget $\varepsilon$ and the data dimension $d$, and it grows exponentially with $d$. As a result, the method incurs

**Table 5.2** Comparative Analysis of Mean Estimation Methods under Local Differential Privacy

| Method name | Advantages | Disadvantages | Communication cost | Asymptotic error bound | Computational overhead |
|---|---|---|---|---|---|
| Laplace | Low sensitivity to the number of users in statistical results | Perturbed values may exceed data bounds | $O(d)$ | $O\left(\frac{2}{(d\varepsilon)^2}\right)$ | Low; only involves noise addition |
| MeanEst | Intuitive perturbation mechanism | High time and space complexity; suitable only for low-dimensional data; large deviation from original values | $O(d)$ | $O\left(\frac{\sqrt{d \log d}}{\varepsilon\sqrt{n}}\right)$ | High; requires enumeration over all variable combinations |
| Harmony | Low time complexity with small publication error and better data utility | Large deviation from original values | $O(d)$ | $O\left(\frac{\sqrt{d \log d}}{\varepsilon\sqrt{n}}\right)$ | Low; only involves mean estimation |

significant time and space overhead when applied to high-dimensional data, making it less suitable for such scenarios.

Building on the work of Duchi et al. [14], the follow-up study [15] proposed a simplified version of the MeanEst method, referred to as **Harmony**, which leverages sampling techniques to reduce communication costs. Specifically, for the $i$th input tuple $t_i \in [-1, 1]^d$, the perturbed output tuple is $t_i^* \in \left[-\frac{e^\varepsilon+1}{e^\varepsilon-1}d,\ 0,\ \frac{e^\varepsilon+1}{e^\varepsilon-1}d\right]^d$.

In the Harmony method, the output tuple is initialized as $t_i^* = \langle 0, 0, ..., 0\rangle$. Then, one dimension $j$ is randomly selected from the $d$ dimensions, and its value is set to either $\frac{e^\varepsilon+1}{e^\varepsilon-1}d$ or $-\frac{e^\varepsilon+1}{e^\varepsilon-1}d$, according to the following sampling rule:

$$P(t_i^*[A_j] = x) = \begin{cases} \frac{t_i[A_j]\cdot(e^\varepsilon-1)+e^\varepsilon+1}{2e^\varepsilon+2}, & x = \frac{e^\varepsilon+1}{e^\varepsilon-1}d \\ \frac{e^\varepsilon+1-t_i[A_j]\cdot(e^\varepsilon-1)}{2e^\varepsilon+2}, & x = -\frac{e^\varepsilon+1}{e^\varepsilon-1}d \end{cases}$$

In the Harmony method, each output tuple has a non-zero value in only one dimension. As a result, its communication cost is reduced to $1/d$ of that of the MeanEst method, while maintaining comparable accuracy in data publication.

In summary, the above discussion introduces mean estimation methods under local differential privacy. Table 5.2 presents a comparative analysis of the primary advantages and disadvantages, communication cost, asymptotic error bounds, and computational overhead for the methods discussed, assuming that each user uploads a numerical data tuple of length $d$.

## 5.3 Privacy Protection for Complex Datasets

With regard to query analysis for simple data types-such as frequency estimation for discrete or set-valued data and mean estimation for numerical data-local differential privacy has been extensively studied. However, with the rapid advancement of big data analytics, there is a growing focus on unstructured and complex data types.

Three major challenges arise in this context:

- Preserving data utility while maintaining inherent data correlations;
- Enhancing the generalizability of privacy protection methods across diverse data types;
- Improving the usability and interpretability of perturbed outputs.

To address these challenges, this section introduces privacy protection mechanisms tailored to three representative types of complex data: key-value data, graph data, and time-series data.

### *5.3.1 Key-Value Data Collection and Estimation*

Key-value data is a fundamental data type in big data analytics. The following examples illustrate common application scenarios:

- **Advertising Video Performance Analysis**: Advertisers target potential user groups through ad placements and evaluate campaign effectiveness by analyzing user interaction data. This data is typically represented as key-value pairs, where the key denotes a specific advertisement and the value indicates the duration a user viewed the corresponding video.
- **Mobile App Usage Analysis**: Mobile device manufacturers and third-party app developers often collect app usage data to improve service quality. For instance, daily active users (DAU) can be identified by optimizing system resource management (e.g., battery or memory usage). The usage data is structured as key-value pairs, where the key is a specific mobile application and the value is the user's screen time for that app.

In both scenarios, data collectors require access to user data for effective analysis. However, such data inherently carries privacy risks, including potential leakage of sensitive personal information such as user preferences or daily routines. To address these concerns under local differential privacy, the first dedicated solution for key-value data, *PrivKV*, was introduced in [16].

**1. Problem Definition**

This section introduces the relevant concepts and problem definitions. Let $\mathcal{K} = \{1, 2, \ldots, d\}$ denote a set of $d$ keys. Each key is associated with a continuous value in the range $[-1, 1]$. Let $\mathcal{U} = \{u_1, u_2, \ldots, u_n\}$ represent a set of $n$ users. Each user holds multiple key-value pairs. Specifically, the $i$th user possesses $l_i$ key-value pairs, denoted as:

$$S_i = \left\{ \langle k_j, v_j \rangle \,\middle|\, 1 \le j \le l_i,\ k_j \in \mathcal{K},\ v_j \in [-1, 1] \right\}.$$

The data collector aims to perform statistical analysis over the key-value data contributed by all users. In this context, we focus on two key statistics: frequency estimation and mean estimation, defined as follows:

- **(1) Frequency Estimation**: For any key $k \in \mathcal{K}$, its frequency $f_k$ denotes the proportion of users who possess at least one key-value pair with key $k$. Formally,

$$f_k = \frac{|\{u_i \mid \exists \langle k, v \rangle \in S_i\}|}{n}.$$

- **(2) Mean Estimation**: For any key $k \in \mathcal{K}$, its mean $m_k$ is the average of all values associated with key $k$ across all users. Formally,

$$m_k = \frac{\sum_{i=1}^{n} \sum_{\substack{j=1 \\ k_j = k}}^{l_i} v_j}{n \cdot f_k}.$$

**2. PrivKV: Benchmark Method for Key-Value Data Collection**

This section introduces **PrivKV**, a key-value data perturbation method under local differential privacy. PrivKV perturbs both keys and values simultaneously while maintaining the usability of data for frequency and mean estimation.

**(1) Correlated Perturbation of Key-Value Pairs**

Since both frequency and mean estimations depend on specific keys, a natural approach is to apply randomized response techniques to perturb the user's key set. To achieve this, it is first necessary to encode each user's key-value pair set.

As shown in Fig. 5.2, for user $u_i$'s original key-value pair set $S_i$, the encoded version is denoted as $S_i'$, which contains exactly $d$ key-value pairs. For each key $k_j \in \mathcal{K}$ , if the user's set $S_i$ includes the pair $\langle k_j, v_j \rangle$, then the $j$th entry in $S_i'$ is encoded as $\langle 1, v_j \rangle$; otherwise, it is set to $\langle 0, 0 \rangle$.

This encoding approach ensures three things. First, each user's key-value pair set has a consistent length after encoding. Second, the index of each key-value pair in the encoded vector implicitly represents the key. Third, the encoding retains all the presence and value information for every key a user holds.

After the above encoding, all keys are represented in a 0/1 format, so the randomized response technique [4] can be directly applied to perturb the keys to satisfy local differential privacy. Specifically, for each key in the 0/1 format, the randomized response technique keeps the value as 0/1 or flips it to 1/0. For each value in the key-value pair, its perturbation method is based on the perturbation result of the corresponding key, which includes the following four cases.

- $1 \rightarrow 1$: A key-value pair that exists both before and after perturbation, where the corresponding value is retained, i.e., $\langle 1, v \rangle \rightarrow \langle 1, v \rangle$.

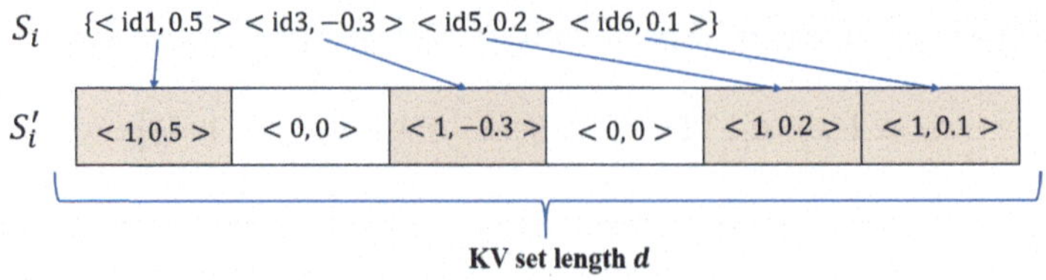


**Fig. 5.2** Key-value pair encoding

- $1 \rightarrow 0$: A key-value pair that existed before perturbation but disappears after perturbation, where the corresponding value should be set to 0 to indicate that the value does not exist, in order to avoid leaking information about the existence of the key-value pair before perturbation, i.e., $\langle 1, v\rangle \rightarrow \langle 0, 0\rangle$.
- $0 \rightarrow 0$: A key-value pair that did not exist before and after perturbation, where the entire key-value pair remains unchanged, i.e., $\langle 0, 0\rangle \rightarrow \langle 0, 0\rangle$.
- $0 \rightarrow 1$: A key-value pair that did not exist before but is newly added after perturbation, where a new value needs to be assigned. Since the user does not know the true value and has no background knowledge, the new value is directly randomly selected from the interval $[-1, 1]$ of the value domain.

The above correlated perturbation method perturbs both keys and values simultaneously, thus ensuring that the association between key-value pairs is not disrupted during the perturbation process. However, this perturbation method still has privacy issues. After the data collector receives the perturbed data sent by many users, they can distinguish between the true values (first case) and the newly assigned values (fourth case) with a high degree of confidence, especially when the data distribution of the true values is significantly different from the uniform distribution in the $[-1, 1]$ interval that the newly assigned values satisfy. Additionally, randomly selecting values from the $[-1, 1]$ interval for assignment, since the mean of these random values is 0, also affects the estimation of the true mean, causing the estimated value to deviate from the true value.

**(2) Perturbation of the Values in Key-Value Pairs**

To address the aforementioned privacy issues, an effective perturbation method is to perturb not only the keys but also the values in a way that satisfies local differential privacy, including both the true values (first case) and the newly assigned values (fourth case).

Based on the Harmony algorithm, PrivKV implements its improved algorithm, referred to as the Value Perturbation Primitive (VPP) algorithm. Compared to the Harmony algorithm, VPP has three main improvements. First, the correction operation for the perturbation results is uniformly centralized at the data collector's end, and the data collector only needs to correct the final mean statistics once, without having to correct each user's data individually, thereby reducing the computational overhead at the user end. Second, the Harmony algorithm needs to amplify the perturbed values by $d$ times in the correction operation to offset the error brought by the sampling operation on the user's key-value pair set. However, simply amplifying the statistical results by $d$ times will also introduce additional data sampling errors. To eliminate such errors, in the VPP algorithm, the data collector will accurately calculate the number of samples for each key and the number of times the key actually exists during sampling, which are used to statistically determine the final frequency and mean. Moreover, due to random errors, the Harmony algorithm may also generate data points outside the value range $[-1, 1]$ during the data perturbation and correction process. In light of this, VPP adds an additional step to correct outlier data points in the correction operation. Specifically, for $N$ users, the count results for keys with values of 0 or 1 must lie within the interval $[0, N]$, so VPP corrects counts less than 0 to 0 and counts greater than $N$ to $N$. The correction step for the correction results improves the accuracy of the statistical results, especially when the privacy budget is relatively small, where the improvement effect is more pronounced.

**(3) Local Perturbation Strategy for Key-Value Pairs**

Combining key perturbation and value perturbation algorithms results in a local perturbation protocol (LPP) for key-value pairs. To reduce the communication cost from $O(d)$ to $O(1)$, LPP employs a sampling method similar to SHist [11], where each user randomly samples one dimension from $d$ dimensions, denoted as $j$. If the user's key-value pair set $S_i$ contains the key-value pair $< k_j, v_j >$, then the value $v_j$ is first perturbed into $v^*$ using the VPP algorithm. Subsequently, based on randomized response technology, the encoded form $< 1, v^* >$ is perturbed, with a probability of $\frac{e^{\varepsilon_1}}{1+e^{\varepsilon_1}}$ to retain $< 1, v^* >$ and a probability of $\frac{1}{1+e^{\varepsilon_1}}$ to perturb it into $< 0, 0 >$. If the user's key-value pair set $S_i$ does not contain the key-value pair $< k_j, v_j >$, then a value $\tilde{m}$ is first randomly selected from the interval $[-1, 1]$. Then, based on the VPP algorithm, $\tilde{m}$ is perturbed into $v^*$, and subsequently, based on randomized response technology, the encoded form $< 0, 0 >$ of the key-value pair $< k_j, v_j >$ is perturbed. When the key 0 is flipped to 1, $v^*$ is used as the newly assigned value. In the LPP algorithm, the perturbation of values is based on the perturbation results of keys, thus ensuring the association between key-value pairs.

Based on the LPP algorithm, [16] designed the overall key-value data protection method PrivKV, which includes perturbation at the user end and correction at the data collector end. At the user end, each user perturbs their key-value pair set based on the LPP algorithm and then sends the sampled and perturbed results to the data collector. At the data collector end, after receiving the perturbed data from all users, the data collector first counts the frequency of each key to obtain the frequency estimation result. Mean estimation is more complex than frequency estimation. The data collector first counts the occurrences of 1 and $-1$ in the values corresponding to each key and then corrects this count. As mentioned above, the main improvement of the value perturbation algorithm VPP compared to Harmony is the correction operation of outlier data points at the data collector end, where outlier data points refer to count values greater than $N$ or less than 0, which should be corrected to $N$ or 0 accordingly.

## 5.3.2 Graph Data Collection and Estimation

Graph data, as a type of unstructured data, is widely used in scenarios such as social networks and knowledge graphs. Graph data analysis typically requires the computation of specific graph metrics, and this computation process may lead to privacy leakage. To protect user privacy, differential privacy technology usually has two approaches. The first is to generate a synthetic graph by simulating the characteristics of a real graph to estimate any graph data metrics, and the process of obtaining this synthetic graph meets certain privacy protection requirements [17]. The second is to design a solution for each specific graph data metric to estimate that metric [18]. The first approach provides a general solution that can be used to estimate any graph metric, but the data usability of the estimation results is generally low, mainly because the adjacency list information is lost in the synthetic graph. The second approach generally provides higher data usability but has low generality, meaning it is usually only applicable to a specific type of graph data and graph metric.

Existing methods are not satisfactory in terms of generality and data usability and are difficult to widely apply in practical graph data analysis tasks. To address this issue, this section introduces the Local Framework for Graph with Differentially Private Release (LF-GDPR) [19], which applies local differential privacy protection technology to the estimation of graph metrics in graph data analysis.

**1. Problem Definition**

This section first introduces the representation of graph data, followed by the formal definition of localized differential privacy techniques applied to graph data.

**(1) Representation of Graph Data**

A graph $G$ can be defined as $G = (V, E)$, where $V = \{1, 2, \dots, n\}$ denotes the set of nodes in the graph, and $n$ is the number of nodes. $E \subseteq V \times V$ represents the set of edges. For a node $i$, $d_i$ denotes its degree, and $\mathbf{B}_i = \{b_1, b_2, \dots, b_n\}$ denotes its adjacency vector. If there exists an edge between node $i$ and node $j$, i.e., $(i, j) \in E$, then $b_j = 1$; otherwise, $b_j = 0$. The adjacency vectors of all nodes in the graph together form the adjacency matrix of the graph, denoted as $M_{n \times n} = \{\mathbf{B}_1, \mathbf{B}_2, \dots, \mathbf{B}_n\}$.

**(2) Localized Differential Privacy for Graph Data**

Depending on the level of protection, localized differential privacy for graph data includes Node Local Differential Privacy (Node LDP) and Edge Local Differential Privacy (Edge LDP). Node LDP ensures that an adversary cannot determine whether any specific node exists in the graph based on the output of a privacy-preserving algorithm. Edge LDP ensures that an adversary cannot determine whether an edge exists between any two nodes based on the algorithm's output. Their formal definitions are given as follows.

**Definition 7** (*$\varepsilon$-Node Local Differential Privacy*) A privacy algorithm $\mathcal{A}$ satisfies $\varepsilon$-Node Local Differential Privacy if and only if for any two adjacency vectors $\mathbf{B}$ and $\mathbf{B}'$, and for any output $s$ of the algorithm $\mathcal{A}$, the following inequality holds:

$$\frac{Pr[\mathcal{A}(\mathbf{B}) = s]}{Pr[\mathcal{A}(\mathbf{B}') = s]} \leq e^{\varepsilon}$$

**Definition 8** (*$\varepsilon$-Edge Local Differential Privacy*) A privacy algorithm $\mathcal{A}$ satisfies $\varepsilon$-Edge Local Differential Privacy if and only if for any two adjacency vectors $\mathbf{B}$ and $\mathbf{B}'$ that differ by at most one bit, and for any output $s$ of the algorithm $\mathcal{A}$, the following inequality holds:

$$\frac{\Pr[M(\mathbf{B}) = s]}{\Pr[M(\mathbf{B}') = s]} \leq e^{\varepsilon}$$

Node Local Differential Privacy is a stricter privacy definition, and its data usability significantly decreases as the number of nodes increases. In contrast, Edge Local Differential Privacy moderately relaxes the privacy constraints, thereby enhancing the usability of the perturbed data. Despite the relaxed constraints, Edge Local Differential Privacy still provides strong protection against edge-level attacks in graph data, which is sufficient for many practical applications and yields high data utility-for instance, in social networks [18]. Similar to existing research [17], this chapter mainly focuses on defending against edge-level attacks, where the goal is to prevent an attacker from determining whether there is an edge between any two nodes.

**2. Graph Data Protection Framework: LF-GDPR**

The implementation process of the LF-GDPR (Local Framework for Graph Data with Differentially Private Release) is illustrated in Fig. 5.3.

First, the data collector specifies a target graph metric $F$ along with the overall privacy budget $\varepsilon$. Then, using a mapping function, the metric $F$ is expressed in terms of the adjacency matrix $\mathbf{M}$ and the degree vector $\mathbf{d}$, i.e., $F = \text{Map}(\mathbf{M}, \mathbf{d})$ (Step ①).

Next, LF-GDPR allocates the total privacy budget $\varepsilon$ into two components, $\varepsilon_1$ and $\varepsilon_2$, based on an optimal allocation strategy ($\varepsilon = \varepsilon_1 + \varepsilon_2$). Here, $\varepsilon_1$ is used for perturbing the adjacency vectors, and $\varepsilon_2$ is reserved for perturbing node degrees (Step ②).

Each user then locally perturbs their adjacency vector and node degree to satisfy $\varepsilon_1$-local differential privacy and $\varepsilon_2$-local differential privacy, respectively (Step ③).

According to the sequential composition property of local differential privacy, the perturbation algorithm executed by each node guarantees $\varepsilon$-local differential privacy. The primary challenge in this step arises from the inherent correlations between node degrees and edge connections. Specifically, for the adjacency vector, the $j$th entry of node $i$'s adjacency vector is equal to the $i$th entry of node $j$'s adjacency vector, due to the symmetry of undirected graphs. Similarly, the existence of an edge between nodes $i$ and $j$ simultaneously influences the degrees of both nodes.

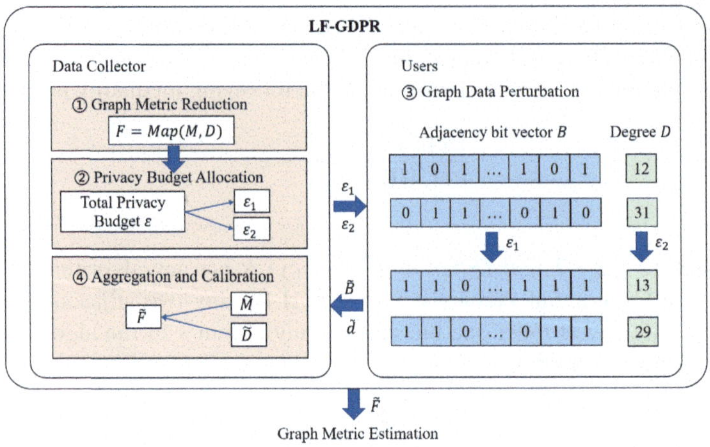


**Fig. 5.3** Graph data protection framework

Finally, after collecting the perturbed adjacency vectors and node degrees from all users, the data collector applies an aggregation algorithm-designed based on the original mapping function-to compute the target graph metric. A correction procedure is then applied to produce the final estimated value $\tilde{F}$ (Step ④), which can be used in downstream graph data analysis tasks.

### *5.3.3 Time Series Data Collection and Estimation*

Time-series data is widely used in a variety of application scenarios, such as health-care monitoring, path tracking, and Internet of Things (IoT) systems. Since much of this data is closely tied to individual behaviors, directly releasing it may lead to privacy breaches. Existing privacy-preserving time-series publishing algorithms generally protect privacy by perturbing the values of the data while preserving the original time order.

However, in many real-world situations, the integrity of the data values must be maintained to ensure usability, and privacy can instead be preserved by perturbing the time dimension. The following examples illustrate this point:

**Example 5-1** (Healthcare Monitoring): Devices such as the Apple Watch, Fitbit, and Omron HeartGuide continuously collect users' physiological data-such as heart rate and blood pressure-for the purpose of health monitoring. The accuracy of this data is critical for clinical diagnosis and thus should not be altered. Compared to the values themselves, the temporal dimension is generally less sensitive; therefore, sudden fluctuations in physiological signals can be hidden by perturbing the time series rather than the values.

**Example 5-2** (Path Tracking): Mobile applications often track users' trajectories to deliver targeted advertisements and personalized services. To accurately infer user preferences (e.g., shopping habits, entertainment, or fitness routines), it is important to retain the fidelity of location data. In contrast, the timing of user movements is often less sensitive, so privacy can be preserved by obfuscating the exact timestamps, thereby preventing real-time tracking without compromising the value data.

**Example 5-3** (IoT Systems): Many IoT systems-such as those used in smart homes and smart cities-deploy a wide range of sensors to monitor environmental parameters, including temperature, humidity, light, sound, and air quality. The accuracy of this sensor data is essential for the proper functioning of such systems and therefore must be preserved. Compared to the data values themselves, the timing of these sensor readings is generally less sensitive. As such, introducing a controlled delay in the time dimension can effectively prevent the exposure of users' real-time locations and activities.

Building on this insight, this section introduces the *temporal perturbation mechanism* [20], which ensures that the release of time-series data satisfies local differential privacy in the temporal dimension-referred to as temporal differential privacy (TDP), or $\varepsilon$-TDP. TDP guarantees that no adversary can reliably infer the true value at any specific point in time based on the published time-series data.

**1. Problem Definition** This section first presents the formal definition of Temporal Differential Privacy (TDP). Based on this definition, it then introduces the notion of *perturbation cost*, which quantifies the cost associated with temporally perturbing each data point.

**(1) Temporal Differential Privacy**

Let $S = \{S_{t_1}, S_{t_2}, \ldots, S_{t_n}, \ldots\}$ denote a time-series dataset defined over a temporal domain $T = \{t_1, t_2, \ldots, t_n, \ldots\}$, where the time series is assumed to be of infinite length. For simplicity, we assume that the timestamps in $T$ are evenly spaced, i.e., $t_2 - t_1 = \ldots = t_n - t_{n-1} = \ldots$. Under this assumption, the time series can be simplified as $S = \{S_1, S_2, \ldots, S_n, \ldots\}$.

Following the approach used in centralized differential privacy, we first introduce the concept of neighboring time-series datasets as a foundation for defining temporal differential privacy.

**Definition 9** (*Neighboring Time-Series Data*) Two time-series datasets $S$ and $S'$ are said to be neighboring if and only if there exist two timestamps $t_i$ and $t_j$ such that the following conditions are satisfied:

① $|i - j| \le k$;

② $S_i = S'_j$ and $S_j = S'_i$;

③ For any timestamp $t_l$ where $l \ne i$ and $l \ne j$, it holds that $S_l = S'_l$.

This definition reflects the temporal nature of the perturbation mechanism, where privacy is preserved by permuting values across time. Specifically, two neighboring datasets differ only by a swap of two values within a maximum time lag of $k$, where $k$ is a system-defined parameter representing the allowed delay in the publication of data values.

**Definition 10** (*Temporal Differential Privacy (TDP)*) Given a privacy budget $\varepsilon$, a privacy-preserving algorithm $\mathcal{A}$ satisfies $\varepsilon$-Temporal Differential Privacy ($\varepsilon$-TDP) if and only if, for any pair of neighboring time-series datasets $S$ and $S'$, and for any possible output $R$ of $\mathcal{A}$, the following condition holds:

$$\Pr(\mathcal{A}(S) = R) \leq e^{\varepsilon} \cdot \Pr(\mathcal{A}(S') = R)$$

Similar to traditional differential privacy, the level of privacy protection in Temporal Differential Privacy (TDP) is controlled by the parameter $\varepsilon$. When publishing time-series data, the objective of privacy-preserving methods is to perturb the real time-series data $\{S_1, S_2, \ldots, S_n, \ldots\}$ such that the resulting perturbed time-series data $\{R_1, R_2, \ldots, R_n, \ldots\}$ satisfies $\varepsilon$-Temporal Differential Privacy.

**(2) Definition of Perturbation Cost**

Given the original time-series data $S = \{S_1, S_2, \ldots, S_n, \ldots\}$ and the perturbed output time-series data $R = \{R_1, R_2, \ldots, R_n, \ldots\}$, along with the sliding window size $k$, this section defines the perturbation cost of the output $R$, considering the following factors: value loss, repetition, emptiness, and delay.

- **Missing Cost** $C_M$: If a value $S_i$ does not appear in the entire sliding window $\{R_i, R_{i+1}, \ldots, R_{i+k-1}\}$ starting from $R_i$, it indicates that the value $S_i$ is missing. The cost associated with this missing value is denoted by $M$.
- **Repetition Cost** $C_N$: If a value $S_i$ appears multiple times within the sliding window $\{R_i, R_{i+1}, \ldots, R_{i+k-1}\}$ starting from $R_i$, a repetition cost is incurred. The cost for each repeated occurrence of a value is denoted by $N$.
- **Empty Cost** $C_E$: If the output value $R_i$ at a given timestamp $t_i$ is empty (i.e., no value is assigned), an empty cost is applied. The empty cost for each empty timestamp is denoted by $E$.
- **Delay Cost** $C_D$: If a value $S_i$ is output at a later time $t_j$ (where $j > i$), a delay cost is incurred. The delay cost is given by $D(j - i)$, where $D$ is the delay cost per timestamp. To avoid double counting, delay costs take precedence over the other three costs. For instance, if a value is repeated, only the repetition cost is considered, and the delay cost is not counted again.

Based on this, there are three temporal perturbation mechanisms that perturb the temporal dimension of each value to satisfy differential privacy protection. The first two mechanisms are called the backward perturbation mechanism (BPM) and the forward perturbation mechanism (FPM). The backward perturbation mechanism refers to the fact that each value to be published is randomly selected from the past $k$ timestamps, while the forward perturbation mechanism means that each value in the original time-series data is randomly assigned to one of the next $k$ timestamps for publication. Since both mechanisms have issues with value loss, repetition, and emptiness, we further introduce a third threshold mechanism that not only solves the problems of value loss, repetition, and emptiness but also alleviates the problem of value delay.

Given a threshold $c_0$, to ensure that the available space for each value stably remains above $c_0$, a "conflict avoidance" constraint can be designed based on the forward perturbation mechanism: for the assignment of value $S_i$, if the current available space size $c > c_0$, then $S_i$ will be randomly assigned to any of the current available timestamps; if $c = c_0$, then first determine whether the current output value $R_i$ is empty. If $R_i$ is empty, then directly assign $S_i$ to $R_i$; otherwise, randomly assign $S_i$ to any of the timestamps in the current available space. Clearly, the above constraint ensures that the available space will not further decrease once it drops from $k$ to $c_0$.

Before assigning the value $S_i$, first calculate the size of the current available space $c$. If $c > c_0$, then randomly assign it to any empty timestamp within the sliding window. If $c = c_0$ and $R_i$ is empty, then assign it to $R_i$; otherwise, randomly select an empty timestamp within the current sliding window for assignment. For any timestamp $t_i$, the algorithm outputs the value $R_i$ immediately after assigning the value $S_i$. Clearly, at this time, $R_i$ may come from any of $\{R_{i-k+1}, R_{i-k+2}, \ldots, R_i\}$.

To ensure that the perturbation mechanism satisfies $\varepsilon$-temporal differential privacy, it is necessary to ensure that the ratio of any two assignment probabilities within the sliding window is less than $e^{\varepsilon/2}$.

## 5.4 Summary

This chapter first elaborates on the fundamental principles of local differential privacy and analyzes its similarities and differences with traditional centralized differential privacy. It then focuses on the applications of local differential privacy in simple datasets, highlighting two basic queries: frequency statistics and mean statistics. For the applications of local differential privacy in complex datasets, it addresses the challenges of data correlation, method generality, and data usability, and provides detailed introductions to three types of problems: key-value data collection, graph data collection, and time-series data collection. Future research directions may include studies on hybrid models based on both local and centralized differential privacy, interactive queries and analysis based on local differential privacy, and high-dimensional data analysis based on local differential privacy.

## References

1. DUCHI J C, JORDAN M I, WAINWRIGHT M J. Local privacy, data processing inequalities, and statistical minimax rates[EB/OL]. (2013-02-13)[2022-08-01]. https://arxiv.org/pdf/1302.3203.pdf
2. DWORK C, MCSHERRY F, NISSIM K, et al. Calibrating noise to sensitivity in private data analysis[C]//Proceedings of Theory of cryptography conference. Berlin: Springer, 2006: 265–284.

3. MCSHERRY F, TALWAR K. Mechanism design via differential privacy[C]//Proceedings of 48th Annual IEEE Symposium on Foundations of Computer Science (FOCS'07). Piscataway, NJ: IEEE, 2007: 94–103.
4. WARNER S L. Randomized response: A survey technique for eliminating evasive answer bias[J]. Journal of the American Statistical Association, 1965, 60(309): 63–69.
5. CHEN R, LI H, QIN A K, et al. Private spatial data aggregation in the local setting[C]//Proceedings of IEEE 32nd International Conference on Data Engineering (ICDE). Piscataway, NJ: IEEE, 2016: 289–300.
6. KIM J W, KIM D H, JANG B. Application of local differential privacy to collection of indoor positioning data[J]. Ieee Access, 2018, 6: 4276–4286.
7. KAIROUZ P, OH S, VISWANATH P. Extremal mechanisms for local differential privacy[J]. The Journal of Machine Learning Research, 2016, 17(1): 492–542.
8. ERLINGSSON Ú, PIHUR V, KOROLOVA A. Rappor: Randomized aggregatable privacy-preserving ordinal response[C]//Proceedings of the 2014 ACM SIGSAC conference on computer and communications security. New York, NY: ACM, 2014: 1054–1067.
9. BLOOM B H. Space/time trade-offs in hash coding with allowable errors[J]. Communications of the ACM, 1970, 13(7): 422–426.
10. TIBSHIRANI R. Regression shrinkage and selection via the lasso[J]. Journal of the Royal Statistical Society: Series B (Methodological), 1996, 58(1): 267–288.
11. BASSILY R, SMITH A. Local, private, efficient protocols for succinct histograms[C]//Proceedings of the forty-seventh annual ACM symposium on Theory of computing. New York, NY: ACM, 2015: 127–135.
12. KAIROUZ P, BONAWITZ K, RAMAGE D. Discrete distribution estimation under local privacy[C]//Proceedings of International Conference on Machine Learning. [S.l.]: PMLR, 2016: 2436–2444.
13. WANG S, HUANG L, WANG P, et al. Mutual information optimally local private discrete distribution estimation[EB/OL]. (2016-07-27)[2022-08-01]. https://arxiv.org/pdf/1607.08025.pdf
14. DUCHI J C, JORDAN M I, WAINWRIGHT M J. Privacy aware learning[J]. Journal of the ACM (JACM), 2014, 61(6): 1–57.
15. DUCHI J C, JORDAN M I, WAINWRIGHT M J. Minimax optimal procedures for locally private estimation[J]. Journal of the American Statistical Association, 2018, 113(521): 182–201.
16. YE Q, HU H, MENG X, et al. PrivKV: Key-value data collection with local differential privacy[C]//Proceedings of IEEE Symposium on Security and Privacy (SP). Piscataway, NJ: IEEE, 2019: 317–331.
17. QIN Z, YU T, YANG Y, et al. Generating synthetic decentralized social graphs with local differential privacy[C]//Proceedings of the 2017 ACM SIGSAC Conference on Computer and Communications Security. New York, NY: ACM, 2017: 425–438.
18. KASIVISWANATHAN S P, NISSIM K, RASKHODNIKOVA S, et al. Analyzing graphs with node differential privacy[C]//Proceedings of Theory of Cryptography Conference. Berlin: Springer, 2013: 457–476.
19. YE Q, HU H, AU M H, et al. LF-GDPR: A framework for estimating graph metrics with local differential privacy[J]. IEEE Transactions on Knowledge and Data Engineering, 2020.
20. YE Q, HU H, LI N, et al. Beyond value perturbation: Local differential privacy in the temporal setting[C]//Proceedings of IEEE INFOCOM 2021-IEEE Conference on Computer Communications. Piscataway, NJ: IEEE, 2021: 1–10.

# Chapter 6
# Hybrid Differential Privacy

The above sections introduce the definitions and methods of two types of differential privacy: centralized and local. The essence of both approaches is to perturb data to ensure that the computation results satisfy the quantified privacy guarantees of differential privacy. However, perturbation inevitably impacts data usability. Local differential privacy (LDP), which perturbs data on the user's side, introduces more noise, resulting in lower usability compared to centralized differential privacy (CDP), which only perturbs the final computation results. The usability of LDP methods is typically reduced by a factor of $O(\sqrt{n})$.

Therefore, this chapter focuses on the trade-off between privacy and usability in differential privacy methods and explores the practical implementation of differential privacy.

There are two primary approaches to enhancing the practicality of differential privacy. The first is to improve the methods themselves by integrating non-perturbation randomization techniques—such as sampling and shuffling—into existing mechanisms, thereby achieving **privacy amplification**. This allows the data to be perturbed less while still satisfying a given privacy guarantee. The second is to combine differential privacy with cryptographic methods, which can ensure full usability of the computation results. Since cryptographic protocols often come with high computational or communication costs, we introduce two concepts: "C4DP" (Cryptography for Differential Privacy) and "DP4C" (Differential Privacy for Cryptography). "C4DP" refers to using cryptographic tools to improve the usability of differentially private computations. "DP4C," on the other hand, means leveraging differential privacy to improve the efficiency or performance of cryptographic protocols. Combining both approaches enhances practicality from different angles.

Finally, this chapter introduces a practical framework that has attracted wide attention in recent years: the Encode-Shuffle-Analyze (ESA) framework. Proposed by Andrea Bittau and Ulfar Erlingsson at Google, this framework incorporates both types of practicality-enhancing methods discussed above, aiming to strike a better balance between data privacy and usability.



X. Meng, *Data Privacy and Data Governance*, Big Data Management,
https://doi.org/10.1007/978-981-95-5787-5_6

## 6.1 Introduction

Differential privacy, which is widely applied today, is often regarded as the "gold standard" for privacy. It protects users' personal information contained in datasets and in the results derived from computations on these datasets by perturbing the data—that is, it ensures *privacy of the results*. However, this distortion of the original data inevitably affects the accuracy and utility of the computation outcomes. Therefore, striking a balance between data privacy and data usability is a core issue in the study of differential privacy mechanisms.

As reviewed in Chaps. 4 and 5 of this book, centralized differential privacy (CDP) and local differential privacy (LDP) differ significantly in their security assumptions and noise-adding strategies, which in turn leads to notable differences in the privacy-utility trade-off of their outputs. CDP assumes the existence of a trusted third party to which the original data is submitted. This party adds noise to the final computation results. This model works well for both small datasets and massive-scale data, typically requiring less noise, thereby achieving high utility in practice. However, its privacy guarantee depends on the assumption that the third party is indeed trustworthy—a condition often hard to satisfy in real-world settings.

In contrast, LDP allows each individual user to perturb their data locally without trusting any external entity. However, this results in an accumulation of noise across the entire system, significantly degrading usability. Under the same privacy parameter $\varepsilon$, for example, to perform frequency estimation (i.e., histogram estimation), LDP mechanisms require $O(\sqrt{n})$ times more noise than CDP mechanisms, thereby reducing the utility by a factor of $O(\sqrt{n})$.

In pursuit of a better privacy-utility balance, researchers seek approaches that minimize perturbation to the original data values without compromising privacy. Here, privacy is measured using $\varepsilon$ or $(\varepsilon, \delta)$-differential privacy. In this chapter, the term "differential privacy" refers broadly to the privacy guarantee itself, not specifically to the perturbation-based mechanisms discussed in Chaps. 4 and 5. Mechanisms aimed at enhancing both privacy and utility fall into two main categories:

The first category focuses on augmenting existing perturbation-based approaches with randomization techniques such as secondary sampling and anonymization to achieve **privacy amplification**. This term refers to the improvement in privacy guarantees, typically resulting in a smaller effective privacy parameter $\varepsilon$, without directly modifying the numerical data values—thus preserving both privacy and utility.

The second category involves integrating differential privacy with cryptographic methods [1]. Cryptographic techniques, such as homomorphic encryption, ensure that the computation process itself does not leak any private information, allowing users to obtain accurate results while keeping the underlying data secure—this is known as *process security*. Applying these techniques to differential privacy enables secure and accurate intermediate computations, enhancing result utility while maintaining strong privacy. This hybrid method is termed **Cryptography for Differential Privacy** (C4DP). However, due to the high computational and communication costs of many cryptographic protocols, an alternative strategy is to apply differential privacy principles to cryptographic systems. This approach, known as **Differential Privacy for Cryptography** (DP4C), aims to reduce overhead and improve the efficiency of privacy-preserving cryptographic protocols.

This chapter provides an overview of the two categories of methods that enhance the practicality of differential privacy. In addition, it introduces a widely studied and practical framework known as the *Encode-Shuffle-Analyze (ESA)* framework. Proposed by Andrea Bittau and Ulfar Erlingsson at Google, ESA integrates secure cryptographic shuffling protocols with perturbation mechanisms by incorporating a semi-honest third party. Through a rigorous analysis of its privacy amplification properties, ESA satisfies formal definitions of differential privacy.

Compared with traditional centralized and local differential privacy schemes, ESA strikes a balance between the high utility of centralized approaches and the strong privacy guarantees of local methods. Furthermore, the framework is easy to deploy and can be layered directly on top of existing local differential privacy systems. Owing to its effectiveness and practicality, ESA has attracted significant interest from major technology companies such as Google and Apple, and it represents the current state-of-the-art in real-world differential privacy deployment.

## 6.2 Privacy and Security

This section introduces the second category of approaches, which integrate differential privacy (DP) with cryptographic techniques. We first present the C4DP method, which leverages cryptography to enhance the utility of differentially private results. While C4DP improves output accuracy, the computational and communication overhead of cryptographic protocols can significantly affect the performance of complex analytical tasks, making them less suitable for large-scale data collection, analysis, and deployment.

To address these limitations, researchers have proposed the DP4C method, which incorporates differential privacy perturbation techniques into cryptographic protocols. This approach reduces computational and communication costs while maintaining robust privacy guarantees.

### *6.2.1 Cryptography for Differential Privacy*

To address the challenge of balancing privacy and utility in differential privacy (DP), researchers have proposed incorporating cryptographic techniques to enhance DP mechanisms. We refer to this class of approaches as "Cryptography for Differential Privacy" (C4DP), defined as follows:

**Definition 11** (*Cryptography for Differential Privacy (C4DP)*) The integration of cryptographic techniques into differential privacy mechanisms to improve both privacy protection and result utility, where the final output continues to satisfy the $(\varepsilon, \delta)$-differential privacy guarantee.

It is important to emphasize that, although cryptographic methods are used to enhance differential privacy, the final output is not necessarily lossless as in standard secure cryptographic protocols. Instead, the output must still conform to the probabilistic privacy guarantees defined by differential privacy.

To achieve this objective, the most straightforward strategy is to replace the trusted third party typically assumed in centralized differential privacy (CDP) with a semi-honest third party using secure computation protocols. In this approach, all computations performed by the third party are executed over encrypted data, thereby enhancing system-level privacy. We refer to this as *Improving Differential Privacy with Secure Computation*.

Alternatively, in the context of local differential privacy (LDP), we can incorporate secure shuffling operations to fully anonymize the locally perturbed user data. By leveraging the combined privacy amplification effects of shuffling and differential privacy, this approach improves the accuracy of the final output. We refer to this method as *Improving Differential Privacy with Secure Shuffling*.

We provide a high-level comparison of these two C4DP approaches against standard centralized and local differential privacy mechanisms in Fig. 6.1. From left to right, the figure illustrates an increasing trend in output utility, accompanied by increasingly stringent security assumptions. Under the same $\varepsilon$-differential privacy guarantee, cryptography-supported differential privacy methods offer a middle ground between CDP and LDP in terms of both data privacy and result usability, thereby achieving a more balanced trade-off. In the following subsections, we provide detailed explanations of these two approaches.

**1. Enhanced Methods Based on Secure Computation**

The method of enhancing differential privacy through secure computation builds upon the framework and principles of centralized differential privacy. It utilizes cryptographic techniques that ensure the *security of the computation process* to replace the trusted third party with an untrusted (typically semi-honest) party. All plain-

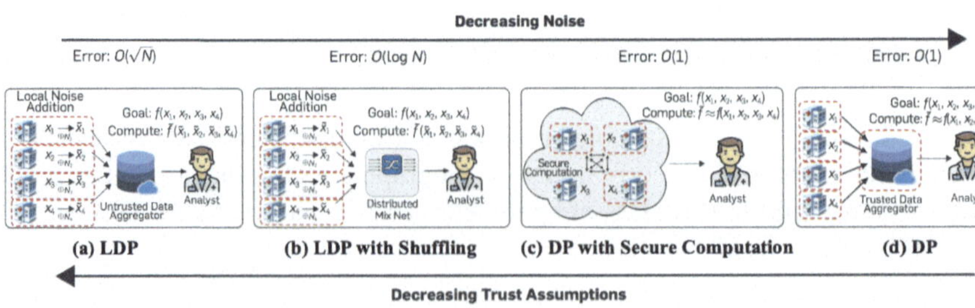


**Fig. 6.1** Comparison of different DP methods

text operations originally performed by this trusted party are substituted with secure ciphertext computations. In doing so, the insecure computation process is merely replaced by secure computation, while the error in the final result remains equivalent to that of centralized differential privacy. As a result, this approach strengthens privacy protection while preserving the utility level of state-of-the-art differential privacy methods.

The specific secure computation techniques used—such as homomorphic encryption or secure multi-party computation—must be chosen based on the nature of the research problem and the practical deployment scenario. However, this requirement also reveals a key limitation of the approach: its lack of generality. Each computation task requires the design of a tailored secure protocol along with a formal security proof. Consequently, a range of differential privacy mechanisms based on secure computation have been proposed to support various data query and analysis tasks. This section illustrates how secure computation can improve differential privacy through the example of DJoin [8].

**Case Scenario**. Suppose participants Alice and Bob each possess a private dataset, and they wish to compute the size of the intersection of their datasets while preserving the privacy of the result–that is, ensuring that it satisfies differential privacy. This operation is a fundamental step in privacy-preserving SQL queries and is particularly essential in join operations.

**Standard Differential Privacy Approach**. A straightforward way to achieve differential privacy in this setting is for Alice and Bob to submit their data to a trusted third party, who then computes the intersection size and adds noise to the result according to a differential privacy mechanism. Although this approach protects the privacy of the final output for Alice and Bob, it exposes their raw data to the third party. In practice, it is often unrealistic to assume the existence of a fully trustworthy third party.

**DJoin: A Differential Privacy Method Based on Secure Computation**. To address this limitation, the DJoin protocol employs secure two-party computation to compute the intersection between Alice's and Bob's datasets. This protocol ensures that neither party learns any information about the other's data, and it eliminates the need for a trusted third party. While secure computation alone does not provide differential privacy guarantees, DJoin incorporates differentially private noise into the secure computation process, thereby ensuring that the final output satisfies differential privacy.

The detailed algorithmic process of the DJoin protocol is illustrated in Fig. 6.2, and is described as follows. First, Alice constructs a polynomial over a finite field whose roots correspond to the elements in her dataset. She then homomorphically encrypts the polynomial's coefficients and sends them, along with the public key $pk$, to Bob.

Upon receiving the encrypted coefficients, Bob evaluates the encrypted polynomial at each of his input values. For each evaluation, he multiplies the result by a newly generated random scalar. The number of zero outputs from this evaluation corresponds to the true size of the intersection between Alice's and Bob's datasets.

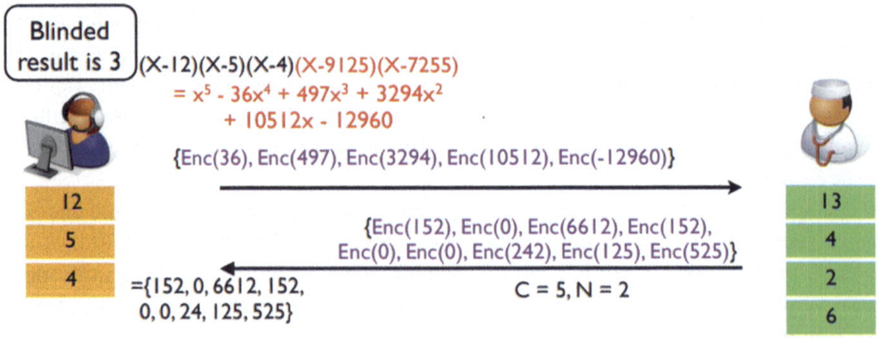


**Fig. 6.2** DJoin: a differential privacy method based on cryptographic computation

To achieve differential privacy, Bob adds a certain number of encrypted zero values to the result. The amount of noise added is calibrated to satisfy the desired differential privacy guarantee. Bob then randomly shuffles the combined true and noisy results and sends them to Alice.

After decrypting and tallying the received values, Alice also adds a number of differentially private zero values, shuffles the results again, and sends them back to Bob. In this protocol, both parties independently inject noise to ensure differential privacy. Since the noise is added directly to the result (similar to centralized differential privacy approaches), the final output can maintain high utility, with an error on the order of $O(1)$.

**2. A Differential Privacy Method Based on Secure Shuffling**

Improving differential privacy with secure shuffling—also known as the shuffled differential privacy method—builds on the framework and methodology of local differential privacy by introducing a semi-honest third party capable of executing a secure shuffling protocol. This third party securely shuffles the data that users have already perturbed locally. Through this shuffling operation, users achieve complete anonymity, making it difficult for the final data analyst to trace any data back to its source. As a result, the output is protected by both local differential privacy and anonymity, thereby achieving what is known as privacy amplification.

A representative approach is the ESA framework, proposed by Andrea Bittau and Ulfar Erlingsson from Google in 2017 [9], along with its implementation in the Prochlo system. This framework can be understood as adding a shuffler component to the local differential privacy pipeline, as illustrated in Fig. 6.3. In this setup, the shuffler refers to a semi-honest third-party server that collects encrypted and perturbed data from users over a designated time window. It then removes any metadata (such as IP addresses and timestamps) and thoroughly randomizes the order of these records using a secure shuffling protocol to ensure complete anonymity.

To better illustrate how shuffled differential privacy enhances data utility, we introduce a representative case example in the next section.

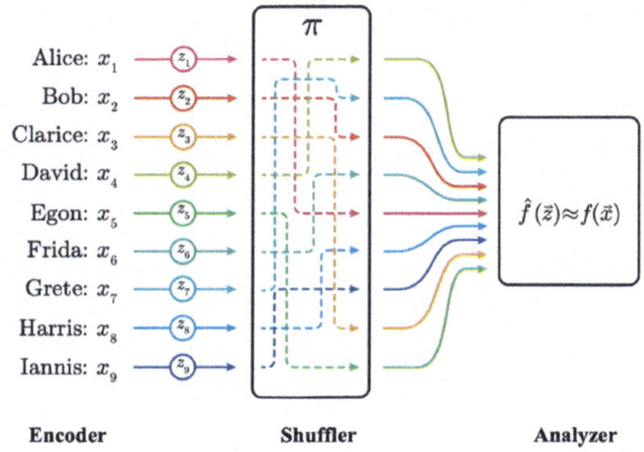


**Fig. 6.3** ESA: shuffle-based differential privacy method

**Case Scenario**: Suppose each user holds a value $x_i \in \{1, 2, \ldots, 100\}$, where each number represents an application ID indicating whether the user has used a specific app (e.g., a dating app). Since the use of such apps may disclose sensitive personal information, such as relationship status, users are reluctant to directly share their data. However, data analysts (e.g., system developers or app operators) are interested in aggregating the number of users who use a particular app.

**Local Differential Privacy Method**: As discussed in previous sections, one can employ the randomized response technique to perturb the data locally. In this approach, each user reports their true value with probability $\frac{e^{\varepsilon}}{e^{\varepsilon}+99}$, and any other value in the domain with equal probability $\frac{1}{e^{\varepsilon}+99}$.

**Shuffled Differential Privacy Method**: In this approach, we still adopt the randomized response mechanism to perturb user data. However, thanks to the introduction of a secure shuffling mechanism, the final computational result benefits from a privacy amplification effect, as discussed in Sect. 6.3.2. Specifically, we can assign a higher probability to reporting the true value and a lower probability to reporting other values, while still maintaining $\varepsilon$-differential privacy for the overall result.

To illustrate this with a concrete example, suppose there are 100,000 users, and we aim for the final result to satisfy $\varepsilon = 0.5$ differential privacy. Under the local differential privacy setting, each user reports their true value with a probability of 24.49% after perturbation. In contrast, under the shuffled differential privacy model, according to Theorem 8, the probability of reporting the true value increases dramatically to 99.84%. This clearly demonstrates that shuffled differential privacy introduces significantly less noise, thereby improving the utility of the result.

We can intuitively understand how shuffling leads to privacy amplification by examining the ESA framework: the data analyst observes only the shuffled, anonymized dataset $\{x_1', x_2', \ldots, x_n'\}$, where the perturbed random values are indistinguishably mixed with the true values. The actual number of true values follows a binomial distribution. This mechanism provides a privacy amplification effect similar to that of uniform subsampling, reducing the estimation error to $O(\log n)$.

### 6.2.2 *Differential Privacy for Cryptography*

The growing popularity of differential privacy methods is largely due to their suitability for large-scale data analysis and processing. However, one of the main challenges in combining cryptographic protocols with differential privacy lies in the high computational and communication overhead of cryptographic techniques, which can significantly hinder system performance. To address this issue, a body of research has emerged that explores how differential privacy can be leveraged to enhance the efficiency of cryptographic protocols. We categorize and define these methods under the term **Differential Privacy for Cryptography (DP4C)** as follows:

**Definition 12** (*Differential Privacy for Cryptography (DP4C)*) Introducing differential privacy into cryptographic protocols to reduce their computational and communication overhead, ensuring that intermediate results satisfy differential privacy and are resistant to inference attacks.

It is important to emphasize that applying differential privacy to improve cryptographic protocols does not guarantee the same level of absolute security as traditional cryptographic approaches. Rather, it ensures that intermediate outputs meet differential privacy guarantees. While this may not prevent all forms of attack, it is sufficient to protect against inference threats and significantly enhances practical performance, making the protocols more applicable to real-world scenarios.

To fully understand this issue, it is important to have some background knowledge about cryptographic protocols. In secure computation or communication protocols based on cryptography, simply encrypting data is not sufficient to guarantee the security of the entire protocol, regardless of how secure the encryption algorithm is. For instance, if encrypted data are stored in a database, they are written to disk one by one. Although an attacker cannot observe the plaintext content during this process, they may still infer sensitive information from the data access patterns. For example, if a specific piece of data is written five times in succession, while others are written only once, the attacker may infer which encrypted record corresponds to the specific data, leading to an inference attack.

To mitigate such inference attacks, cryptographic protocols typically introduce fake ciphertexts during secure computation to obscure the size of intermediate results. Similarly, in secure communication, dummy messages may be introduced to conceal communication patterns. Building on this idea, researchers have proposed two methods: ciphertext padding via perturbation and virtual communication via perturbation. Both approaches ensure that the sizes of intermediate results satisfy differential privacy, eliminating the need to pad up to the maximum possible size as in traditional secure protocols. Since every padded ciphertext must undergo the same computation as real data, these methods can reduce overall computational and communication overhead. In the following, we will explain each of these two approaches in detail.

**1. Improving Ciphertext Padding with Perturbation**

The core idea behind improving ciphertext padding with perturbation is to insert dummy data such that the size of intermediate results during ciphertext computations satisfies differential privacy, thereby defending against inference attacks. To illustrate how this method is applied, we take Shrinkwrap [10] as a representative example.

**Case Scenario**: Executing secure SQL queries on encrypted databases. For example, consider the query: "the number of patients with heart disease who have taken aspirin." Although all the data involved are encrypted, an attacker can still infer sensitive information by observing the sizes of intermediate results during query execution. As shown in the query plan tree in Fig. 6.4a, unprotected selection and join operations can reveal, for instance, the number of patients with heart disease or those who have taken aspirin, simply based on how much data is processed at each stage.

**Secure Ciphertext Computation Method**: To conceal the selectivity of each operation (e.g., selection, join, projection), it is necessary to add dummy ciphertexts–ciphertexts with empty plaintexts—so that the result of each query step is padded to its maximum possible size, which equals the size of the input data. As shown in the query plan tree in Fig. 6.4a, assume that the number of tuples in the input tables "diagnosis", "medication," and "demographic" is $N$. To obscure the selectivity rate, the result of the selection operation $\sigma_{diag=hd}$ must also be padded to size $N$. All intermediate results follow the same rule, leading to a final output size of $N^3$. If the actual selectivity is only 0.01%, then this padding results in 1000 times more encrypted data, drastically increasing the computational overhead.

**Differential Privacy-Based Ciphertext Computation Method**: The Shrinkwrap protocol incorporates differential privacy to mitigate this overhead. Instead of padding every result to the maximum size, each operation injects Laplace noise in accordance with the differential privacy mechanism—specifically, by adding a number of fake ciphertexts sampled from a Laplace distribution. In practice, the size of the noisy output is calculated by adding Laplace noise to the true intermediate result size, and this determines how many fake ciphertexts are appended. Although this approach does not guarantee absolute security, it provides a rigorous differential privacy guarantee that prevents adversaries from precisely inferring intermediate result sizes. As illustrated in Fig. 6.4c, this significantly reduces the overall computational cost of secure query execution.

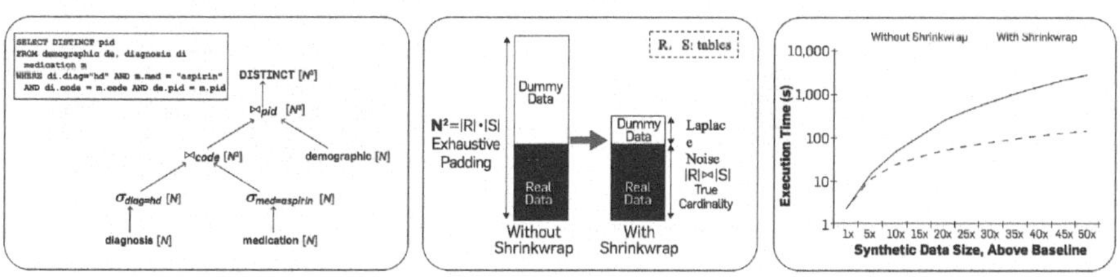


(a) Encrypted query syntax tree (b) Intermediate results with DP (c) Efficiency

**Fig. 6.4** Shrinkwrap: secure SQL query

**2. Improving Virtual Communication with Perturbation**
The basic idea of improving virtual communication with perturbation is to add fake communication messages such that the total volume of communication satisfies differential privacy guarantees. This helps conceal the actual number of real communications and resists inference attacks. We illustrate this method using the example of Vuvuzela [11].

**Case Scenario**: Vuvuzela is a secure, anonymous messaging network, as illustrated in Fig. 6.5a. When using this network, an adversary should not be able to distinguish whether "Alice is not communicating with anyone", "Alice is communicating with Bob", or "Alice is communicating with Charlie" based on observable network behavior.

The Vuvuzela network consists of $n$ servers $s_i$ and several "dead drops." Each server $s_i$ receives encrypted messages from users, shuffles the order of these messages to hide the linkage between messages and senders, and then forwards them to the next server $s_{i+1}$. Eventually, the messages arrive at the intended "dead drop." Only legitimate users can retrieve messages from a dead drop, so communicating users must agree on a shared dead drop to exchange messages. However, an adversary may infer communication by simply observing the number of messages processed at a dead drop during a given time interval. For instance, if the number of messages is even, it suggests that communication is occurring between users; if the number is odd, it may indicate that no real communication is taking place—thus enabling an inference attack.

**Secure Communication Protocol**: To protect users' communication privacy, both users who are actively communicating and those who are not send messages to the "dead drop" at each time interval. This masks users' communication status by inflating the total volume of communications through virtual messages. However, this approach comes at the cost of significantly increased communication overhead.

**Differential Privacy-Based Secure Communication Method**: Differential privacy offers a more efficient way to determine the amount of virtual communication needed. At each moment, the actual number of communications is first determined, and then noise drawn from a differential privacy mechanism is added to this count. Based on the perturbed total, a corresponding number of virtual messages are

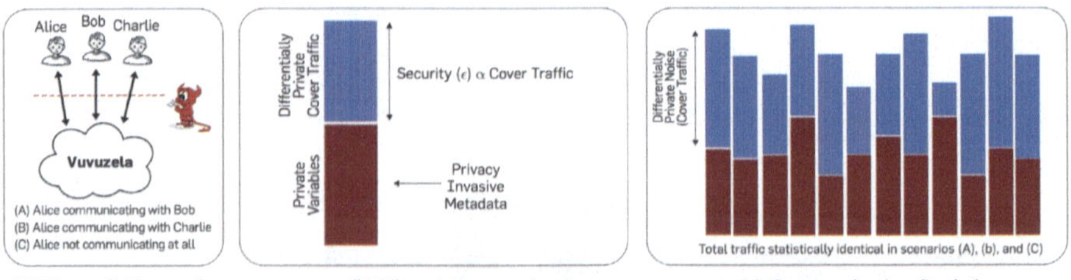


(a) Vuvuzela Protocol (b) Virtual Communication (c) Communication Statistics

**Fig. 6.5** Vuvuzela: a secure communication protocol

generated. As shown in Fig. 6.5c, this method effectively conceals communication patterns at the "dead drop," thereby preventing attackers from inferring users' communication status.

## 6.3 Privacy Amplification

This section introduces the first category of methods for enhancing the practicality of differential privacy—privacy amplification techniques and their underlying theoretical foundations. Privacy amplification refers to strategies that improve the privacy guarantees of a differential privacy mechanism through additional randomization operations. It is important to note that the techniques employed for privacy amplification, such as uniform random sampling and anonymization, do not themselves satisfy differential privacy. Rather, they amplify the privacy level when used in conjunction with a differential privacy mechanism.

In particular, this section focuses on two widely studied privacy amplification techniques: amplification by subsampling [2] and amplification by shuffling [3–5]. These methods are introduced in detail, including their formal guarantees, practical implementations, and privacy bounds.

Additionally, the section provides a brief overview of other emerging privacy amplification techniques, such as those based on iterative procedures [6] and randomized user check-ins [7].

For clarity, we assume the existence of a baseline mechanism $\mathcal{M}$ that satisfies $(\varepsilon_0, \delta_0)$-differential privacy. After applying privacy amplification operations, the mechanism's output satisfies an improved privacy guarantee of $(\varepsilon_{pa}, \delta_{pa})$, where $\varepsilon_{pa} \leq \varepsilon_0$. This reduction reflects the amplification effect, offering stronger privacy guarantees without increasing the amount of noise added.

### *6.3.1 Privacy Amplification via Subsampling*

Subsampling is one of the most fundamental and widely used privacy amplification methods, particularly in the context of centralized differential privacy. This method involves randomly selecting $m$ records from a dataset of $n$ items before applying random perturbation, thereby amplifying the privacy guarantee. Based on the literature [2], this section presents Theorem 6 along with its proof.

**Theorem 6** (Privacy Amplification via Subsampling) *Given a dataset $x \in \mathcal{X}^n$, let $m \in \{0, 1, \dots, n\}$, and let $\bar{x} \in \mathcal{X}^m$ denote a randomly sampled subset of $m$ records from $x$. Suppose $M : \mathcal{X}^m \to \mathcal{R}^m$ is a randomized algorithm that satisfies $(\varepsilon, \delta)$-differential privacy. Define algorithm $M'(x) : \mathcal{X}^n \to \mathcal{R}^m$ as performing perturbation on the random subset $\bar{x}$, that is, $M' = M(\bar{x})$. Then, the algorithm $M'(x)$ satisfies $\left(\frac{(e^{\varepsilon}-1)m}{n}, \frac{\delta m}{n}\right)$-differential privacy.*

***Proof*** Let $T \subseteq \{1, \ldots, n\}$ denote the set of indices corresponding to the randomly selected subset of size $m$. The randomness of the algorithm $M'$ thus includes both the randomness from the choice of $T$ and the internal randomness of the algorithm $M$. Let $\tilde{x}$ and $x'$ be neighboring datasets, and let $x_T$ (or $x'_T$) denote the subset of records in $x$ (or $x'$) indexed by $T$. Let $S$ denote any possible output of the algorithm $M'$. For convenience, let $p = m/n$ represent the probability of sampling a single item. According to the definition of differential privacy, to show that the algorithm $M'(x)$ satisfies $(p(\mathrm{e}^{\varepsilon} - 1), p\delta)$-differential privacy, it suffices to prove:

$$\begin{aligned}
&\frac{\Pr\left[M'(x) \in S\right] - p\delta}{\Pr\left[M'\left(x'\right) \in S\right]} \\
&= \frac{p \Pr\left[M\left(x_T\right) \in S \mid i \in T\right] + (1-p)\Pr\left[M\left(x_T\right) \in S \mid i \notin T\right] - p\delta}{p \Pr\left[M\left(x'_T\right) \in S \mid i \in T\right] + (1-p)\Pr\left[M\left(x'_T\right) \in S \mid i \notin T\right]} \\
&\leq \mathrm{e}^{p(\mathrm{e}^{\varepsilon}-1)}
\end{aligned}$$

To facilitate the discussion of scenarios involving different records being randomly sampled and perturbed, we abbreviate these probabilities as follows:

$$\begin{aligned}
C &= Pr[M(x_T) \in S|i \in T] \\
C &= Pr[M(x'_T) \in S|i \in T] \\
D &= Pr[M(x_T) \in S|i \notin T] = Pr[M(x'_T) \in S|i \notin T]
\end{aligned}$$

Therefore,

$$\begin{aligned}
&\Pr\left[M'(x) \in S\right] \\
&= pC + (1-p)D - p\delta \\
&\leq p(\mathrm{e}^{\varepsilon} min\{C', D\} + \delta) + (1-p)D - p\delta \\
&= p((\mathrm{e}^{\varepsilon} - 1)min\{C', D\} + min\{C', D\}) + (1-p)D \\
&\leq p((\mathrm{e}^{\varepsilon} - 1)min\{C', D\} + C') + (1-p)D \\
&\leq p((\mathrm{e}^{\varepsilon} - 1)(pC' + (1-p)D) + C') + (1-p)D \\
&= (p(\mathrm{e}^{\varepsilon} - 1) + 1)(pC' + (1-p)D) \\
&\leq \mathrm{e}^{p(\mathrm{e}^{\varepsilon}-1)}(pC' + (1-p)D) \\
&= \mathrm{e}^{p(\mathrm{e}^{\varepsilon}-1)} \Pr\left[M'\left(x'\right) \in S\right]
\end{aligned}$$

In the above formula, since algorithm $M$ satisfies $(\varepsilon, \delta)$-differential privacy, we have $C \leq \mathrm{e}^{\varepsilon} \min\{C', D\} + \delta$, so the first inequality holds. For any $0 < \alpha < 1$, it holds that $\min\{x, y\} \leq \alpha x + (1-\alpha)y$, which ensures the third inequality. Moreover, since $x + 1 \leq \mathrm{e}^{x}$, the fourth inequality also holds. This completes the proof. □

### 6.3.2 Privacy Amplification via Shuffling

Privacy amplification based on shuffling, also known as privacy amplification based on anonymity, can transform local differential privacy into centralized differential privacy. The mechanism of this privacy amplification is that users locally perturb their data using a local differential privacy algorithm satisfying $\varepsilon_0$, and then a shuffler anonymizes all user data completely, thereby satisfying centralized $\varepsilon_{pa}$ differential privacy. This section provides a general theorem for privacy amplification based on shuffling under both interactive and non-interactive mechanisms, as well as a specific theorem for privacy amplification under the Randomized Response algorithm. Given the complexity of the proof, this section skips it and instead demonstrates the effect of privacy amplification through the analysis of experimental results.

**Theorem 7** (Privacy Amplification under the General Interactive Mechanism Based on Shuffling [3]) *Given n users, each corresponding to a record $x_i$ and running a randomized encoding protocol R locally. For any $n > 1000$ and $\delta \in (0, 1/100)$, if the protocol R satisfies $\varepsilon_0$-local differential privacy with $\varepsilon_0 \in (0, 1/2)$, then the protocol $S(R^n)$ indicates that the n outputs corresponding to the shuffled randomly perturbed data satisfy $(\varepsilon_{pa}, \delta)$-differential privacy, where*

$$\varepsilon_{pa} = 12\varepsilon_0\sqrt{\ln(1/\delta)/n} \tag{6.1}$$

**Theorem 8** (Privacy Amplification under the General Non-Interactive Mechanism Based on Shuffling [5]) *Given n users, each corresponding to a record $x_i$ and running a randomized encoding protocol R locally. For any $n \in \mathbb{N}$, $\delta \in [0, 1]$, and $\varepsilon_0 \in \left(0, \frac{1}{2}\log\left(\frac{n}{\ln\frac{1}{\delta}}\right)\right]$, if the protocol R satisfies $\varepsilon_0$-local differential privacy, then the protocol $S(R^n)$ indicates that the n outputs corresponding to the shuffled randomly perturbed data satisfy $(\varepsilon_{pa}, \delta)$-differential privacy, where*

$$\varepsilon_{pa} = O\left((e^{\varepsilon_0} - 1)\sqrt{(\ln 1/\delta)/n}\right) \tag{6.2}$$

Based on the privacy amplification theorems mentioned above, setting $\delta = 10^{-9}$, the following tables show the results of privacy amplification. Let $n$ denote the number of trustworthy users participating in the computation. Table 6.1 presents the values of $\varepsilon_{pa}$ obtained after privacy amplification of $\varepsilon_0$ according to Eq. (6.1). Table 6.2 shows the values of $\varepsilon_0$ before amplification corresponding to $\varepsilon_{pa}$ calculated according to Eq. (6.2). From these tables, it can be intuitively observed that through privacy amplification, it is easy to add noise satisfying a larger $\varepsilon_0$ at the user's local end, while obtaining a smaller $\varepsilon_{pa}$ differential privacy guarantee at the analyzer end. Moreover, the effect of privacy amplification increases with the number of participating users. It is important to note that since the privacy amplification under the interactive mechanism restricts $\varepsilon_0 \in (0, 1/2)$, for data analysts (i.e., data collectors), the value of $\varepsilon_{pa}$ is often less than 0.2, and sometimes even less than 0.01, which is usually not required in practical scenarios. Therefore, the privacy amplification

**Table 6.1** Privacy amplification results under the general interactive mechanism based on shuffling ($\varepsilon_{pa}$)

| $n$ | $\varepsilon_0 = 0.1$ | $\varepsilon_0 = 0.2$ | $\varepsilon_0 = 0.3$ | $\varepsilon_0 = 0.4$ |
|---|---|---|---|---|
| 1e+4 | 0.0546 | 0.1092 | 0.1638 | 0.2185 |
| 1e+5 | 0.0172 | 0.0345 | 0.0518 | 0.0691 |
| 1e+6 | 0.0054 | 0.0109 | 0.0163 | 0.0218 |
| 1e+7 | 0.0017 | 0.0034 | 0.0051 | 0.0069 |
| 1e+8 | 0.0005 | 0.0010 | 0.0016 | 0.0021 |

**Table 6.2** Reverse privacy amplification results under the general Non-interactive mechanism based on shuffling ($\varepsilon_0$)

| $n$ | $\varepsilon_{pa} = 0.1$ | $\varepsilon_{pa} = 0.3$ | $\varepsilon_{pa} = 0.5$ | $\varepsilon_{pa} = 0.7$ | $\varepsilon_{pa} = 0.9$ |
|---|---|---|---|---|---|
| 1e+4 | 1.16 | 2.03 | 2.48 | 2.80 | 3.03 |
| 1e+5 | 2.07 | 3.08 | 3.58 | 3.90 | 4.15 |
| 1e+6 | 3.13 | 4.20 | 4.71 | 5.04 | 5.29 |
| 1e+7 | 4.26 | 5.34 | 5.85 | 6.19 | 6.44 |
| 1e+8 | 5.40 | 6.49 | 7.00 | 7.34 | 7.59 |

theorem under the general non-interactive mechanism is more widely applied, and efficient privacy amplification theorems under the interactive mechanism still need further exploration.

To achieve more effective privacy amplification, researchers have developed more precise privacy amplification theorems tailored to specific differential privacy mechanisms. A notable example is the Randomized Response algorithm discussed in Sect. 5.1.3.

**Theorem 9** (Privacy Amplification Theorem for Shuffled Randomized Response Algorithm [4]) *Given $n$ users, each corresponding to a record $x_i \in \{0, 1\}$ and running a randomized encoding protocol $R$ locally. For any $n \in \mathbb{N}$, $\delta \in [0, 1]$, and $\lambda \in \left(\frac{14\ln(4/\delta)}{n}, 1\right]$, if the protocol $R$ outputs values uniformly from $\{0, 1\}$ with probability $\lambda$ and the true value with probability $1 - \lambda$, then the protocol $S(R^n)$ indicates that the $n$ outputs corresponding to the shuffled randomly perturbed data satisfy $(\varepsilon_{pa}, \delta)$-differential privacy, where*

$$\varepsilon_{pa} = \sqrt{\frac{32n \cdot \log\frac{4}{\delta}}{\lambda - \sqrt{2\lambda n \cdot \log\frac{2}{\delta}}}} \cdot \left(1 - \frac{\lambda - \sqrt{2\lambda n \log\frac{2}{\delta}}}{n^2}\right) \tag{6.3}$$

In this theorem, when $\lambda = \frac{2}{e^{\varepsilon_0}+1}$, the Boolean Randomized Response mechanism satisfies $\varepsilon_0$ local differential privacy. Substituting this expression into Eq. (6.3) and simplifying, we obtain the following relaxed privacy amplification effect. That is,

**Table 6.3** Privacy amplification results under the random response algorithm based on shuffling

| $n$ | $\varepsilon_{pa} = 0.1$ | $\varepsilon_{pa} = 0.3$ | $\varepsilon_{pa} = 0.5$ | $\varepsilon_{pa} = 0.7$ | $\varepsilon_{pa} = 0.9$ |
|---|---|---|---|---|---|
| 1e+4 | None | None | 0.57 | 1.24 | 1.74 |
| 1e+5 | None | 1.85 | 2.87 | 3.54 | 4.05 |
| 1e+6 | 1.96 | 4.15 | 5.17 | 5.85 | 6.35 |
| 1e+7 | 4.26 | 6.46 | 7.48 | 8.15 | 8.65 |
| 1e+8 | 6.56 | 8.76 | 9.78 | 10.45 | 10.96 |

when $0 < \varepsilon_0 \leq \log n - \log(14 \log(4/\delta)), \varepsilon_{pa} = \sqrt{64 \cdot \mathrm{e}^{\varepsilon_0} \log(4/\delta)/n}$. Based on this formula, this section provides the values of $\varepsilon_0$ given $n$ and $\varepsilon_{pa}$, as shown in Table 6.3. Here, "None" indicates that the given conditions do not meet the above theorem and effective privacy amplification cannot be performed. From this table, it can be observed that privacy amplification for specific algorithms yields significantly better results than general privacy amplification theorems.

### 6.3.3 Other Privacy Amplification Methods

In addition to the two basic privacy amplification methods mentioned above, privacy amplification methods based on iteration [6] and random check-ins [7] are also widely used. The privacy amplification method based on iteration enhances privacy protection by avoiding the release of all intermediate results during the iteration process through the idea of compressing iterations, and is suitable for convex optimization problems. The privacy amplification method based on random check-ins breaks through the limitation of uniform sampling of all user data required in subsampling techniques, decentralizes the data sampling process to the user end, and allows users to decide whether to participate in a round of machine learning training, thereby enhancing privacy effects. This method is suitable for distributed computing tasks such as federated learning.

The essence of privacy amplification methods is to add random data processing steps on the basis of differential privacy algorithms to increase the randomness of the results and thereby enhance privacy protection. It is worth noting that typical privacy amplification methods are completed through randomization processing methods such as sampling and shuffling, which do not disturb or disturb the data values themselves as little as possible. In this way, while amplifying the degree of privacy protection, less noise can be introduced compared to differential privacy methods, thereby improving the usability of the results. Privacy amplification methods provide direction and pathways for the integration and enhancement of differential privacy methods with other randomness methods, and also lay the foundation for the proposal of new privacy protection methods.

## 6.4 "Encode-Shuffle-Ananlyze" Framework

By integrating the two types of frameworks discussed above that enhance the practicality of differential privacy, we arrive at a unified and practical privacy framework known as Encode-Shuffle-Analyze (ESA). This framework was proposed by Andrea Bittau and Ulfar Erlingsson from Google in 2017 and has since received widespread attention. In this chapter, we provide a detailed overview of the ESA framework and define *shuffled differential privacy* in its context. We then explain the roles played by cryptographic protocols and privacy amplification within this process and introduce several representative methods for privacy-preserving data collection and analysis built on this framework.

### 6.4.1 ESA Framework and Definition

In this section, we introduce the overall structure of the ESA framework and define shuffled differential privacy within this context. This framework can be seen as a type of differential privacy framework. By comparing it with traditional differential privacy frameworks, such as centralized and local, we highlight the superior properties of this framework in terms of both privacy and usability.

**1. ESA Framework Structure**

The ESA framework, as shown in Fig. 6.6, mainly consists of an encoder, a shuffler, and an analyzer, and it assumes that these three parties cannot collude.

**Encoder**: It primarily runs on the user's local client and is generally considered trustworthy. Its role is to encode user data to control the scope, granularity, perturbation level, and randomization degree of the data publication, thereby protecting user data privacy without relying on any trust assumptions [7].

The encoder can be categorized into single-encoding mode and multi-encoding mode based on the number of output messages. In single-encoding mode, the user

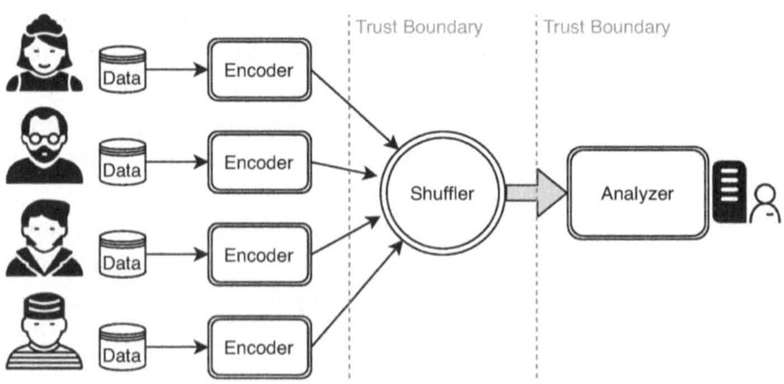


**Fig. 6.6** ESA framework

encodes the data into a single message, which can be a value, a tuple, or an array, with each message being the smallest unit for subsequent processing. In multi-encoding mode, the user encodes the data into multiple messages that can be processed separately, such as multiple values, tuples, and arrays. For the same input, multi-encoding mode typically carries more information, which helps the analyzer obtain more accurate results.

The specific implementation of the encoder can be achieved through data generalization, data partitioning, encryption, and the addition of differential privacy noise to eliminate or reduce the privacy information contained in the data.

**Shuffler**: The shuffler is an independent semi-honest server capable of performing secure shuffling operations without knowledge of the data content, and it serves as the core component of the ESA framework. Its role is to receive encoded data from users, remove associated metadata (such as reception time, order, and IP addresses), and shuffle the data (i.e., randomize the order) to achieve anonymity. To ensure sufficient privacy protection, the shuffler needs to wait for a certain period to gather enough user data before performing the shuffling. Additionally, data meeting a particular threshold is published. When the volume of data is sensitive, noise satisfying differential privacy can be added to this threshold for perturbation, or the shuffler can randomly discard data to ensure the volume adheres to differential privacy, thus protecting the privacy of the data volume.

Regarding the shuffler's mode, it can be divided into **single-shuffler mode** and **multi-shuffler mode**. In **single-shuffler mode**, all the data output by the encoders are shuffled together, meaning a single shuffler is used for the process. In **multi-shuffler mode**, the data output by the encoders are categorized based on attributes or other features, and multiple shufflers are used to shuffle the data within each category separately. Multi-shuffler mode is typically employed when the attributes or classification features are not sensitive, and it is combined with encoders in multi-output mode. However, the multi-shuffler mode does not correspond directly to the multi-encoding mode in the encoder; messages with multiple encodings can still utilize a single shuffler in the single-shuffler mode. While the single-shuffler mode provides higher privacy by shuffling all data together, multi-shuffler mode offers greater usability for cases where classification features in multi-output messages are not sensitive.

It should be specifically noted that the two shuffling modes mentioned above do not correspond one-to-one with the number of shufflers in the specific implementation. These two shuffling modes are defined from the logical aspect of privacy. The multi-shuffler mode can be implemented using a single shuffler, by adding labels for each category and shuffling the data belonging to different labels separately. Both of these shuffling modes can also be implemented using multiple shufflers based on existing secure protocols to avoid single-point failure.

Here, to prevent the third-party "shuffler" introduced for shuffling from becoming a new source of privacy leakage, we need to perform **secure shuffling**. Secure shuffling ensures that the shuffler, while performing a uniform shuffling operation, knows nothing about the data it collects or the intermediate results it generates, and cannot peek into user privacy. The specific implementation of the shuffler can be based on the deployment conditions of the model, using existing secure shuffling protocols, and can be completed through trusted hardware, homomorphic encryption, or secure multi-party computation.

**Analyzer**: The analyzer is run by the data collector and is considered an untrusted server. Its role is to receive the data published by the shuffler, analyze and correct the data according to the corresponding encoding and shuffling rules, and obtain the final statistical results. The privacy of the data in this framework is primarily aimed at protecting against the analyzer, meaning that the analyzer is treated as a potential data snooper.

**2. ESA Assumption**

The ESA framework assumes that the encoder, shuffler, and analyzer do not collude with each other. However, if any two of them collude, the final privacy effect obtained by the model will be significantly reduced. Assuming the analyzer is the attacker, the privacy protection level obtained by the model is denoted as $\mathcal{A}_c$ when none of them collude, $\mathcal{A}_s$ when the analyzer colludes with the shuffler, and $\mathcal{A}_e$ when the analyzer colludes with the encoder. The relationship between these three levels of privacy protection should satisfy $\mathcal{A}_c > \mathcal{A}_e \geq \mathcal{A}_s$. The specific analysis is as follows:

When the analyzer colludes with the shuffler, the user data can only obtain the protection brought by the encoder, i.e., $\mathcal{A}_s$. Specifically, when the final goal of privacy protection in this framework is to achieve differential privacy, and the encoder uses the local differential privacy method for encoding, the user can obtain a relatively weaker local differential privacy protection compared to $\mathcal{A}_c$.

When the analyzer colludes with the encoder, the effect of $\mathcal{A}_e$ varies depending on the number of colluding encoders. When only part of the encoders collude, the shuffling effect will be weakened, but it will still provide a privacy protection level greater than $\mathcal{A}_s$ and less than $\mathcal{A}_c$. In the extreme case, when all but one of the encoders collude, the shuffler becomes ineffective, and at this point, the user can only obtain a privacy protection effect of $\mathcal{A}_s$.

**3. Shuffled Differential Privacy**

Under normal circumstances, researchers combine the ESA framework with the strictly defined differential privacy to ensure that the final output obtained by the analyzer satisfies the definition of differential privacy, thereby guaranteeing and measuring data privacy. This combination is called shuffled differential privacy. According to the post-processing invariance of differential privacy, if the data processed by the randomized encoder and the shuffler in the ESA framework satisfies differential privacy, then the final result will also satisfy differential privacy. The privacy effect of this result is independent of the analyzer, whose main role is to compute the perturbed data and correct the estimated results. Therefore, this section provides the formal definition of shuffled differential privacy:

**Definition 13** (*Shuffled Differential Privacy*) Given $n$ trusted users, each corresponding to a record $x_i$. Let $R : X \rightarrow Y^m$ denote the randomized encoder, where $m$ represents the number of messages after encoding; $S : Y^m \rightarrow \Pi(Y^m)$ represents the shuffling operation; and the algorithm $A : \Pi(Y^m) \rightarrow Z$ is the analysis function,

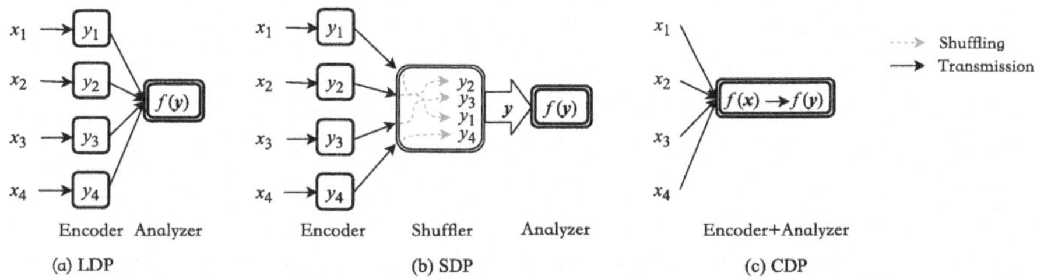


**Fig. 6.7** Comparison of DP methods under different frameworks

where $\Pi$ denotes the permutation. Then, the shuffled differential privacy protocol can be represented as $P = (R, S, A)$. According to the post-processing invariance, if $S(R^n) = S(R(x_1), \ldots, R(x_n)) = \Pi(R(x_1), \ldots, R(x_n))$ satisfies $(\varepsilon, \delta)$-differential privacy, then the protocol $P$ satisfies $(\varepsilon, \delta)$-differential privacy.

Intuitively, we can compare shuffled differential privacy with local differential privacy and centralized differential privacy, as shown in Fig. 6.7.

Compared to local differential privacy, shuffled differential privacy shares a high degree of similarity with it and can use the same encoder to achieve differential privacy for user-local data. The shuffled differential privacy method can be seen as an extension of the local differential privacy framework with the addition of a shuffler, which relies on a semi-honest security assumption. Compared to the local differential privacy framework that has no trust dependency, the security of this framework is somewhat reduced. However, the anonymization operation performed by the shuffler can effectively enhance privacy, meaning that under the same $\varepsilon$-differential privacy protection, the shuffled differential privacy framework can add less noise through the encoder to improve the usability of the final data.

Compared to centralized differential privacy, which uses a centralized privacy protection framework integrating the analyzer and encoder into a trusted third party (the data collector), the shuffled differential privacy method, although it adds more noise to user data and loses some data usability, breaks free from the strong reliance on a trusted server.

Overall, in terms of the model's dependency on trust assumptions, local differential privacy < shuffled differential privacy < centralized differential privacy, that is, local differential privacy has the smallest trust assumption. Aiming for the same $\varepsilon$-differential privacy, in terms of the usability of the analysis results, centralized differential privacy > shuffled differential privacy > local differential privacy, that is, centralized differential privacy has the highest result usability. It can be seen that the shuffled differential privacy method lies between local and centralized differential privacy in terms of privacy and usability, achieving a better balance.

### 6.4.2 Applications

The improvement in the usability of computational results in the ESA framework is attributed to the privacy amplification effect brought by shuffling. Intuitively, the anonymization of user data through shuffling enhances data privacy beyond what is achieved through local encoding and perturbation alone. As analyzed in Sect. 6.3.2, the privacy amplification effect can be quantified. Based on these theoretical foundations, shuffled differential privacy achieves a result error that is $O(\sqrt{n})$ times smaller than that of local differential privacy methods.

For example [12], consider 100,000 users, each holding an integer $x_i \in [1, 100]$. Users perturb their data locally following the ESA framework and local differential privacy mechanisms, and a data collector performs frequency estimation based on the perturbed data. For comparison, assume both approaches use $k$-ary randomized response (i.e., $kRR$; see Sect. 5.2.1), and the published results satisfy differential privacy with a privacy budget of $\varepsilon = 0.5$ from the data collector's perspective.

Under the local differential privacy approach, users perturb their data with a local privacy budget of $\varepsilon = 0.5$, resulting in only 24.49% of the perturbed data reflecting the true value, while the remainder consists of randomized noise. In contrast, using the ESA framework, the privacy amplification effect of shuffling allows users to apply perturbation with a much higher privacy budget of $\varepsilon = 10.5$, thereby preserving the true value in 99.84% of the perturbed data.

This comparison clearly demonstrates that the ESA framework can retain substantially more of the original data while still offering the same differential privacy guarantees, thereby significantly enhancing data usability.

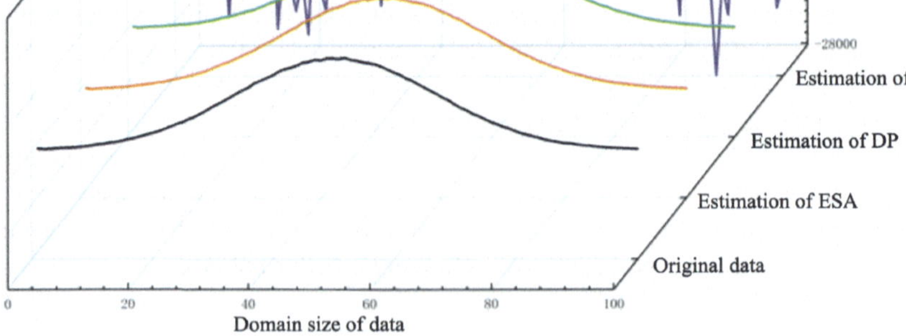


**Fig. 6.8** Comparison of results from different methods

Figure 6.8 shows the distribution of frequency estimates obtained by the data collector in the example scenario. The estimates perturbed using the ESA framework are notably closer to the original data, whereas those derived from the local differential privacy (LDP) method deviate significantly from the true values. Interestingly, in this case, the results from the ESA framework are approximately equivalent to those obtained using the centralized differential privacy (CDP) method.

It is important to highlight that the CDP method relies on the assumption that the data collector is fully trusted (or that a trusted third party exists), and achieves privacy by directly adding Laplace noise to the histogram computed from users' true data. In contrast, the ESA framework achieves a similar level of accuracy while requiring noise to be added independently at each user's end, a total of $n$ times, thus eliminating the need for a trusted central authority.

### *6.4.3 Shuffle Based Differential Privacy*

After introducing the foundational principles of the ESA framework and shuffled differential privacy, this section presents several specific methods based on shuffled differential privacy. The focus is on statistical problems oriented toward basic data collection, including count estimation, frequency estimation, and sum estimation.

**1. Count Estimation: Problem and Method**

The count estimation problem serves as the foundation for a wide range of statistical estimation tasks. In this setting, each user holds a binary value $x_i \in \{0, 1\}$, and the analyzer aims to estimate the total number of users holding the value 1, that is, to compute $\sum_{i=1}^{n} x_i$. This problem is also referred to as Boolean summation or binary summation.

Albert Cheu applied the basic randomized response mechanism within the ESA framework to estimate the values $x_i \in \{0, 1\}$ held by users [4], achieving centralized differential privacy guarantees through anonymity-based privacy amplification.

Similar to the standard randomized response technique, each user outputs a randomized response $y_i \in \{0, 1\}$ with probability $\lambda$, and reports their true value $y_i = x_i$ with probability $1 - \lambda$. The shuffler anonymizes and shuffles these values before passing them to the analyzer. The analyzer then performs an unbiased estimation using Eq. (6.4), where $\hat{n}$ denotes the estimated number of users with value 1, $n^*$ is the count observed from the shuffled data, and $N$ is the total number of users.

$$\hat{n} = \frac{n^* - \frac{1}{2}N\lambda}{1 - \lambda} \tag{6.4}$$

According to Theorem 3, when $\delta \in (0, 1)$, $n > 14 \log \frac{4}{\delta}$, and $\varepsilon \in \left(\frac{\sqrt{3456}}{n \log \frac{4}{\delta}}, 1\right)$, the algorithm satisfies $(\varepsilon, \delta)$-differential privacy provided that $\lambda$ meets the condition given in Eq. 6.5.

$$\lambda = \begin{cases} \frac{64}{\varepsilon^2} \log \frac{4}{\delta}, & \text{if } \varepsilon \geq \sqrt{\frac{192}{n} \log \frac{4}{\delta}} \\ n - \frac{\varepsilon n^{\frac{3}{2}}}{\sqrt{432 \log \frac{4}{\delta}}}, & \text{otherwise} \end{cases} \tag{6.5}$$

In addition, Victor Balcer proposed a shuffled differential privacy method under the multi-message encoder model in [13], where each user encodes their numerical value into at most two perturbed messages. However, the final result obtained through this method is not unbiased. Later, in [14], the scenario where users are not fully trustworthy was further considered, and robust differential privacy was achieved under such assumptions. Furthermore, Ghazi [15] developed a technique that links perturbation messages associated with user inputs to noise that is independent of those inputs, ensuring that the probability densities of the output distributions for adjacent datasets differ by only a small multiplicative factor at every point—thus achieving pure differential privacy with $\delta = 0$.

**2. Frequency Estimation: Problem and Method**

In the frequency estimation problem, it is assumed that each user holds a discrete value $x_i \in \{1, \ldots, d\}$. The goal of the analyzer is to estimate the frequency count$(j)$ for each value $j \in \{1, \ldots, d\}$ based on anonymized and perturbed user data, essentially reconstructing a histogram of user inputs.

Balle [5] proposed a frequency estimation method based on the $k$-ary randomized response mechanism under the local differential privacy model. This approach is one of the most straightforward and intuitive methods for frequency estimation. Specifically, each user reports a value $y_i \in \{1, \ldots, d\}$, where with probability $\lambda$ the value is drawn uniformly at random from the domain, and with probability $1 - \lambda$, the user reports their true value, i.e., $y_i = x_i$.

The shuffler receives these reports, strips identifying metadata, and randomly permutes the messages before forwarding them to the analyzer. The analyzer then applies Eq. (6.6) to produce an unbiased estimate of the frequency for each domain value $j \in \{1, \ldots, d\}$.

Throughout this process, the local differential privacy guarantee with privacy loss $\varepsilon_0$ is transformed into a centralized differential privacy guarantee with a reduced privacy loss $\varepsilon$, thanks to the privacy amplification effect achieved through anonymization and shuffling.

$$\hat{n} = \frac{n^* - \frac{1}{k} N \lambda}{1 - \lambda} \tag{6.6}$$

In [5], Borja Balle introduces the concept of the *Privacy Blanket*, referring to the $\lambda n$ randomly generated values contributed by users. After the shuffling process, these random values serve as a protective layer, enhancing the privacy of each individual user's true value. Building upon this idea, the author presents a rigorous and elegant analysis of both the privacy guarantees and the estimation error of the proposed method.

When the parameter $\lambda$ is selected according to Eq. (6.7), the data collected by the analyzer satisfies $(\varepsilon, \delta)$-differential privacy. Meanwhile, the local perturbation performed at the user side satisfies $\varepsilon_0$-local differential privacy, where

$$\varepsilon_0 = \log\left(\frac{(n-1)\varepsilon^2}{14\log\frac{2}{\delta}} - d + 1\right).$$

This formulation illustrates the trade-off between local privacy parameters, global privacy amplification, and estimation accuracy enabled by the ESA framework and shuffling.

$$\lambda = \max\left\{\frac{14k\log\frac{2}{\delta}}{(n-1)\varepsilon^2}, \frac{27k}{(n-1)\varepsilon}\right\} < 1 \tag{6.7}$$

To further reduce the error in frequency estimation, researchers have proposed various advanced frequency estimation schemes. Tianhao Wang, building upon the Optimized Local Hashing (OLH) method [16], introduced the Shuffler-Optimal Local Hashing (SLH) mechanism [17], which incorporates privacy amplification theory. Although SLH achieves error bounds that are independent of the value domain size $d$, it requires each user to employ a distinct hash function during the perturbation process. Consequently, the analyzer must traverse all individual hash functions during frequency estimation, leading to substantial computational overhead at the analyzer side.

Ghazi [18], leveraging the multi-message encoder model, proposed a method that retains both true values and randomly generated values forming the *Privacy Blanket* in the user's output, achieving frequency estimation with logarithmic or polynomial error bounds. Additionally, to address different randomization strategies used by users, two algorithms were proposed: *private-coin* and *public-coin*. In the private-coin model, users independently generate random values, while in the public-coin model, users share the randomness generation algorithm with the analyzer to reduce communication overhead. However, the increased complexity of these perturbation mechanisms imposes significant computational costs on both the user and analyzer sides.

**3. Summation Estimation Problem and Methods**

Summation estimation primarily targets real-valued data, assuming each user holds a value $x_i \in [0, 1]$. The analyzer estimates the total sum $\Sigma_n x_i$ based on anonymized and perturbed user data. If real values can be encoded into discrete representations, the summation problem can be reduced to the aforementioned counting or frequency estimation problems. A commonly used approach for this transformation is the *randomized rounding* algorithm, which encodes real numbers into discrete values using randomization.

Cheu [4] proposed mapping user values $x_i$ to vectors $\hat{b_i} = \{b_{i1}, \ldots, b_{ip}\} \in \{0, 1\}^p$ via randomized rounding in an unbiased manner. Specifically, the number of 1s in $\hat{b_i}$ is determined by $\lfloor x_i p \rfloor + \mathrm{Ber}(x_i p - \lfloor x_i p \rfloor)$, where $\mathrm{Ber}(\cdot)$ denotes a Bernoulli random variable and $\lfloor\cdot\rfloor$ is the floor function. This mechanism essentially estimates $x_i \times p$ based on the number of ones in $\hat{b_i}$, with $p$ controlling the precision of the rounding—effectively scaling $x_i \in [0, 1]$ into an integer range $[0, p]$.

For example, if a user holds the value $x_i = 0.732$ and the precision is set to $p = 10$, then with probability 0.32, the user encodes the value as a vector with 8 ones and 2 zeros, and with probability 0.68, as 7 ones and 3 zeros.

Each bit $b_{ij}$ of these binary vectors is then independently perturbed using the counting estimation algorithm proposed in [4], and the total privacy budget $\varepsilon$ is allocated across all $p$ bits using the advanced composition theorem [19]. Let $b'_j$ denote the perturbed and shuffled vector for dimension $j$. If each $b'_j$ satisfies $\left(\frac{\varepsilon}{\sqrt{8p\log\frac{4}{\delta}}}, \frac{\delta}{2p}\right)$-differential privacy, then the final estimated sum satisfies $(\varepsilon, \delta)$-differential privacy. To maintain an unbiased estimate, the final summation result must be divided by the amplification factor $p$.

More directly, Balle [5] scales each user value $x_i$ by a factor of $p$ and applies randomized rounding to obtain $\hat{x_i} = \lfloor x_i p\rfloor + \mathrm{Ber}(x_i p - \lfloor x_i p\rfloor)$. This allows the direct application of the $k$-value randomized response algorithm to perturb each $\hat{x_i}$, with the perturbed value denoted as $x'$. The final sum estimate is then computed as $\frac{\Sigma_n x'/p - \lambda n/2}{1-\lambda}$.

Furthermore, to improve estimation accuracy and reduce errors introduced by randomized rounding, Balle [20] encodes each user value into multiple values based on $m$ fixed precision levels and independently applies randomized response to each encoded value, thereby maximizing the privacy protection offered by the shuffler.

Additionally, Ghazi [15] encodes real numbers owned by users in binary form and perturbs each bit separately, achieving $\delta = 0$ differential privacy.

## 6.5 Summary

This chapter discusses two approaches from the perspective of differential privacy and practical utility: privacy amplification methods and methods that combine cryptography with differential privacy. We propose that when integrating cryptographic methods with differential privacy, two aspects—"C4DP" and "DP4C"—should be considered. "C4DP" primarily leverages the security of cryptographic protocols to enhance the privacy of differential privacy methods while also improving the usability of computational results. "DP4C" focuses on using the concepts of differential privacy to limit redundant computations and communication rounds, thus improving the overall performance of the algorithm. Only by addressing both the utility issue of differential privacy and the efficiency issue of cryptographic protocols can a practical privacy-preserving solution be achieved. Subsequently, we introduced the practical framework ESA. The solutions discussed in this chapter all aim to protect the privacy of results while minimizing the perturbation of data as much as possible. How to further improve upon this, and whether there are better privacy protection methods that allow minimal data disturbance while balancing privacy, efficiency, and utility, remains an open question worthy of further thought.

# References


1. WAGH S, HE X, MACHANAVAJJHALA A, et al. DP-cryptography: marrying differential privacy and cryptography in emerging applications[J]. Communications of the ACM, 2021, 64(2): 84–93.
2. ULLMAN J. Cs7880: Rigorous approaches to data privacy[EB/OL]. [2022-01-07]. https://www.ccs.neu.edu/home/jullman/cs7880s17/HW1sol.pdf
3. ERLINGSSON Ú, FELDMAN V, MIRONOV I, et al. Amplification by shuffling: From local to central differential privacy via anonymity[C]//Proceedings of the Thirtieth Annual ACM-SIAM Symposium on Discrete Algorithms. Philadelphia, PA: SIAM, 2019: 2468–2479.
4. CHEU A, SMITH A, ULLMAN J, et al. Distributed differential privacy via shuffling[C]//Annual International Conference on the Theory and Applications of Cryptographic Techniques. Berlin: Springer, 2019: 375–403.
5. BALLE B, BELL J, GASCÓN A, et al. The privacy blanket of the shuffle model[C]//Annual International Cryptology Conference. Berlin: Springer, 2019: 638–667.
6. FELDMAN V, MIRONOV I, TALWAR K, et al. Privacy amplification by iteration[C]//Proceedings of the IEEE 59th Annual Symposium on Foundations of Computer Science (FOCS). Piscataway,NJ: IEEE, 2018: 521–532.
7. BALLE B, KAIROUZ P, MCMAHAN B, et al. Privacy amplification via random check-ins[J]. Advances in Neural Information Processing Systems, 2020, 33: 4623–4634.
8. NARAYAN A, HAEBERLEN A. DJoin: Differentially Private Join Queries over Distributed Databases[C]//Proceedings of the 10th USENIX Symposium on Operating Systems Design and Implementation (OSDI 12). Berkeley, CA: USENIX Association, 2012: 149–162.
9. BITTAU A, ERLINGSSON Ú, MANIATIS P, et al. Prochlo: Strong privacy for analytics in the crowd[C]//Proceedings of the 26th symposium on operating systems principles. New York, NY: ACM, 2017: 441–459.
10. BATER J, HE X, EHRICH W, et al. Shrinkwrap: efficient SQL query processing in differentially private data federations[J]. Proceedings of the VLDB Endowment, 2018, 12(3): 307–320.
11. VAN DEN HOOFF J, LAZAR D, ZAHARIA M, et al. Vuvuzela: Scalable private messaging resistant to traffic analysis[C]//Proceedings of the 25th Symposium on Operating Systems Principles. New York, NY: ACM, 2015: 137–152.
12. WANG L, MENG X.ESA: A Novel Privacy Preserving Framework[J]. Journal of Computer Research and Development, 2022, 59(01): 144–171.
13. BALCER V, CHEU A. Separating Local & Shuffled Differential Privacy via Histograms[C]//Proceedings of the 1st Information-Theoretical Cryptography Conference (ITC). Germany: Schloss Dagstuh-Leibniz-Zentrum für Informatik, 2020: 1:1–1:14.
14. BALCER V, CHEU A, Joseph M, et al. Connecting robust shuffle privacy and pan-privacy[C]//Proceedings of the 2021 ACM-SIAM Symposium on Discrete Algorithms (SODA). Philadelphia, PA: SIAM, 2021: 2384–2403.
15. GHAZI B, GOLOWICH N, KUMAR R, et al. Pure Differentially Private Summation from Anonymous Messages[C]//Proceedings of the 1st Information-Theoretical Cryptography Conference (ITC). Germany: Schloss Dagstuhl-Leibniz-Zentrum für Informatik, 2020: 15:1–15:23.
16. WANG T, BLOCKI J, LI N, et al. Locally differentially private protocols for frequency estimation[C]//Proceedings of the 26th USENIX Security Symposium (USENIX Security 17). Berkeley, CA: USENIX Association, 2017: 729–745.
17. WANG T, DING B, XU M, et al. Improving utility and security of the shuffler-based differential privacy[J]. Proceedings of the VLDB Endowment, 2020, 13(13): 3545–3558.

18. GHAZI B, GOLOWICH N, KUMAR R, et al. On the power of multiple anonymous messages: Frequency estimation and selection in the shuffle model of differential privacy[C]//Proceedings of Annual International Conference on the Theory and Applications of Cryptographic Techniques. Berlin: Springer, 2021: 463–488.
19. DWORK C, ROTH A. The algorithmic foundations of differential privacy[J]. Foundations and Trends ® in Theoretical Computer Science, 2014, 9(3-4): 211–407.
20. BALLE B, BELL J, GASCÓN A, et al. Private summation in the multi-message shuffle model[C]//Proceedings of the 2020 ACM SIGSAC Conference on Computer and Communications Security. New York,NY: ACM, 2020: 657–676

# Part III
# AI Data Privacy

With the boost of the Internet, big data, and machine learning, artificial intelligence (AI) technology is evolving rapidly. Facial recognition payments, assisted diagnosis, personalized services, and more are gradually entering the public eye and profoundly changing the way humans produce and live. However, behind these seemingly brilliant intelligent products, a vast amount of personal sensitive data such as users' biometric characteristics, medical records, and social networks are being collected by various companies and institutions at all times. Large-scale data collection can drive the improvement of machine learning performance, achieving a win-win situation for economic and social benefits, but it poses greater risks and challenges to individual privacy protection.

To implement privacy protection in machine learning, in addition to the constraints of laws and regulations, it also requires researchers to design, train, and deploy models with privacy protection as the primary premise, ensuring that personal sensitive information in the data will not be directly or indirectly obtained by unauthorized personnel. This part outlines the current privacy issues in machine learning and reviews and summarizes existing privacy protection research work. Firstly, it discusses the algorithm design of differential privacy protection under centralized learning for both traditional machine learning and deep learning. Then, it outlines the privacy issues and protection methods in federated learning, illustrating the main challenges faced in current machine learning privacy protection research.

# Chapter 7
# Privacy Protection in Machine Learning

As a key AI technology, machine learning aims to learn from data to predict and decide on real-world events. In the big data era, large-scale data collection has greatly improved machine learning algorithms' performance, achieving economic and social benefits. But it also poses greater privacy-protection risks and challenges.

Machine learning training architectures are categorized into centralized and distributed learning based on training data storage locations. Centralized learning, widely used in the industry, is easy to deploy and allows long-term data storage for analysis. However, it faces significant data security and privacy risks if the database is directly or indirectly attacked. Distributed learning, on the other hand, trains local models on dispersed data nodes and passes parameters to a server. While it avoids direct attacks from centralized data collection, it still can't fully defend against indirect privacy attacks from external attackers.

From the algorithmic perspective, existing privacy-protection technologies for machine learning can be categorized into three main lines: encryption-based (e.g., homomorphic encryption), perturbation-based (e.g., differential privacy), and collaborative-computation-based (e.g., secure multi-party computation and federated learning). This chapter will focus on privacy protection in centralized learning, while the next chapter will discuss the privacy-protection issues in distributed learning, especially federated learning.

## 7.1 Introduction

Machine learning is a collective term for data-analysis algorithms. They can analyze and mine patterns from existing data, then classify or predict new data. Formally, given a finite training dataset with independent and identically distributed samples, it uses an evaluation criterion and learning strategy. It selects an optimal model $f$ from an unknown hypothesis space $\mathcal{F}$. This model should be accurate and generalize well,



X. Meng, *Data Privacy and Data Governance*, Big Data Management,
https://doi.org/10.1007/978-981-95-5787-5_7

capturing the input-output mapping. Machine learning aims not only to fit existing data but also to perform well on new data. When evaluating a model, apart from prediction accuracy, security and privacy are crucial factors to consider.

Privacy issues in machine learning mainly lie in two aspects:

1. Direct privacy breaches from large-scale data collection: Untrustworthy data collectors illegally gather, share, and trade data without authorization.
2. Indirect privacy leaks due to insufficient model generalization: Malicious data analysts interact with models multiple times to inversely deduce sensitive attributes of unknown data.

This book focuses on indirect privacy leaks in machine learning, specifically various privacy attacks on models. These attacks allow adversaries to infer trained models or reconstruct samples without compromising model integrity or usability. Such attacks stem from overfitting, where models excessively learn training data details, reducing prediction accuracy on new samples. Adversaries exploit this to deduce sensitive training data or reconstruct samples. Common attacks include membership inference, model inversion, and model extraction. The first two target training samples, while the latter targets the model itself, as shown in Table 7.1.

To achieve privacy-protected machine learning, apart from legal constraints, researchers must prioritize privacy in model design, training, and deployment. This prevents unauthorized third-parties from directly or indirectly obtaining personal sensitive information. Traditional machine learning architectures involve centralized data collection by data collectors, followed by model training by data analysts.

Once user data is collected, users largely lose control over it and remain unaware of its specific uses and destinations.

Numerous studies have been done to solve the privacy-protection issue in machine learning. This chapter focuses on privacy-algorithm design in supervised learning, a key and widely-used ML method. Its common strategy is **empirical risk minimization** (ERM).

Numerous studies have been done to solve the privacy-protection issue in machine learning. This chapter focuses on privacy-algorithm design in supervised learning, a key and widely-used ML method. Its common strategy is **empirical risk minimization** (ERM). In essence, it is an unconstrained optimization problem. The most

**Table 7.1** Privacy attacks in machine learning

| Type | Attack target | Attack condition |
|---|---|---|
| Membership inference attack [1] | Infer whether a specific sample was used for model training | The attacker needs to have specific background knowledge of the model or training data |
| Model inversion attack [2, 3] | Reconstruct training samples | Few training samples |
| Model extraction attack [4] | Reconstruct the target model | The model is simple, with few parameters |

commonly used solution method is gradient descent (GD) and its improved versions, including stochastic gradient descent (SGD) and mini-batch gradient descent (MBGD). The core idea of these methods is to iteratively update model parameters in the direction of the steepest descent of the objective function, starting from any point in the model hypothesis space. In summary, when designing privacy-protection mechanisms for machine learning, most approaches focus on three aspects: the model, the strategy, and the algorithm. Appropriate privacy-protection methods are introduced to ensure that the machine learning process is not vulnerable to external privacy attacks.

From the algorithmic perspective, existing privacy-protection technologies in machine learning can be categorized into three main lines: **encryption** techniques represented by **homomorphic encryption** (HE), **perturbation** techniques represented by **differential privacy** (DP), and **collaborative-computation** frameworks represented by **secure multi-party computation** (SMPC) and **Federated Learning**.

1. **Encryption techniques**: These use cryptographic algorithms to encode plaintext data into ciphertext, readable only by specific individuals. They ensure data confidentiality during storage, computation, and transmission, and are fundamental data-security methods. While accurate, they're limited by supporting few algebraic operations and high computational costs.
2. **Perturbation techniques**: These introduce randomness into model training by adding noise, creating a deviation between output and true results. This thwarts malicious inference by attackers. Unlike encryption, they have no extra computational overhead [5], but can somewhat reduce model usability.
3. **Collaborative-computation frameworks**: In these, data isn't sent to a central server but kept locally. Parties collaborate decentrally to train models, preventing direct and indirect privacy leaks.

In addition to privacy concerns, machine learning faces numerous security challenges. The main difference between privacy and security issues in machine learning is that privacy issues may lead to direct or indirect training data leakage without attacking the model itself. In contrast, security issues involve malicious manipulation or destruction of the model's internal logic, preventing it from functioning as intended. Security attacks on machine learning can occur during both model training and application stages. Although this issue has received significant attention over the years, it is not the focus of this book, so we will not delve into it further here.

## 7.2 Core Techniques

This section focuses on homomorphic encryption and differential privacy mechanisms and their applications in machine-learning privacy protection. The next chapter will cover collaborative-computation-framework applications.

### 7.2.1 *Homomorphic Encryption*

Homomorphic encryption allows computations on ciphertexts to generate encrypted results that, when decrypted, match the results of similar operations performed on plaintexts. If an encryption function only preserves addition or multiplication, it's called semi-homomorphic or somewhat-homomorphic encryption. For example, Paillier and DGK encryption support additive homomorphism, while RSA and EL-Gamal support multiplicative homomorphism. In contrast, fully homomorphic encryption (FHE) supports both operations. A notable FHE example is Gentry's ideal lattice-based scheme.

The advantage of encryption methods lies in their ability to ensure the correctness of computational results. However, data encryption and decryption processes often involve substantial computations. For machine learning models with numerous nonlinear computations, the algorithmic overhead is significantly high. This is why encryption methods have been controversial in terms of effectiveness and practicality, and have not been widely adopted in real-world applications.

### 7.2.2 *Differential Privacy*

Differential privacy is a key perturbation technique. Unlike cryptography, it adds random noise to data for easy deployment. However, unlike homomorphic encryption which ensures accurate results, differential privacy affects model usability.

For machine learning tasks, model training involves frequent access to the training dataset for processes like data preprocessing, loss function calculation, and iterative optimization. Thus, the overall privacy loss across the entire training process must be minimized. However, differential privacy methods vary significantly between statistical machine learning and deep learning models and need distinct considerations during design. This is primarily due to the following reasons:

1. Traditional statistical machine learning models are structurally simple and can achieve approximate optimal solutions with fewer iterations.
2. Deep learning models are complex with numerous parameters and non-linear elements, resulting in non-convex objective functions. This requires more iterations to find an approximate optimal solution and makes balancing model usability and privacy protection challenging.

This chapter will discuss privacy-protection algorithm design in statistical learning in Sect. 7.3 and focus on deep-learning algorithms in Sect. 7.4.

## 7.3 Privacy Protection in Statistical Learning

This chapter focuses on machine learning algorithm design under differential privacy protection. As mentioned in Sect. 7.1, empirical risk minimization is the most commonly used model learning strategy. Its core idea is to find the optimal model that minimizes the risk across the entire model hypothesis space $\mathcal{F}$. Given an input dataset $\mathcal{D} = \{(x_i, y_i) \in (\mathcal{X}, \mathcal{Y})\}_{i\in[n]}$ and a loss function $\ell : \mathcal{X} \rightarrow \mathcal{Y}$, the learning objective is to obtain the optimal model parameters $f^* \in \mathcal{F}$ that minimize the empirical risk shown below:

$$\mathcal{L}(\mathbf{w}, \mathcal{D}) = \frac{1}{n}\sum_{i=1}^{n} \ell(f(\mathbf{w}; x_i), y_i) + \lambda N(f) \tag{7.1}$$

Here, $L(\cdot)$ is the objective function, $\mathbf{w}$ represents the model parameters, $n$ is the number of samples, and $N(\cdot)$ is a regularizer related to model complexity. This regularizer "punishes" complex models to enhance their generalization ability and prevent overfitting. $\lambda$ is the regularization coefficient.

**Empirical Risk Minimization Does Not Satisfy Differential Privacy**. For traditional machine learning, the optimal model from empirical risk minimization is often closely related to some training samples near the decision boundary (such as support vectors in support vector machines). According to the definition of differential privacy, if the set of these samples is added, deleted, or modified, it may completely change the model. In this case, the information of the training samples will be easily inferred. For deep learning, since most models are non-linear, this situation will be more severe, as shown in Fig. 7.1.

For most machine learning tasks, if the empirical risk minimization process satisfies differential privacy, the model can achieve a certain level of privacy protection.

Differential privacy perturbation methods can be categorized into four types based on the stages at which perturbations are applied in the optimization process: input perturbation, objective perturbation, gradient perturbation, and output perturbation.

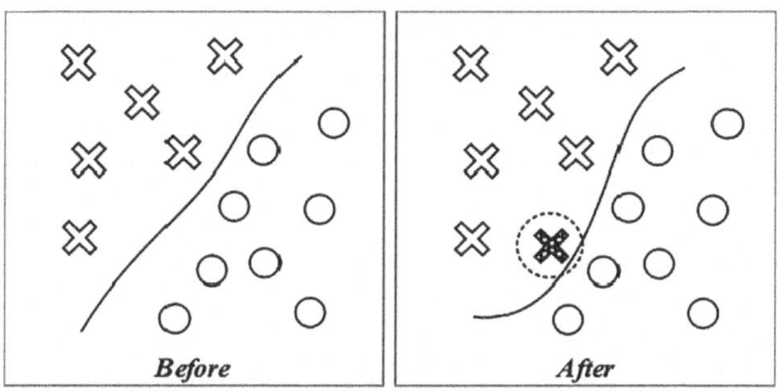


**Fig. 7.1** Empirical risk minimization does not satisfy differential privacy

**1. Input Perturbation**: This involves adding noise to raw data to prevent the model from directly accessing real data. There are two scenarios: global privacy, where data is centrally collected and perturbed before release; and local privacy, where individuals perturb their data locally before sending it to the collector. Early research showed significant limitations in the global approach. Since users don't know each other's data, global sensitivity-based perturbation isn't suitable. Local differential privacy (LDP) has been introduced and is now a mainstream privacy-protection method, with extensive research on various data types [8], data-mining tasks, and simple machine-learning models like linear and logistic regression.

**2. Output Perturbation**: This involves adding noise to the optimal model parameters obtained from empirical risk minimization. The noise level is closely related to the sensitivity of the objective function. When the objective function $\mathcal{L}(\mathbf{w}, \mathcal{D})$ is continuous, differentiable, and convex, its sensitivity is proven to be $\frac{2}{n\lambda}$, and the algorithm satisfies $\epsilon$-differential privacy. The output perturbation process is shown in Algorithm 1.

---

**Algorithm 1:** Output Perturbation

---

**Input** : Training dataset $\mathcal{D} = \{(x_i, y_i)\}_{i \in [n]}$
**Output** : Optimal private model parameters $\tilde{\mathbf{w}}^*$

```
// Solve for optimal model parameters
```
1 $\mathbf{w}^* = \arg\min_{\mathbf{w}} \mathcal{L}(\mathbf{w}, \mathcal{D})$
```
// Add random noise to optimal model parameters
```
2 $\tilde{\mathbf{w}}^* = \mathbf{w}^* + \mathbf{z}$, where $\rho(\mathbf{z}) \propto \exp(-\frac{n\epsilon\lambda}{2}\|\mathbf{z}\|)$
3 **return** $\tilde{\mathbf{w}}^*$

---

The above conditions impose significant limitations. Specifically, this method is inapplicable when the regularizer or loss function is non-convex. Moreover, since the added noise follows a certain probability distribution, attackers can still infer the true algorithm output by analyzing the noise distribution from repeated identical queries.

**3. Objective Perturbation**: This involves introducing a random term into the *objective function* of empirical risk minimization and solving for the optimal model based on the perturbed objective function. The objective perturbation process is shown in Algorithm 2.

---

**Algorithm 2:** Objective Perturbation

---

**Input** : Training dataset $\mathcal{D} = \{(x_i, y_i)\}_{i \in [n]}$
**Output** : Optimal private model parameters $\tilde{\mathbf{w}}^*$

```
// Add noise to the objective function
```
1 $\hat{\mathcal{L}}(\mathbf{w}, \mathcal{D}) = \mathcal{L}(\mathbf{w}, \mathcal{D}) + \mathbf{z}$, where $\rho(\mathbf{z}) \propto \exp(-\frac{n\epsilon\lambda}{2}\|\mathbf{z}\|)$
```
// Solve for optimal model parameters of the perturbed
   objective function
```
2 $\tilde{\mathbf{w}}^* = \mathrm{argmin}_{\mathbf{w}} \hat{\mathcal{L}}(\mathbf{w}, \mathcal{D})$
3 **return** $\tilde{\mathbf{w}}^*$

---

Objective perturbation also requires the objective function to be continuous, differentiable, and convex to prove differential privacy, which significantly limits its applicability. Zhang et al. [9] proposed a polynomial approximation method. They used Taylor series expansion to approximate the objective function's polynomial form and added Laplace noise to the coefficients. Although successfully applied to logistic regression, this method is only suitable for specific objective functions and thus hard to generalize to broader models.

**4. Gradient Perturbation**: This involves adding noise to the computed *gradient* during gradient descent and updating the model parameters using the perturbed gradient. To maintain computational efficiency, mini-batch gradient descent (MBGD) is often used in practice, where only a small batch of samples is used for parameter updates in each iteration. The gradient perturbation process is shown in Algorithm 3.

**Algorithm 3:** Gradient Perturbation

**Input** : Training dataset $\mathcal{D} = \{(x_i, y_i)\}_{i\in[n]}$; mini-batch sample $B_t$ and learning rate $\eta_t$ at the $t$-th iteration

**Output** : Optimal private model parameters $\tilde{\mathbf{w}}^*$

```
Initialize model parameters w_0;
for t = 0 to T − 1 do
    Randomly sample mini-batch B_t;
    // Add noise to the gradient
    ∇̃L(w_t) = (1/b)(Σ_{(x_i,y_i)∈B_t} ∇ℓ(w_t, (x_i, y_i)) + z_t), where ρ(z_t) ∝ exp(−(nελ/2)‖z‖);
    // Perform gradient descent using the perturbed gradient
    w_{t+1} = w_t − η_t ∇̃L(w_t);
return w̃*_T
```

$$\tilde{\nabla}\mathcal{L}(\mathbf{w}_t) = \frac{1}{b}\left(\sum_{(\mathbf{x}_i, y_i)\in B_t} \nabla\ell(\mathbf{w}_t, (\mathbf{x}_i, y_i)) + \mathbf{z}_t\right), \text{ where } \rho(\mathbf{z}_t) \propto \exp(-\tfrac{n\epsilon\lambda}{2}\|\mathbf{z}\|)$$

$$\mathbf{w}_{t+1} = \mathbf{w}_t - \eta_t\tilde{\nabla}\mathcal{L}(\mathbf{w}_t)$$

**Example 1** Below, we illustrate the differences in adding noise under output perturbation, objective perturbation, and gradient perturbation using Logistic Regression as an example.

Logistic Regression is a classic classification model in machine learning, formulated as a parameterized logistic distribution. For a binary classification task, given the training samples $\mathcal{D} = \{(\mathbf{x}_i, y_i)\}_{i\in[n]}$ with $y_i \in [1, -1]$, Logistic Regression can be represented by the following probability distribution:

$$\begin{aligned} P(Y = y_i|X = \mathbf{x}_i) = \sigma(y_i\mathbf{w}^\top\mathbf{x}_i) &= \frac{\exp(y_i\mathbf{w}^\top\mathbf{x}_i)}{1 + \exp(y_i\mathbf{w}^\top\mathbf{x}_i)} \\ &= \sqrt{\sigma(y_i\mathbf{w}^\top\mathbf{x}_i)^{(1+y_i)} + (1 - \sigma(y_i\mathbf{w}^\top\mathbf{x}_i))^{(1-y_i)}} \end{aligned} \tag{7.2}$$

where $\sigma(\cdot)$ denotes the Logistic function (also known as the Sigmoid function). The log-likelihood function for the samples is constructed using maximum likelihood estimation:

$$\log L(\mathbf{w}) = \log \prod_{i\in[n]} P(Y = y_i|X = \mathbf{x}_i) \\ = \sum_{i\in[n]} \left[ -\log(1 + \exp^{-y_i \mathbf{w}^\top \mathbf{x}_i}) \right] \tag{7.3}$$

The objective function for empirical risk minimization is set as the negative log-likelihood function, with the average loss calculated to avoid sample size effects. To ensure the objective function is convex, the $L_2$ norm is chosen as the regularizer, as shown in formula (7.4):

$$\mathcal{L}(\mathbf{w}) = \frac{1}{n} \sum_{i\in[n]} \log\left(1 + \exp^{-y_i \mathbf{w}^\top \mathbf{x}_i}\right) + \frac{\lambda}{2} \|\mathbf{w}\|_2^2 \tag{7.4}$$

As proved in [10], when $\|\mathbf{x}_i\|_2 \leq 1$,

- The sensitivity of the objective function output is $\frac{n\lambda}{2}$. Thus, output perturbation satisfies differential privacy when the random noise $\mathbf{z}$ follows a distribution with parameter $\beta = \frac{n\lambda\epsilon}{2}$;
- The sensitivity of the objective function is $\frac{n}{2}$. Hence, objective perturbation meets differential privacy when the random noise $\mathbf{z}$ follows a distribution with parameter $\beta = \frac{n\epsilon}{2}$;
- The sensitivity of the objective function's gradient is $\frac{n}{2}$. Therefore, gradient perturbation satisfies differential privacy when the random noise $\mathbf{z}_t$ added at each iteration follows a distribution with parameter $\beta = \frac{n\epsilon}{2}$.

## 7.4 Privacy Protection in Deep Learning

Compared to traditional ML models with simple structures, DL models often have a complex non-linear structure. Therefore, the objective function is non-convex, and the gradient descent method is used to solve the optimal model. Not only are there issues such as a large number of parameters, slow algorithm convergence, and local optimality, but the iterative optimization process inevitably requires frequent access to training data. The *over-parameterized* model structure is more likely to generate over-fitting problems, making privacy protection in DL face greater challenges.

### *7.4.1 Privacy Algorithm Design*

**1. Output perturbation**: Papernot et al. [11] proposed the PATE (private aggregation of teacher ensemble) framework based on knowledge transfer, which utilizes the output disturbance mechanism based on constructing an ensemble model, thereby achieving privacy protection in DL. The main approach of this method is to introduce a *student* model and multiple *teacher* models, achieving the isolation of underlying data from user access interfaces. This method can be specifically summarized in 3 steps: first, the training dataset is divided into $N$ non-intersecting subsets, and $N$ *teacher* models are independently trained; Second, for any test sample, the prediction result of each *teacher* model is considered as a vote, and noise is added to the voting results during the voting process. The prediction result with the highest vote count is obtained based on the noisy results; Finally, the *student* model is trained with the dataset labeled by the *teacher* models, and this *student* model is ultimately used for subsequent prediction tasks.

PATE achieves the indirect training of a public model without exposing sensitive data, thereby effectively defending against model inversion attacks. However, in some special cases, such as when the prediction results of the majority of *teacher* models are consistent, the output perturbation mechanism is not sufficient to effectively defend against individual privacy leaks.

**2. Gradient perturbation**: Compared with the gradient perturbation in traditional machine learning discussed in the previous section, it is often ensured that DL algorithms satisfy differential privacy by adding random noise from a Gaussian distribution to the gradient during the iterative process of SGD. The most representative of these is the differentially private stochastic gradient descent (DPSGD) [14], as shown in Algorithm 4,

**Algorithm 4:** Differentially Private Stochastic Gradient Descent (DPSGD)

**Input** : Training dataset $\mathcal{D} = \{(\mathbf{x}_i, y_i)\}_{i\in[N]}$; mini-batch samples $B_t$ and learning rate $\eta_t$ at the $t$-th iteration

**Output** : Optimal private model parameters $\mathbf{w}_T$

Initialize model parameters $\mathbf{w}_0$

**for** $t = 0$ *to* $T - 1$ **do**

  Randomly draw mini-batch samples $B_t$ with a sampling probability of $L/N$

  **for** $\mathbf{x}_i \in B_t$ **do**

    // Calculate the gradient for each record $\mathbf{x}_i$ in the mini-batch sample

    $\mathbf{g}_t(\mathbf{x}_i) \leftarrow \nabla_{\mathbf{w}_t}\mathcal{L}(\mathbf{w}_t, \mathbf{x}_i)$

    // Gradient clipping

    $\bar{\mathbf{g}}_t(\mathbf{x}_i) \leftarrow \mathbf{g}_t(\mathbf{x}_i)/\max(1, \frac{\|\mathbf{g}_t(\mathbf{x}_i)\|}{C})$, where $C$ is a given maximum gradient norm threshold

  // Gradient perturbation

  $\tilde{\mathbf{g}}_t \leftarrow \frac{1}{L}(\sum_i \bar{\mathbf{g}}_t(\mathbf{x}_i) + \mathcal{N}(0, \sigma^2 C^2 \mathbb{I}))$

  // Gradient descent

  $\mathbf{w}_{t+1} = \mathbf{w}_t - \eta_t \tilde{\mathbf{g}}_t$

**return** $\tilde{\mathbf{w}}_T$

### *7.4.2 Privacy Risk Analysis*

For deep learning, training involves greater difficulty in balancing data privacy risks and model usability. Specifically, if each iteration meets differential privacy, the cumulative privacy loss over the entire training process, according to the basic composition theorem of differential privacy, will be proportional to the number of iterations. This implies an extremely large overall privacy budget, which undermines the purpose of privacy protection. Conversely, to keep the privacy budget within a small range, more noise must be added at each iteration, which compromises model usability. One solution is to relax the definition of differential privacy, moderately reducing the standards for privacy requirements. This allows for less noise to be added while keeping the cumulative privacy loss constant, thereby enhancing model usability.

This chapter introduces several common relaxations of differential privacy, all derived from $\epsilon$-differential privacy. These definitions enable a more rigorous privacy risk analysis of deep learning algorithms.

**Definition 14** (*($\epsilon, \delta$)-Differential Privacy*) For any two neighboring datasets $D, D' \in \mathcal{D}$, given a randomized algorithm $f : \mathcal{D} \to \mathbb{R}$ and any output $S \in \mathbb{R}$, if

$$\max_S \ln \left[ \frac{\Pr[f(D) \in S] - \delta}{\Pr[f(D') \in S]} \right] \leq \epsilon \tag{7.5}$$

then algorithm $f$ satisfies $(\epsilon, \delta)$-differential privacy.

$(\epsilon, \delta)$-differential privacy [12] is the first relaxed DP definition. It introduces a small non-zero $\delta$ to represent the probability of DP violation. This allows $(\epsilon, \delta)$-DP to have lower privacy loss with the same noise level, as it permits a small probability $\delta$ of not satisfying the privacy guarantee. In practice, $\delta$ is often set to the reciprocal of the training sample size.

**Definition 15** (*KL Differential Privacy*) For any two neighboring datasets $D, D' \in \mathcal{D}$, given a randomized algorithm $f : \mathcal{D} \to \mathbb{R}$ and any output $S \in \mathbb{R}$, if the following inequality holds:

$$D_{KL}(f(D)||f(D')) = \max_S \ln \left[ \frac{\Pr[f(D) \in S] - \delta}{\Pr[f(D') \in S]} \right] \leq \epsilon \tag{7.6}$$

then algorithm $f$ satisfies KL differential privacy.

KL differential privacy is proposed based on $(\epsilon, \delta)$-differential privacy and KL-divergence (relative entropy), which measures the difference between two probability distributions. Compared with $(\epsilon, \delta)$-differential privacy, KL differential privacy relaxes the privacy requirement by limiting the expected privacy loss rather than the maximum privacy loss.

**Definition 16** (*Concentrated Differential Privacy (CDP)*) For any two neighboring datasets $D, D' \in \mathcal{D}$ and a randomized algorithm $f : \mathcal{D} \rightarrow \mathbb{R}$, let $D_{subG}$ be the sub-Gaussian divergence. If the following inequality holds:

$$D_{subG}(f(D)||f(D')) \leq (\mu, \tau) \tag{7.7}$$

then algorithm $f$ satisfies $(\mu, \tau)$-concentrated differential privacy.

In the CDP definition, privacy loss is regarded as a random variable following a sub-Gaussian distribution. Here, parameters $\mu$ and $\tau$ determine the mean and variance (concentration level) of this distribution. Analysis shows that if an algorithm satisfies $\epsilon$-DP, it will meet $(\frac{\epsilon(e^{\epsilon}-1)}{2}, \epsilon)$-CDP, but the converse is not true.

**Definition 17** (*Zero Concentrated Differential Privacy (zCDP)*) For any two neighboring datasets $D, D' \in \mathcal{D}$ and a randomized algorithm $f : \mathcal{D} \rightarrow \mathbb{R}$, let $D_\alpha$ be the $\alpha$-Rényi divergence with $\alpha \in (1, \infty)$. If the following inequality holds:

$$D_\alpha(f(D)||f(D')) \leq \xi + \rho\alpha \tag{7.8}$$

then algorithm $f$ satisfies $(\xi, \rho)$-zero concentrated differential privacy.

zCDP is a variant of CDP where privacy loss tightly concentrates around zero mean. Analysis shows that if an algorithm satisfies $\epsilon$-DP, it meets $\frac{\epsilon^2}{2}$-zCDP. Since Rényi divergence allows direct mapping from zCDP to DP, it can be further deduced that if an algorithm satisfies $\rho$-zCDP, it will satisfy $(\rho + 2\sqrt{\rho \ln(1/\delta)}, \delta)$-DP.

**Definition 18** (*Rényi Differential Privacy (RDP)*) For any two neighboring datasets $D, D' \in \mathcal{D}$ and a randomized algorithm $f : \mathcal{D} \rightarrow \mathbb{R}$, let $D_\alpha$ be the $\alpha$-Rényi divergence with $\alpha \in (1, \infty)$. If the following inequality holds:

$$D_\alpha(f(D)||f(D')) \leq \epsilon \tag{7.9}$$

then algorithm $f$ satisfies $(\alpha, \epsilon)$-Rényi differential privacy.

Compared with CDP and zCDP, RDP allows for more precise calculations of privacy loss. If an algorithm satisfies $\epsilon$-DP, then it satisfies $(\alpha, \epsilon)$-RDP. Conversely, if an algorithm satisfies $(\alpha, \epsilon)$-RDP, then it satisfies $(\epsilon + \frac{\ln(1/\delta)}{\alpha-1}, \delta)$-DP, where $0 < \delta < 1$.

Combining the above relaxed DP definitions can further reduce the upper bound of cumulative privacy loss in deep learning model training, enabling stricter composition analysis. A typical study is the advanced composition theorem proposed by Dwork et al. [13] and the MA (moments accountant) mechanism based on RDP proposed by Abadi et al. [14]. However, it should be noted that the cost of protection methods based on relaxed DP definitions is the increased privacy leakage risk when the model is subjected to membership inference attacks or model inversion attacks.

## 7.5 Summary

This chapter first outlines privacy issues in machine learning, including direct and indirect privacy leaks. From the algorithm perspective, existing privacy-protection technologies can be categorized into three main types: encryption techniques (e.g., homomorphic encryption), perturbation techniques (e.g., differential privacy), and collaborative-computation frameworks (e.g., secure multi-party computation and federated learning). The chapter then focuses on differential privacy techniques, discussing the design and analysis of privacy-preserving machine learning methods in both statistical machine learning and deep learning contexts. Unlike simple statistical queries, machine learning tasks that require multiple iterations to find optimal models face greater challenges in balancing cumulative privacy loss and model usability. Current research typically addresses this by first analyzing privacy loss theoretically, designing reasonable noise-adding mechanisms to ensure differential privacy in empirical risk minimization. It also involves developing more relaxed differential privacy definitions and deriving stricter upper bounds on cumulative privacy loss.

Differential privacy has certain inapplicability in specific situations. For instance, it can only protect single-point privacy. If records are correlated, attackers can still launch inference attacks on algorithms that satisfy differential privacy. For example, in a social network, if user A has multiple connections to other users, these relationships are stored as multiple records. Differential privacy can only protect each record in isolation, not all of user A's records collectively to fully conceal their presence in the network. In reality, true individual privacy protection is only achieved when the attacker cannot deduce whether an individual participated in data generation.

## References

1. SHOKRI R, STRONATI M, SONG C, et al. Membership inference attacks against machine learning models[C]//Proceedings of the 38th IEEE Symposium on Security and Privacy. Piscataway:IEEE, 2017:3-18.
2. FREDRIKSON M, LANTZ E, JHA S, et al. Privacy in pharmacogenetics: An end-to-end case study of personalized warfarin dosing[C]//Proceedings of the 23rd USENIX Security Symposium. Berkeley:USENIX Association, 2014:17-32.
3. FREDRIKSON M, JHA A, RISTENPART T. Model inversion attacks that exploit confidence information and basic countermeasures[C]//Proceedings of the 2015 ACM SIGSAC Conference on Computer and Communications Security. New York: ACM, 2015:1322-1333.
4. TRAMÈR F, ZHANG F, JUELS A, et al. Stealing machine learning models via prediction APIs[C]//Proceedings of the 25th USENIX USENIX Security Symposium. Berkeley:USENIX Association, 2016:601-618.
5. ZHANG Q, SWORD J. Towards [C]//Proceedings of the 2014 ACM SIGSAC Conference on Computer and Communications Security. New York: ACM, 2014.
6. ZHANG X, MENG X. Differential privacy in data publication and analysis [J]. Chinese Journal of Computers, 2014, 37(4):927-949.

7. DUCHI J C, JORDAN M I, WAINWRIGHT M J. Local privacy and statistical minimax rates[C]//Proceedings of the 54th IEEE Annual Symposium on Foundations of Computer Science, Piscataway:IEEE, 2013, 429-438.
8. YE Q, MENG X, ZHU M, et al. A review of localized differential privacy research [J]. Journal of Software, 2018, 29(7):1981-2005.
9. ZHANG J, ZHANG Z, XIAO X, et al. Functional mechanism: regression analysis under differential privacy[J]. Proceedings of the VLDB Endowment, 2012, 5(11): 1364-1375.
10. CHAUDHURI K, MONTELEONI C, SARWATE A D. Differentially private empirical risk minimization[J]. Journal of Machine Learning Research, 2011, 12(2):1069-1109.
11. PAPERNOT N, ABADI M, ERLINGSSON U, et al. Semi-supervised Knowledge Transfer for Deep Learning from Private Training Data[C/OL]//Proceedings of the 5th International Conference on Learning Representations. 2017[2022-09-07]. https://openreview.net/pdf?id=HkwoSDPgg
12. DWORK C, KENTHAPADI K, MCSHERRY F, et al. Our data, ourselves: Privacy via distributed noise generation[C]//Proceedings of the 25th Annual International Conference on the Theory and Applications of Cryptographic Techniques. New York:Springer, 2006:486-503.
13. DWORK C, ROTHBLUM GN, VADHAN S. Boosting and differential privacy[C]//Proceedings of the 51st IEEE Annual Symposium on Foundations of Computer Science. Piscataway:IEEE, 2010:51-60.
14. ABADI M, CHU A, GOODFELLOW I, MCMAHAN H B, et al. Deep learning with differential privacy[C]//Proceedings of the 2016 ACM SIGSAC Conference on Computer and Communications Security. New York: ACM, 2016:308-318.

# Chapter 8
# Privacy Protection in Federated Learning

Traditional machine learning architectures require data to be centrally stored before model training, which is easy to implement and remains the mainstream application architecture in the industry. However, with the growing capabilities of big data analysis, privacy issues caused by centralized data collection have become more prominent. On one hand, untrustworthy data collectors may leak user data either actively or passively. On the other hand, once collected, user data is no longer under their control, making it difficult to trace and hold accountable in case of a data breach.

Building on the previous chapter, this one delves into federated learning and its privacy-protection issues. It starts with an introduction to the federated learning framework and the privacy-leakage risks it faces, then outlines two privacy-protection methods: differential-privacy-based and secure-aggregation-based federated learning. Federated learning has inherent data-privacy-protection characteristics. Its training data isn't centrally stored, thus avoiding direct privacy leaks from large-scale data collection. However, studies indicate that even though federated learning gives users control over their personal data, it still can't fully prevent potential indirect privacy attacks.

## 8.1 Introduction

With the rapid development of mobile internet and mobile smart devices (such as mobile phones, tablet computers, etc.), future mobile devices will become the main battlefield for technological innovation and personal privacy protection. As data contains more and more personal sensitive information, the early method of centrally storing data in a single node for machine learning is no longer feasible. This is because, on the one hand, storing and computing massive data places extremely high demands on servers; on the other hand, once personal data is centrally collected,



X. Meng, *Data Privacy and Data Governance*, Big Data Management,
https://doi.org/10.1007/978-981-95-5787-5_8

people lose their right to know and control it. To address these issues, Google proposed the concept of **federated learning** [1, 2] in 2017, aiming to keep user data on local devices while still being able to train a globally usable model, as shown in Definition 19. Currently, federated learning has been applied in Google's GBoard input method for functions such as word association and smart suggestions [3, 4].

**Definition 19** (*Federated Learning*) $N$ edge nodes jointly train a global model $\mathbf{w} \in \mathbb{R}^d$ using their respective local datasets $D_1, \ldots, D_N$. During this process, local data from each edge node doesn't flow to other nodes. Instead, they interact by uploading local model parameters to a central node. The central node aggregates the information, updates the global model parameters, and sends them back to the edge nodes for the next round of training. This cycle repeats until the global model parameters converge.

From the system-architecture perspective, federated learning resembles early distributed machine learning data parallelism. As shown in Fig. 8.1, it involves a central node and multiple edge nodes with different training data. Each edge node independently trains using the global model from the central node and uploads updated model information. The central node aggregates these updates into the global model and redistributes it. This iterative process continues until the central model converges.

However, from the system-deployment perspective, federated learning and data-parallel distributed machine learning differ significantly in four main aspects:

1. **Data Heterogeneity**. Traditional data-parallel training involves uniformly slicing central-node data and distributing it to edge nodes, yielding independent and identically distributed (I.I.D.) data. In federated learning, edge nodes locally generate and collect data in a non-I.I.D. fashion. This leads to significant differences in data quantity and distribution across nodes, driven by participant diversity and thus uncontrollable. For instance, in input-method applications, user-generated data varies by attributes like nationality, age, and occupation, posing a challenge for training effective input-word association models.

**Fig. 8.1** Federated learning framework

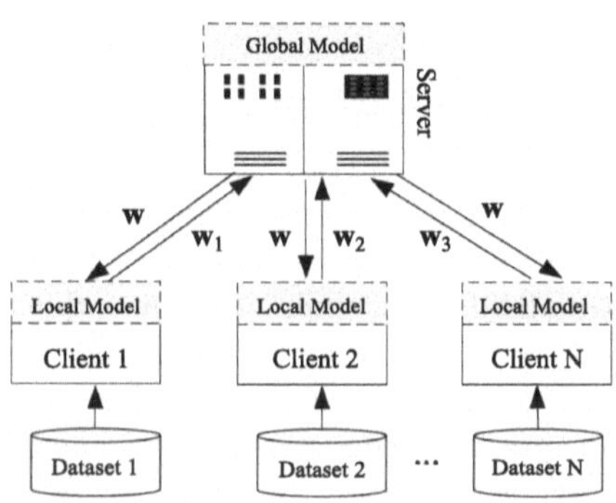

2. **System Heterogeneity**. In federated learning, each edge node's storage, computing, and communication capabilities are heterogeneous due to differences in hardware (CPU, memory), network connections (3G, 4G, 5G, WIFI), and power sources (battery level). Moreover, only a small fraction of all edge nodes are active during training, and they may drop out suddenly due to connectivity or power constraints. This necessitates higher fault tolerance and robustness in federated learning systems.
3. **Communication Constraints**. Federated learning faces communication challenges similar to traditional distributed machine learning. Additionally, hardware limitations often impose higher communication demands in mobile scenarios. For instance, devices can only participate in model training when connected to a wireless network and charging.
4. **Ultra-Large-Scale Distributed Network**. With the growing penetration of mobile devices, popular apps like Facebook and WeChat now have over 1 billion monthly active users. In such scenarios, the number of nodes in a distributed network far exceeds the amount of data stored per node, a scale that is difficult for traditional distributed machine learning to achieve.

Federated learning can be categorized based on participant types into cross-device and cross-institution (or cross-silo) federated learning [1], as shown in Table 8.1.

Federated learning can also be categorized into horizontal federated learning (HFL), vertical federated learning (VFL), and federated transfer learning based on training data samples and features [5], as shown in Fig. 8.2.

**Table 8.1** Comparison between Cross-device and Cross-institution FL

| Differences | Cross-silo FL | Cross-device FL |
|---|---|---|
| Type of clients | Enterprises, organizations or institutions, local datasets are generally composed of individual data from its user community, with a larger sample size | Smartphones, tablets and other mobile devices, local datasets are generally composed of usage data from device users, with a smaller sample size |
| Scale of clients | 2–100 clients | Highly parallelized, up to 1 billion clients |
| Device stability | Strong stability, almost guaranteed to be stable online | Poor stability, only a small part of participants remain online at a certain period, and prone to sudden disconnection issues |
| Addressability | Addressable, i.e., generally assigning unique identifiers to individual clients, allowing the server to perform specific access | Non-addressable, i.e., generally not assigning unique identifiers to individual clients, thus the service provider cannot specifically access a certain client |
| System Bottleneck | Computational cost and communication constraints | More reflected in communication constraints |

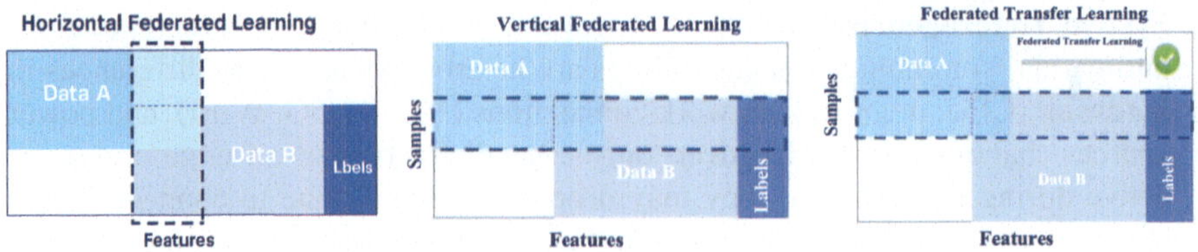


**Fig. 8.2** Federated learning classification

- **Horizontal Federated Learning**: Edge nodes have highly overlapping or identical data features but different samples. Their data can be seen as obtained by horizontal slicing of a 2D master table, hence the name Sample-Partitioned Federated Learning. For instance, a bank's financial data across different regions typically has consistent features but low customer overlap.
- **Vertical Federated Learning**: Edge nodes have low feature overlap but high sample overlap. Their data resembles vertical slicing of a 2D master table, hence the term Feature-Partitioned Federated Learning. For example, different banks in the same area often share a high degree of customer overlap but have significant differences in financial data features.
- **Federated Transfer Learning**: Edge nodes have low overlap in both data features and training samples. The goal of transfer learning is to minimize the prediction error rate when using the labels of the original feature domain to predict the labels of the target domain.

Privacy protection is both the starting point and a key research focus of federated learning. Although decentralized data collection reduces direct data leakage, indirect leakage risks remain during gradient-sharing. This chapter discusses federated learning's privacy issues in Sect. 8.2, and introduces two privacy-protection methods in Sects. 8.3 and 8.4: differential-privacy-based and secure-aggregation-based federated learning.

## 8.2 Privacy-Enhancing Frameworks

Federated learning abandons the traditional process of data collection in datasets, sharing model update information (such as gradients) through various clients, thereby greatly alleviating the problem of direct data leakage. However, the risk of indirect privacy leakage still exists. Similar to the privacy issues in machine learning introduced in the previous chapter, the privacy issues in federated learning also manifest in two aspects:

(1) During the model training phase, data privacy leaks can occur due to parameter interactions within the system. In a federated learning framework, both participants and service providers may potentially act as attackers to steal the private

information of other participants. If the central node is curious or malicious, once the participant uploads the local model parameters to the server of the central node, it can infer the local data features or other implicit information of the participant through these parameters. If other participants are curious or malicious, they can monitor or steal the global model by receiving the aggregated information sent by the service provider, or they can damage the usability of the global model through data poisoning attacks. Furthermore, malicious participants can conspire with other participants or even the server to jointly infer the data information of other participants.

(2) During the model prediction phase, data privacy leaks can occur due to the model's insufficient generalization ability. If a machine learning model has weak generalization capabilities, it will produce significantly different output results when encountering some data that has appeared in the training set compared to data that has not appeared in the training set. Untrustworthy users can identify whether a record belongs to the training set through multiple rounds of interaction with the model. If the training set data is sensitive (for example, the training set is a dataset of patients with a certain disease), it can lead to personal data privacy leaks.

Before delving into the design of privacy-protected federated learning architectures, let's first understand the formal representation of federated learning and one of its classic algorithms-Federated Averaging (FedAvg).

As mentioned in the previous chapter, the commonly used empirical risk minimization strategy in machine learning model training can also be applied to find the optimal model in federated learning. However, the objective function is no longer the empirical risk on a centralized training dataset but the weighted average of the empirical risks on each edge node's local dataset. Let $D = \cup_{i \in [N]} D_i$ represent all the training data logically. The federated learning objective function is shown in Eq. 8.1.

$$\begin{aligned} \mathcal{L}(\mathbf{w}, D) &= \sum_{i=1}^{N} p_i \mathcal{L}_i(\mathbf{w}, D_i) \\ \mathcal{L}_i(\mathbf{w}, D_i) &= \mathbb{E}_{(\mathbf{x}, y) \sim \mathcal{P}_i} [\ell(f(\mathbf{w}, \mathbf{x}), y)] \\ &= \frac{1}{|D_i|} \sum_{(\mathbf{x}_j, y_j) \in D_i} \ell(f(\mathbf{w}, \mathbf{x}_j), y_j) \end{aligned} \tag{8.1}$$

Thus, by minimizing the average empirical risk, we can obtain the optimal global model $\mathbf{w}^* = \text{argmin}_{\mathbf{w}} \mathcal{L}(\mathbf{w}, D)$. Here, $\ell(f(\mathbf{w}, \mathbf{x}), y)$ represents the loss function used to evaluate the model, such as squared loss or cross-entropy loss. $\mathcal{P}_i$ denotes the local data distribution of the $i$th edge node. In practice, $\mathcal{P}_i$ varies across edge nodes. However, for research simplicity and ease of analysis, it is often assumed that the data is independent and identically distributed, meaning all nodes share the same $\mathcal{P}_i$.

Solving the empirical risk minimization problem in federated learning can also employ gradient descent, with Federated Averaging being a typical example. Its core idea is that the central node updates the global model by calculating the weighted average of the model parameters or parameter updates from each edge node, based on their respective training data, as shown in Algorithm 5. Since the Federated Averaging algorithm is the most widely accepted federated learning method and has given rise to many variants, unless specified otherwise, subsequent sections assume that federated learning is implemented based on the Federated Averaging algorithm.

**Algorithm 5:** Federated Averaging [2]

**Input** : Training dataset $D_i$ of the $i$-th edge node $C_i$; mini-batch sample $B_t$ and learning rate $\eta_t$ at the $t$-th iteration; global training rounds $T$; local iterations $K$ per round; number of edge nodes $M$ per round

**Output** : Optimal global model parameters $\mathbf{w}^*$

**Central Node** `Global Coordination`**:**

  $\mathbf{w}_0 \leftarrow$ (Randomly initialize global model parameters)

  **for** $t = 0$ *to* $T - 1$ **do**

    `// Randomly sample participants for this round`

    $\mathcal{S}_t \leftarrow$ (Set of $M$ edge nodes participating in this round)

    `// Local model updates at each edge node`

    **foreach** $C_i \in \mathcal{S}_t$ **do** *in parallel*

      $\Delta \mathbf{w}_t^i \leftarrow$ **Local Update**($\mathbf{w}_t$)

    `// Aggregate and update global model parameters`

    $\Delta \bar{\mathbf{w}}_{t+1} \leftarrow \frac{1}{|\mathcal{S}_t|} \sum_{C_i \in \mathcal{S}_t} \Delta \mathbf{w}_t^i$

  **return** $\mathbf{w}_T$

**Edge Node** $C_i$ `Local Update`**:**

  $\mathbf{w}_{t,0} \leftarrow \mathbf{w}_t$

  **for** $k = 0$ *to* $K - 1$ **do**

    Randomly sample mini-batch $B_k$ from $D_i$

    `// Gradient Descent`

    $\mathbf{w}_{t,k+1} = \mathbf{w}_{t,k} - \eta_t \nabla \mathcal{L}_m(\mathbf{w}_t, B_k)$

  **return** $\mathbf{w}_{t,K}$

Currently, various privacy-protection architectures for federated learning have been proposed in academia. Among them, the most representative are differential privacy-based and secure aggregation-based federated learning. Both architectures are designed under the assumption that the central node is semi-trusted or untrusted, as shown in Fig. 8.3.

- Differential Privacy-based Federated Learning [6, 7]: Relying on noise-addition mechanisms, each edge node adds randomly-distributed noise to model information before uploading it to the central node, ensuring differential privacy for the entire training process. Research focuses on reducing noise impact on the global model's convergence and usability while maintaining privacy protection.

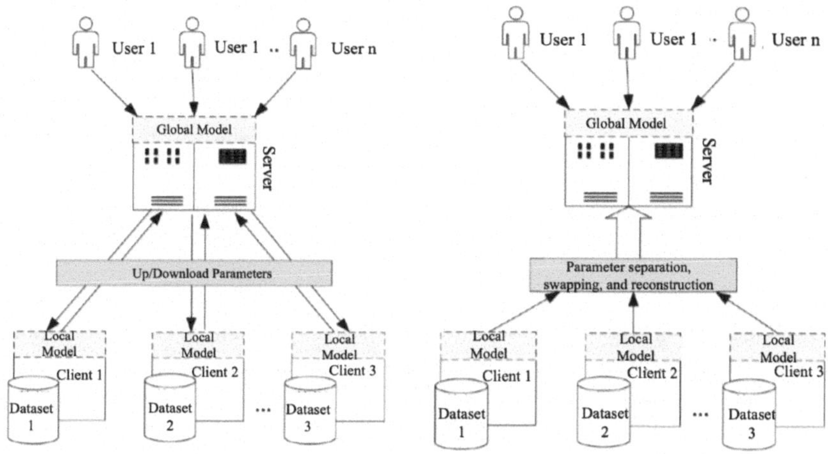


(a) Privacy-Protection Federated Learning Based on Differential Privacy

(b) Privacy-Protection Federated Learning Based on Secure Aggregation

**Fig. 8.3** Architectures of privacy-protection federated learning

- Secure Aggregation-based Federated Learning [8]: Using secret-sharing mechanisms, a trusted entity splits, exchanges, and recombines edge nodes' model parameters before sending them to the central node. Given the numerous communication rounds in federated learning, research emphasizes communication-cost reduction.

## 8.3 Differential Privacy in Federated Learning

Implementing differential privacy based federated learning essentially continues the differential privacy protection methods for centralized machine learning introduced in Sect. 7.4. As raw data stays on edge nodes, the risk of direct data leakage is significantly reduced. Moreover, since the central and edge nodes primarily exchange model parameters, input and output perturbation are no longer research focuses. Instead, researchers mostly leverage gradient perturbation to design and implement privacy-preserving federated learning frameworks.

Assuming the central node is trustworthy, random noise can be added to the aggregated local model results to prevent malicious edge nodes from inferring other nodes' local data using the global model. When the central node isn't trustworthy, noise addition must occur at the edge nodes to ensure local data isn't inferred from transmitted model information by the central node or other edge nodes, as shown in Fig. 8.4. In the figure, $P$ represents participants, $\mathbf{w}$ denotes the parameters of local models, and $\eta$ indicates the random noise added by participants.

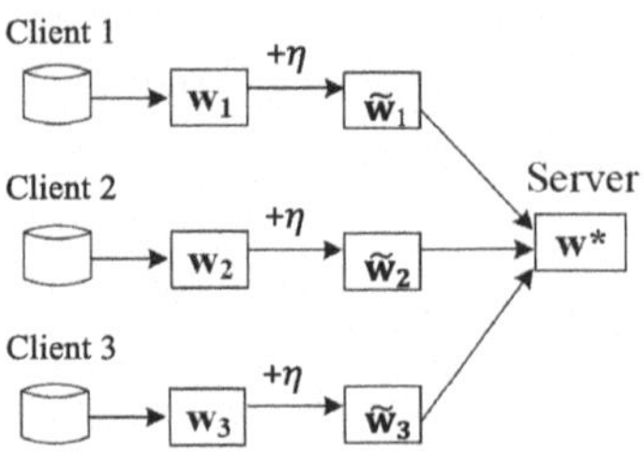


**Fig. 8.4** Federated learning architecture based on differential privacy

Since the FedAvg algorithm essentially parallelizes gradient descent across nodes, the design and analysis of noise-addition mechanisms are similar to those in centralized machine learning, as discussed in Sect. 7.4. Here, key points include:For each participant, privacy loss throughout training should be analyzed using the sequential composition theorem, i.e., it increases with more iterations. For the entire federated learning process, total privacy loss should be analyzed via the parallel composition theorem, i.e., it equals the maximum privacy loss among all participants.

Differential privacy-based federated learning is simple to design and easy to deploy with low computational overhead. However, the added noise can slow down the model's convergence and reduce its usability. Thus, a key research challenge is to minimize the noise while maintaining the same level of local parameter privacy protection.

## 8.4 Secure Aggregation in Federated Learning

Unlike differential privacy-based federated learning, secure aggregation-based methods mainly rely on homomorphic encryption or secret sharing. They allow parameters to circulate in encrypted or split form without adding extra noise, ensuring the accuracy of aggregated results at the central node.Thus, this method doesn't affect model usability.

**(1) Homomorphic Encryption for Secure Aggregation of Parameters**
Section 7.2 introduces the basics of homomorphic encryption (HE). Essentially, HE is a cryptographic function that ensures computations on ciphertext yield results equivalent to those from computations on plaintext.

Figure 8.5a presents the FL architecture for secure parameter aggregation using HE. In general, achieving this secure aggregation in FL involves four main steps:

1. Key Generation: Each participant randomly selects their private key and computes the public key.
2. Model Training: Each participant trains a local model on their data to obtain gradient values.

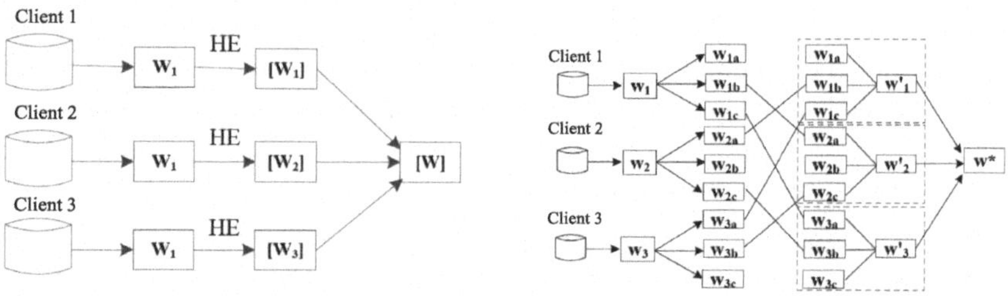


(a) Implementing secure parameter aggregation using homomorphic encryption

(b) Implementing secure parameter aggregation using secret sharing

**Fig. 8.5** Federated learning architecture based on secure aggregation

3. Data Processing: Gradient values are encrypted using Paillier or another homomorphic encryption scheme.
4. Parameter Aggregation: The server aggregates the encrypted parameters and distributes the aggregated parameters to the participants.

Homomorphic encryption can effectively ensure the confidentiality of parameters when edge nodes upload them to the central node in federated learning. However, as mentioned in Sect. 7.2, homomorphic encryption has significant drawbacks in computational overhead, making it difficult to implement in practice.

**(2) Secret Sharing for Secure Parameter Aggregation**

Secret Sharing (SS) is a common technology for Secure Multiparty Computation (MPC), as defined below.

**Definition 20** (*Secret Sharing*) A secret $s$ is split into $n$ shares, such that $s$ can be reconstructed only when at least $t$ shares are combined. Any $t-1$ or fewer shares provide no information about $s$.

The main process of implementing secure parameter aggregation via secret sharing technology is illustrated in Fig. 8.5b. In general, this method consists of three primary steps:

1. Each edge node decomposes the locally trained model parameters $\mathbf{w}_i$ into multiple shares, represented as vectors $\{\mathbf{w}_{ia}, \mathbf{w}_{ib}, \mathbf{w}_{ic}, \ldots\}$;
2. Each edge node exchanges shares pairwise to ensure that each holds one of its own shares.
3. Each edge node performs local aggregation on the held shares and sends the result to the central node, which then conducts global aggregation to obtain $\mathbf{w}^*$.

In addition to the above method, one-time masks can also be used to encrypt local models. Let the random variable $\mathbf{s}_{u,v}$ be the encryption parameter for any pair of edge nodes $(u, v)$, where node $u$ adds this random vector to its local model parameters $\mathbf{w}_u$, and node $v$ subtracts it from its local model parameters $\mathbf{w}_v$. This ensures that the sum of the encrypted parameters received by the server for each pair of edge nodes equals the sum of the true parameter values. Formula (8.2) shows the process of the encrypted model parameters $\mathbf{y}_u$ sent by edge node $u$ to the server, and the aggregation result $\mathbf{z}$ obtained by the central node after aggregating the encrypted parameters.

$$
\begin{aligned}
\mathbf{y}_u &= \mathbf{w}_u + \sum \mathbf{s}_{u,v} - \sum \mathbf{s}_{u,v} (\text{mod } R) \\
\mathbf{z} &= \sum_{u \in U} \mathbf{y}_u = (\mathbf{w}_u + \sum \mathbf{s}_{u,v} - \sum \mathbf{s}_{v,u}) = \sum_{u \in U} \mathbf{w}_u (\text{mod } R)
\end{aligned}
\tag{8.2}
$$

Although the above method can ensure high parameter privacy in federated learning, it has two obvious drawbacks: first, high communication overhead. Each round of federated learning training requires each pair of edge nodes to exchange parameter shares or encrypted parameters, resulting in significant communication costs; second, poor fault tolerance. In federated learning, edge nodes often go offline randomly. If a node goes offline after exchanging information with others and fails to send its parameters to the central node, a correct aggregation result cannot be obtained. Moreover, if there is a malicious node uploading fraudulent model parameters, it will severely undermine the model's usability.

## 8.5 Personalized Privacy in Federated Learning

In privacy protection research, different sources and types of data lead to varying privacy protection needs among data owners. Applying uniform privacy protection to all data has two major flaws.

First, uniform privacy protection cannot meet the needs of data with different sensitivity levels. In data collection, sensitive attributes such as diseases and geographical locations can be generalized through a tree-like classification system like the one shown in Fig. 8.6 to blur original attribute values. For example, "influenza" can be generalized to "respiratory disease", and "AIDS" to "immune-system disease". However, most people don't think influenza, a common disease, is very sensitive. In contrast, AIDS is so sensitive that even when generalized to "immune-system disease", sufficient privacy isn't guaranteed.

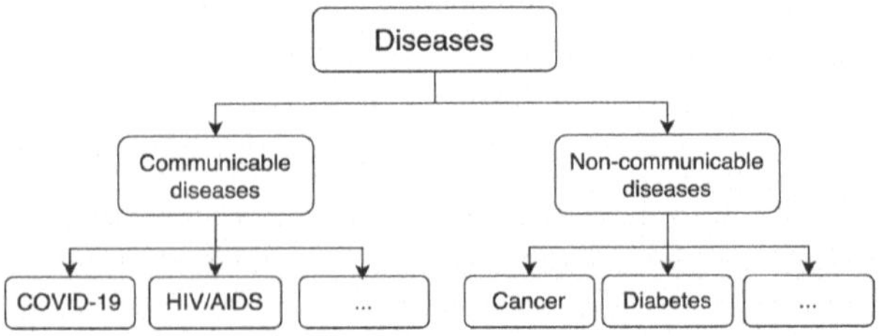


**Fig. 8.6** A hierarchy of diseases

Second, uniform privacy protection can't satisfy data owners' diverse privacy preferences. Service providers like Google and Apple, which use differential privacy, let users set privacy parameters. However, to ensure result usability, providers usually don't set overly high privacy protection levels, falling short of most data owners' privacy requirements.

The FL framework based on distributed architecture enables data owners to control their personal data, creating conditions for personalized privacy protection in machine learning. The combination of personalized privacy protection and FL gives rise to three key research questions: personalized privacy-protected FL, privacy-protected personalized FL, and doubly personalized FL with privacy protection. Personalized FL aims to train individual models for each participant based on their local data distribution. This chapter will introduce relevant knowledge of personalized privacy protection in Sect. 8.5.1. Due to the lack of effective solutions for the latter two problems at present, this chapter will focus on the first problem in Sect. 8.5.2.

### *8.5.1 Personalized Privacy Protection*

Personalized privacy, as the name suggests, allows each data owner to independently set their own privacy preferences. Early research proposed a personalized privacy protection method based on $k$-anonymity [9]. Yet, due to many privacy-leakage risks of $k$-anonymity, it's been phased out academically, so this section doesn't discuss it but focuses on differential-privacy-based personalized privacy protection methods.

Research on personalized differential privacy protection allows each data owner to set their own differential privacy parameter, $epsilon$, to safeguard their personal data. In data publishing, the service provider's main task is to perform statistical analysis on the collected data, such as generating histograms. This section introduces two personalized privacy definitions for this scenario: personalized differential privacy and personalized local differential privacy. The difference lies in whether the data perturbation occurs on the local device.

**(1) Personalized Differential Privacy**

Jorgensen et al. [10] first introduced personalized differential privacy (PDP), as defined in Definition 21. This definition ensures that during the data-publishing phase, the data of any data owner $u \in U$ in the dataset meets specific differential privacy protection.[1]

[1] Here, it is assumed that one user in the dataset corresponds to only one data record. Also, to avoid symbol redundancy, $u$ represents both the user and their data record.

**Definition 21** (*Φ-Personalized Differential Privacy* (Φ-PDP)) Given the privacy preferences $\Phi = \{\epsilon_1, \ldots, \epsilon_n\}$ of $n$ data owners, for any data owner $u \in U$ and adjacent datasets $D$, $D' \in \mathcal{D}$, $D' = D \cup \{u\}$, if the random algorithm $f : \mathcal{D} \rightarrow \mathbb{R}$ and any output result $S \in \mathbb{R}$ satisfy

$$\Pr[f(D) \in S] \leq e^{\Phi^u} \Pr[f(D') \in S] \tag{8.3}$$

the algorithm $f$ is said to satisfy Φ-Personalized Differential Privacy. Here, $\Phi^u$ is the privacy preference of $u$.

A simple way to achieve personalized differential privacy is the minimum mechanism, where all data owners meet the "strongest privacy", i.e., each data record satisfies $\epsilon_{min}$-differential privacy with $\epsilon_{min} = \min_i \epsilon_i$. However, this doesn't truly personalize protection and reduces output usability for data needing only weak protection due to excessive perturbation. Another approach is the threshold mechanism, which selects a subset of data owners with privacy preferences above a threshold $\epsilon_T$ and applies differential privacy mechanisms to this subset for analysis.

Jorgensen et al. [10] proposed an improved sampling mechanism based on the threshold mechanism. They set a privacy threshold $\epsilon_T$ and sample data records according to the probability in Eq. 8.4, then apply differential privacy to the subset to get the final output. The key challenge is determining a suitable threshold. A large threshold results in sampling few data points, causing significant "sampling error." Conversely, a small threshold leads to the minimum mechanism's "noise error."

$$p_j = \begin{cases} 1 & \epsilon_j \geq \epsilon_T \\ \frac{e^{\epsilon_j} - 1}{e^{\epsilon_T} - 1} & \epsilon_j < \epsilon_T \end{cases} \tag{8.4}$$

**(2) Personalized Local Differential Privacy**

Chen et al. [11] first defined personalized local differential privacy (PLDP), as shown in Definition 22. This definition, built on local differential privacy (LDP), involves data owners perturbing their data to varying degrees before sending it to untrusted collectors.

**Definition 22** (*(τ, ϵ)-Personalized Local Differential Privacy*, (τ, ϵ)-PDP) Given any data owner $u \in U$ with privacy preference $(\tau, \epsilon)$, for any two attribute values $d, d' \in \tau$, if the random algorithm $f : \tau \rightarrow \mathbb{R}$ and any output result $S \in \mathbb{R}$ satisfy

$$\Pr[f(d) \in S] \leq e^{\epsilon} \Pr[f(d') \in S] \tag{8.5}$$

the algorithm $f$ is said to satisfy $(\tau, \epsilon)$-personalized local differential privacy. Here, $\tau$ is referred to as the safe region of the data owner $u$.

Note that this definition only applies to data attribute domains that meet the classification system structure shown in Fig. 8.6. For instance, for an "address" attribute, a classification system can be built based on the "country-province-city-district-street" relationship, and the real location can be perturbed to a larger area in the upper level to protect privacy. Chen et al. [11] proposed a spatial data aggregation framework PSDA (Private Spatial Data Aggregation) to realize personalized local differential privacy. This framework integrates a clustering strategy based on user-specific safe regions and a personalized local perturbation mechanism to better balance data privacy and output usability.

Machine learning is essentially a complex process of iteratively solving for optimal model parameters over multiple rounds, contrasting with traditional statistical tasks in data publishing. Training models on perturbed data within a centralized learning framework can significantly impact model utility, and currently, there are no effective personalized privacy protection methods for this. However, the distributed architecture of federated learning allows data owners to control their personal data, paving the way for personalized privacy protection in machine learning. The next section will focus on implementing personalized differential privacy methods within federated learning.

### 8.5.2 Personalized Privacy Protection in Federated Learning

In traditional federated learning frameworks (see Fig. 8.1), the service provider updates the global model by aggregating local model parameters (updates) from participants and redistributes it until convergence. Throughout this process, local data of participants (data owners) remains on their devices.One intuitive way to achieve personalized differential privacy in federated learning is through a gradient perturbation mechanism. This mechanism ensures that each participant meets different levels of differential privacy during local training by adding Gaussian random noise with varying parameters to their local model parameters. Liu et al. [12] formalized this as heterogeneous differential privacy in federated learning, as shown in Definition 23. However, this approach can introduce significant bias to the globally aggregated model, making it difficult to converge and severely impacting model utility.

**Definition 23** (*Heterogeneous Differential Privacy in Federated Learning*) Given $n$ data owners' privacy preferences $\Phi = \{(\epsilon_1, \delta_1), \ldots, (\epsilon_n, \delta_n)\}$ and their local datasets $D_u \in \mathcal{D}$, if the random algorithm $f : \mathcal{D} \rightarrow \mathbb{R}$ satisfies $(\epsilon_u, \delta_u)$-differential privacy for any data owner $u \in U$, then the entire federated learning process meets $\Phi$-heterogeneous differential privacy.

The key to addressing the above challenge lies in reducing the bias caused by heterogeneous noise in the aggregated model. Liu et al. [12] proposed a projected federated averaging (PFA) framework to reduce noise and enhance model utility by projecting noisy parameters into a low-dimensional subspace. The algorithm considers that users can be categorized into "conservative" and "open" groups based on privacy preferences or external incentives. "Open" users accept weaker privacy protection, resulting in less noisy local model parameters. Thus, a low-dimensional subspace is constructed using the less noisy parameters from the "open" group.

The noisy parameters from the "conservative" group are then projected into this subspace for aggregation. Experimental results show that this method ensures model convergence and significantly improves prediction accuracy compared to the basic federated averaging algorithm.

## 8.6 Summary

This chapter delves into federated learning and its privacy protection issues. Privacy protection is one of the key motivations behind federated learning. While distributed data storage reduces direct privacy leakage, sharing local model information among participants still poses indirect privacy risks. This chapter presents two privacy-protection methods for federated learning: differential-privacy-based and secure-aggregation-based. Each has pros and cons. The former struggles to balance model privacy and usability, while the latter, though highly private, suffers from high communication costs and poor fault tolerance. Exploring solutions to balance efficiency, privacy, and usability in federated learning is a major research focus. Lastly, this chapter introduces federated learning with personalized privacy protection.

## References

1. KAIROUZ P, MCMAHAN H B, AVENT B, et al. Advances and Open Problems in Federated Learning[J/OL]. Foundations and Trends® in Machine Learning, 2021, 14(1-2):1-210(2021-06-23)[2022-09-09]. http://dx.doi.org/10.1561/220000008
2. MCMAHAN B, MOORE E, RAMAGE D, et al. Communication-efficient learning of deep networks from decentralized data[C/OL]//Proceedings of the 20th International Conference on Artificial Intelligence and Statistics. 2017:1178-1187(2017-04-10)[2022-09-07]. http://proceedings.mlr.press/v54/tian17a
3. YANG T, ANDREW G, EICHNER H, et al. Applied federated learning: Improving Google keyboard query suggestions[EB/OL]. (2018-12-07)[2022-09-06]. https://arxiv.org/abs/1812.02903
4. HARD A, RAO K, MATHEWS R, et al. Federated learning for mobile keyboard prediction[EB/OL]. (2018-11-08)[2022-09-09]. https://arxiv.org/abs/1811.03604
5. YANG Q, LIU Y, CHEN T, TONG Y. Federated machine learning: Concept and applications[J]. ACM Transactions on Intelligent Systems and Technology, 2019, 10(2):1-9.
6. GEYER R C, KLEIN T, NABI M. 2017. Differentially private federated learning: A client level perspective[EB/OL]. (2017-12-20)[2022-09-09]. https://arxiv.org/abs/1712.07557
7. GIRGIS A, DATA D, Diggavi Suhas, et al. Shuffled Model of Differential Privacy in Federated Learning[C/OL]//Proceedings of the 24th International Conference on Artificial Intelligence and Statistics. 2021:2521-2529(2021-03-18)[2022-09-07]. https://proceedings.mlr.press/v130/girgis21a.html
8. BONAWITZ K, IVANOV V, KREUTER B, et al. Practical secure aggregation for privacy-preserving machine learning[C]//Proceedings of the 2017 ACM SIGSAC Conference on Computer and Communications Security. New York: ACM, 2017:1175-1191.
9. XIAO X and TAO Y. Personalized privacy preservation[C]//Proceedings of the ACM SIGMOD International Conference on Management of Data. New York: ACM, 2006:229-240.

10. JORGENSEN Z, YU T, CORMODE G. Conservative or liberal? Personalized differential privacy[C]//Proceedings of the IEEE 31st International Conference on Data Engineering. Piscataway:IEEE, 2015:1023-1034.
11. CHEN R, LI H, QIN A K, et al. Private spatial data aggregation in the local setting[C]//Proceedings of the IEEE 32nd International Conference on Data Engineering. Piscataway:IEEE, 2016:289-300.
12. LIU J, LOU J, XIONG L, et al. Projected Federated Averaging with Heterogeneous Differential[J]//Proceedings of 48th International Conference on Very Large Data Bases, 2022, 15(4): 828-840.

# Chapter 9
# Machine Unlearning

In today's digital era, digital applications permeate every aspect of daily life and production. As information technology advances and becomes more widely applied, data has become inextricably linked to people's lifestyles. The rapid growth of the internet has made life more convenient but has also introduced significant risks to personal information security. For example, the collection of user personal information by mobile applications during their operation can lead to privacy breaches, posing risks to users. If large—scale personal data is stolen and misused, it can endanger user safety.

This chapter delves into machine unlearning and its privacy—protection issues. It first highlights the importance of "data forgetting" for personal privacy and the related privacy—leakage risks. Then, it focuses on the method of machine unlearning.

## 9.1 Introduction

As digital applications rapidly spread, data has become tightly linked to people's lives, making personal information protection increasingly important. In 2012, the European Commission first introduced the right to be forgotten, which allows individuals to legally request that their data be deleted by data collectors for legitimate reasons. This concept emphasizes granting users legal rights to manage their private data. Many countries have begun to pay more attention to privacy issues in the big data era. China's Information Security Technology Personal Information Security Specification, effective since 2020, states that users should have the right to delete their personal data [1]. In 2018, the EU's General Data Protection Regulation (GDPR) came into force. It stipulates that automated algorithms, including machine learning systems, must ensure users' right to be forgotten. To meet the needs of the right to be forgotten, machine unlearning has emerged, aiming to erase both the data itself and its influence.



X. Meng, *Data Privacy and Data Governance*, Big Data Management,
https://doi.org/10.1007/978-981-95-5787-5_9

**Definition 24** (*Machine Unlearning*) Given a model $M$, original dataset $D$, data to be forgotten $x^*$, cost function $Cost(M)$, and similarity function $Sim(M_1, M_2)$ (which is always positive and decreases as $M_1$ and $M_2$ become more similar), we aim to achieve two goals. First, the cost of the unlearned model $M_{unlearn}$ obtained via machine unlearning should be less than the cost of the model $M_{retrain}$ retrained on the remaining data $D\backslash x^*$. Second, the similarity between $M_{unlearn}$ and $M_{retrain}$ should approach zero, indicating they are nearly identical. In mathematical terms, we strive to satisfy $Cost(M_{unlearn}) < Cost(M_{retrain})$ and $Sim(M_{unlearn}, M_{retrain}) \to 0$.

On measuring the similarity between $M_{retrain}$ and $M_{unlearn}$, existing literature varies: some use model parameter distance, where smaller norm differences imply closer models [2, 3]; others use model output distribution distance, deeming similarity sufficient when it's below a threshold [4, 5]. Enhancing similarity is a key goal of machine unlearning. Currently, similarity definitions differ across papers, with each method achieving unlearning under its own definition.

Data cleaning and continual learning are fields closely related to machine unlearning. This paper distinguishes their relationships with machine unlearning. Data cleaning removes "dirty" data with missing or abnormal values from raw data [6]. In real datasets, such data increases the model's training burden and may harm its performance. The difference between data cleaning and machine unlearning is that data cleaning happens before model training, improving model performance by enhancing data quality; machine unlearning occurs after training, aiming to erase the impact of specific data from the model. However, after model training, machine unlearning can also be used to eliminate the influence of dirty data on the model. In this case, both machine unlearning and data cleaning aim to improve model performance.

Continual learning studies how models learn continuously across tasks. When learning a new task, the model can't access prior task data. Its goal is to minimize forgetting of old data and maximize the use of prior knowledge for new tasks [7].

Machine unlearning differs from continual learning in two main ways:

1. Granularity: Machine unlearning targets individual data samples, while continual learning targets entire learning tasks.
2. Objective: Machine unlearning aims to make the model forget specific data and related knowledge, whereas continual learning aims to make the model remember prior knowledge.

Paradoxically, machine unlearning can enhance continual learning. By strategically forgetting less important or outdated knowledge, the model can free up capacity to learn new information, ensuring flexibility and adaptability in dynamic learning environments.

Machine unlearning can be categorized into three types based on design concepts and key technologies: training—based, editing—based, and generation—based. These will be detailed in Sects. 9.2, 9.3, and 9.4.

## 9.2 Training Based Unlearning Methods

Training—based unlearning refers to achieving unlearning through model retraining. These methods partition the retraining process, either partially retraining on some data or starting from a specific epoch, to reduce costs while maintaining model similarity to fully retrained models. Training—based unlearning mainly includes three sub—methods: continued computation, model decomposition, and hybrid methods. Table 9.1 lists their requirements, costs (in time and space), and pros/cons. The requirements indicate what needs to be known to apply these methods.

### *9.2.1 Continued Computation*

Continued computation involves saving intermediate results from training model $M_0$, and resuming training from these results upon a forgetting request. These methods save intermediates like sample counts in Naive Bayes or gradients in deep learning. When forgetting is needed, they continue computing from these saved points to reduce time costs, though with extra space costs. The key is to identify reusable data during model training, save it, and modify it when a forgetting request occurs. Continued computation methods are used in classification algorithms like Naive Bayes and ridge regression, clustering algorithms like K-means, and in deep learning.

In K-means clustering, data points are assigned to the nearest of $k$ clusters, with centers $c_1, \ldots, c_k$. Points are initially assigned to the closest center, and centers are updated based on the mean of cluster points. This repeats until centers stabilize. The unlearning method for K-means converts cluster center calculation into cumulative data operations [8]. Forgetting a point $x_u$ involves removing its contribution from

**Table 9.1** Training-based unlearning methods

| Category | Requirements | Time cost | Space cost | Advantages | Disadvantages |
|---|---|---|---|---|---|
| Continued computation | Intermediate results | Cost of computing from intermediates | Cost of storing intermediates | Fast | Specific to certain algorithms; may not fully unlearn in deep learning |
| Model decomposition | Subset-data to submodel mapping | Cost of retraining submodels | None (no intermediate storage) | No intermediate storage needed | Specific to certain algorithms |
| Hybrid approach | Subset-data to submodel mapping and intermediates | Cost of mid-training submodel training | Cost of storing intermediates | Better unlearning effect | High space cost |

these cumulative results. Specifically, using functions $g_{ci,j}(x)$ (outputting the minimum distance when $x$ is closest to $c_i$) and $g'_{ci,j}(x)$ (outputting 1 when $x$ is closest to $c_i$), each iteration of cluster centers is calculated as $\sum g_{ci,j}(x)/\sum g'_{ci,j}(x)$. Forgetting $x_u$ entails removing its contributions from these sums and reiterating until convergence.

DeltaGrad is a continued computation method for deep learning [9]. During $M_0$ training, it saves intermediate results like training datasets, hyperparameters, and gradients. To maintain model usability during unlearning, it precisely calculates gradients on $D\backslash x^*$ for some epochs and approximates gradients using saved intermediates for others. This reduces overall training time while ensuring model utility.

### *9.2.2 Model Decomposition*

Model decomposition breaks down the training of a large model into several submodels. When a forgetting request occurs, only the sub—models related to the data to be forgotten are retrained, reducing training time. Unlike continued computation, model decomposition involves partitioning the dataset.

Compared to continued computation, model decomposition doesn't require extra storage for intermediate results. However, it raises questions about how to partition the model and aggregate sub—model results. The key is converting the large model into sub—models. If the partitioning is too fine—grained, sub—models might perform poorly due to limited data, affecting overall performance. If it's too coarse—grained, retraining sub—models may involve large datasets, potentially increasing training time. Model decomposition is used in unlearning methods for ensemble tree models [10, 11], regression models [9], and clustering models [12].

Taking K-means clustering as an example again, DC–k–means (Divide—and—Conquer k–means) is a model—decomposition—based unlearning method for K–means [12]. It divides $D$ into several subsets, runs the K–means algorithm on each subset independently, and then recursively merges the results.

DC-k-means is tree-based. The original dataset is divided into leaf nodes. Each leaf node determines its dataset's centroid via clustering. When merging leaves into a parent node, the new dataset of the parent includes all centroids of the leaves. DC–k–means then computes new centroids for the parent node using a clustering algorithm and repeats this process up the tree. By leveraging the tree's hierarchy, DC–k–means modularizes centroid and dataset dependencies. When a forgetting request occurs, only the clustering computations from the corresponding leaf node up to the root need to be redone. Compared to the continued—computation method Q-k-means from the previous section, DC–k–means offers slightly better clustering results but is slower.

### 9.2.3 *Hybrid Method*

Hybrid approaches combine continued computation and model decomposition for machine unlearning. These methods first decompose the model into smaller submodels and save intermediate training results. Upon a forgetting request, they resume training from the relevant submodel's intermediate results, avoiding the computational cost of retraining the entire submodel. A typical example is the SISA (sharded, isolated, sliced, and aggregated) framework [13], widely discussed for its applicability to deep learning. As shown in Fig. 9.1, SISA exemplifies the basic ideas, optimization methods, and application scenarios of hybrid approaches in machine unlearning.

In the SISA framework, dataset $D$ is divided into multiple non—overlapping shards, with each data point residing in only one shard. SISA trains submodels on each shard and limits the influence of individual data points on the submodels. When a forgetting request arrives, only the affected submodel needs retraining. Since shards are smaller than the entire training set, this reduces training time. However, it also decreases the data available for each submodel, potentially weakening their predictive power.

To accelerate training, SISA further divides each shard into slices. When training a submodel, SISA incrementally adds slices instead of using the entire shard at once. Before adding a new slice, the current model state is saved. When a data point to be forgotten is identified within a slice, training can resume from the last saved state before that slice was added. This approach, similar to checkpointing in databases, reduces training time. During final prediction, the model owner can aggregate predictions from submodels using strategies like majority voting.

SISA's unlearning speed is directly related to the size of the shards and slices. Smaller shards and slices mean fewer data points for retraining and less time. However, smaller training sets can weaken the submodels' predictive power and impact overall model performance.

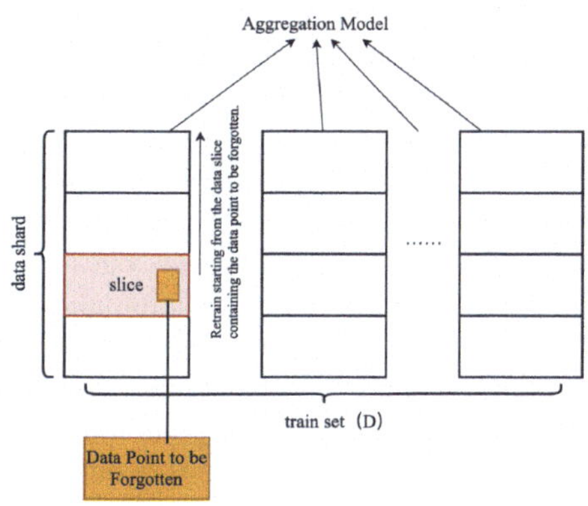


**Fig. 9.1** The framework of SISA

The ARCANE framework [14] improves upon SISA's data partitioning by creating shards based on labels. It preserves more detailed model states during training and places data with higher probability of being forgotten in later slices to reduce the number of slices needed for training. Additionally, DeepObliviate builds on SISA by simplifying the continued computation process [15].

## 9.3 Editing Based Unlearning Methods

Methods of unlearning based on editing involve editing $M_0$ to achieve unlearning, given $M_0$ or $D$. These methods use information like $x^*$ and $D \backslash x^*$ to modify $M_0$ and obtain $M_{unlearn}$. Unlike training—based methods, editing—based methods don't partition the training process. Instead, they directly alter the model's input, parameters, or output to approximate the retrained model. Depending on the editing target, these methods can be categorized into input editing, parameter editing, and output editing.

### *9.3.1 Input Editing*

Input editing involves altering input data (including modifying labels or features) to influence the model's decision—making and achieve unlearning. Unlike training—based methods, it doesn't require partitioning the training process. Instead, it directly affects the model's input, aiming to make the edited model behave similarly to a retrained one. Input editing methods can be categorized into label editing and feature noising.

Label editing modifies the labels of input data. In traditional machine learning, Parne et al. [16] researched how to forget specific emails using decision trees and random forests for spam classification. Attackers can add spam content to benign samples to pollute the model. To make the model forget such malicious samples, the model owner can modify the labels of samples containing spam information, reducing their impact on the model. In deep learning, Class Clown [17] implements unlearning by modifying input data labels. For a data point, the model's confidence in its label is related to the point's distance to the decision boundary. By changing the loss function space distribution and distorting the decision boundary, the model can be made to "believe" the data point wasn't used during training. Kim et al. [18] also modified input data labels but introduced adversarial learning. Their method involves two steps: neutralization and distillation. Neutralization tampers with the correct labels of the data to be forgotten and trains a "student model" on it, making the student model's predictions nearly random. Distillation continues training the student model using the original model ($M_0$) as a "teacher model," with the student model taking the teacher model's outputs as inputs, thereby accelerating training and stabilizing the process.

Feature noising modifies the features of input data by adding noise. Huang et al. [19] proposed a feature—noising method for deep learning. They added noise to the features of input data so that models trained on these data cannot learn the underlying knowledge. By learning the relationship between the added noise and labels, the model can generate noise that confuses the labels and achieves unlearning. This learning process can be viewed as a bi—level optimization problem: the outer optimization minimizes the model loss function to maintain model performance, while the inner optimization minimizes the noise to reduce changes to the model.

### 9.3.2 Parameter Editing

Parameter editing uses mathematical knowledge or dataset information to directly compute the parameters of $M_{\text{unlearn}}$. This method often requires knowledge of the original model parameters $M_0$, and dataset information (such as the original dataset $D$ or the remaining dataset $D \backslash x^*$). Sometimes, it also requires recording gradients from training $M_0$. These methods adjust $M_0$ directly, avoiding large—scale data iterations, thus being faster. This section introduces four parameter—editing approaches: Taylor expansion, gradient updating, optimization solving, and residual updating.

**1. Taylor Expansion**
Taylor expansion approximates function values around a point using polynomials. To approximate $M_{\text{unlearn}}$, especially when $D$ and $D \backslash x^*$ are similar and $M_0$ is known, Taylor expansion calculates the product of the loss function's Hessian inverse and the gradient vector. However, Hessian inverse computation is complex. Several papers have improved this process. For instance, some use the Fisher matrix to approximate the Hessian matrix [20, 21], employ the BFGS method for Hessian—vector product approximation [21], or apply LCODEx to reduce Hessian computation parameters. Others transform Hessian solutions into optimization problems [22]. These approaches sacrifice some precision to reduce computation time. For example, CR is about 1000 times faster than full retraining and supports forgetting up to 10,000 data points [23].

**2. Gradient Updating**
Gradient updating leverages $M_0$'s training gradients to update its parameters and obtain $M_{\text{unlearn}}$. Suitable for gradient—descent—based optimization (like deep learning), this method requires knowing the gradients of the data to be forgotten during training. Liu et al.'s Forsaken method also updates $M_0$ using gradients but differs from [24] by altering the loss function for gradient computation.

**3. Optimization Solving**
Optimization—solving methods frame $M_{\text{unlearn}}$ computation as an optimization problem. The solution to this problem is $M_{\text{unlearn}}$. The key lies in constructing the optimization problem, which characterizes the dataset's impact on the model. When a forgetting request arrives, the method subtracts the target data's influence from the optimization problem and solves it to yield $M_{\text{unlearn}}$.

**4. Residual Updating**

Residual updating edits parameters using synthetic data. Unlike previous methods, Izzo et al.'s projective residual update (PRU) [25] synthesizes $M_{\text{unlearn}}$'s predictions via a leave—one—out method based on $M_0$'s predictions. PRU then updates parameters using the distance between synthesized and $M_0$'s predicted values. PRU's time complexity is linear to the size of data to be forgotten and independent of the entire dataset $D$.

### *9.3.3 Output Editing*

Output editing involves adjusting the model's output to align with that of $M_{\text{retrain}}$. Currently, the only known method in this category is Linear Filtration, proposed by Baumhaumer et al. [26]. This method is applicable to models where outputs are label—based and represent confidence distributions across labels. In Linear Filtration, when the model outputs a confidence—distribution vector for a data point across labels, this vector is multiplied by a filter matrix. The resulting vector excludes the dimension corresponding to the label to be forgotten, effectively removing that label from the model's output. Filter matrix construction can use methods like normalization or randomization. Linear Filtration alters the model's output to exclude the target label without changing the model's internal structure.

## 9.4 Generation-Based Unlearning Method

Generation-based unlearning creates $M_{\text{unlearn}}$ using generative models. Common generative models include Naive Bayes and MCMC in traditional machine learning, and GANs in deep learning [27]. These models simulate data—generation probabilities and, in the context of unlearning, infer the parameter probabilities of $M_{\text{unlearn}}$. This section covers both traditional machine learning and deep learning approaches to generating $M_{\text{unlearn}}$.

### *9.4.1 Machine Learning*

In traditional machine learning, MCMC can be used to generate $M_{\text{unlearn}}$. MCMC is a sampling algorithm that constructs a Markov chain with the target distribution as its stationary distribution. As the number of state transitions increases, the obtained distribution approaches the target distribution. MCMC is suitable for models with fewer parameters, such as logistic regression and linear regression.

Nguyen et al. [28] proposed generating $M_{\text{unlearn}}$ parameters using MCMC. First, MCMC generates a set of candidate parameters for $M_{\text{unlearn}}$, which are then expanded (e.g., via probability unfolding). Finally, these parameters are weighted and averaged to form the final model parameters. Ullah et al. [29] also used MCMC but focused on modeling the distribution of model latent states before and after data deletion as the start and end points of a Markov chain. They constructed a Markov chain for the noisy stochastic gradient descent process to achieve unlearning. Beyond MCMC, Nguyen et al. [30] treated logistic regression as a variational inference problem. Variational inference optimizes the distance between simple and complex distributions, enabling the simple distribution to approximate the complex one.

### *9.4.2 Deep Learning*

GANs, introduced in 2014, are deep—learning frameworks consisting of two neural networks: a generator and a discriminator. The generator produces samples, which the discriminator evaluates. The generator aims to increase the discriminator's error rate. If the discriminator cannot distinguish between generated and real samples, the generated samples are deemed usable.

Chen et al. [31] utilized GANs to generate $M_{\text{unlearn}}$, offering a method applicable to various machine—learning models, including non—convex ones. In their approach, the generator produces $M_{\text{unlearn}}$, while the discriminator ensures that the output distribution of $M_{\text{unlearn}}$ matches that of $M_{\text{retrain}}$ on unseen third—party data. Similarly, Kim et al. [18] and Chunwadat et al. [32] employed generative models to obtain $M_{\text{unlearn}}$, but they additionally considered the accuracy of $M_{\text{unlearn}}$. OptLearn uses a deep neural network to predict $M_{\text{unlearn}}$ [33], but it is limited to models with convex loss functions, such as SVMs. OptLearn consists of an offline—training phase and an online—estimation phase. During offline training, the deep neural network is trained with a loss function that includes KKT regularizers and model—usability regularizers to ensure the predicted model meets the optimality conditions for its loss function. In the online—estimation phase, the trained neural network predicts the parameters of $M_{\text{unlearn}}$.

### *9.4.3 Evaluation Metrics for Machine Unlearning*

From a performance evaluation perspective, machine unlearning differs from machine learning. While the performance of machine learning models can be assessed by comparing the model's predictions on a test set with the true labels, machine unlearning requires a different set of considerations. Specifically, it involves evaluating the time required for the unlearning process, the similarity between $M_{\text{retrain}}$ and $M_{\text{unlearn}}$, and the prediction accuracy of $M_{\text{unlearn}}$. Various studies have proposed different metrics for evaluating machine unlearning. In this paper, we summarize these metrics into three main categories: unlearning speed, unlearning usability, and unlearning completeness.

**1. Speed Metrics**
Unlearning speed is measured by the reduction in time achieved by obtaining $M_{\text{unlearn}}$ compared to the time required for retraining $M_{\text{retrain}}$. It is evaluated by comparing the training times of $M_{\text{retrain}}$ and $M_{\text{unlearn}}$ and calculating the speedup ratio of the unlearning process relative to full retraining. A higher speedup ratio indicates a faster unlearning process. Formally, speedup is defined as follows:

**Definition 25** (*Speedup*) is defined as the ratio of the time required for retraining $M_{\text{retrain}}$ to the time required for obtaining $M_{\text{unlearn}}$ through the unlearning process. Specifically, if the time for retraining is $T_{\text{retrain}}$ and the time for unlearning is $T_{\text{unlearn}}$, then the speedup is given by Speedup $= T_{\text{retrain}}/T_{\text{unlearn}}$.

**2. Usability Metrics**
The usability of machine unlearning refers to the ability of $M_{\text{unlearn}}$ to make correct predictions, i.e., to accurately identify the true labels of samples. If the accuracy of $M_{\text{unlearn}}$ on a test set is significantly lower than that of $M_{\text{retrain}}$, it indicates that the model's prediction capability is subpar and thus the usability of the model is considered to be too low. The usability of unlearning is typically compared and measured by evaluating the accuracy of both $M_{\text{retrain}}$ and $M_{\text{unlearn}}$ on the test set. The formal definition of accuracy on the test set is provided below:

**Definition 26** (*Accuracy on the Test Set*) is defined as the ratio of the number of correctly predicted samples by the model $M$ to the total number of samples in the test set. If $n$ is the total number of samples in the test set and $c$ is the number of samples correctly predicted by the model, then the accuracy of the model on the test set is given by ACC $= c/n$.

**3. Completeness Metrics**
The completeness of machine unlearning is measured by the similarity between $M_{\text{retrain}}$ and $M_{\text{unlearn}}$. Higher similarity indicates higher completeness. This comparison can be approached in multiple ways, which are categorized here into three main methods: comparing output distributions, comparing parameter distances, and data—inference evaluation.

Comparing Output Distributions involves using a set of samples to generate predictions with both $M_{\text{retrain}}$ and $M_{\text{unlearn}}$, and then comparing the differences in their output distributions. Methods to measure the distance between distributions include calculating the Kullback-Leibler divergence [20], computing the ratio of output probabilities [34], and applying the Kolmogorov-Smirnov test [35].

In addition to directly calculating the distance between probability distributions, external classifiers can be introduced to determine whether the outputs of two models are indistinguishable. Baumhauer et al. [26] employed a Bayesian classifier to see if it could differentiate between the outputs of $M_{\text{retrain}}$ and $M_{\text{unlearn}}$. If the classifier's accuracy is close to random guessing, the outputs are considered highly similar.

Data Inference Evaluation assesses the effectiveness of machine unlearning by determining whether a sample was part of the training set. If inference methods can determine that a sample was in the training set, unlearning completeness is low; if not, it's high. This evaluation includes membership inference attacks and adding "triggers" to data, both applicable for black—box testing where users lack model—specific knowledge.

Membership inference attacks aim to determine whether a sample was in a model's training data. To train a membership inference attack model, multiple shadow models are created. These models mimic the target model's behavior but are trained on datasets constructed by the attacker, who knows which data is in each shadow model's training set. The attacker labels the outputs of these shadow models as "in the dataset" or "not in the dataset" and uses them to train an attack model. Once trained, this attack model can infer whether the target model was trained on a specific sample based on its output.

## 9.5 Summary

This chapter delves into privacy protection in machine unlearning, focusing on training—based, editing—based, and generation—based unlearning methods. It elaborates on the concepts and optimizations of each method and makes horizontal comparisons between them.

## References

1. SHOKRI R, STRONATI M, SONG C, et al. Membership inference attacks against machine learning models[C]// Proceedings of the 2017 IEEE Symposium on Security and Privacy. IEEE, 2017: 3–18.
2. GUO C, GOLDSTEIN T, HANNUN A, et al. Certified data removal from machine learning models[C]//Proceedings of the 37th International Conference on Machine Learning. PMLR, 2020: 3832–3842.
3. LIU X, TSAFTARIS S A. Have you forgotten? a method to assess if machine learning models have forgotten data[C]// Proceedings of Medical Image Computing and Computer Assisted Intervention–MICCAI 2020, 23rd International Conference. Springer, 2020: 95–105.
4. GOLATKAR A, ACHILLE A, SOATTO S. Eternal sunshine of the spotless net: selective forgetting in deep networks[C]// Proceedings of the 2020 IEEE/CVF Conference on Computer Vision and Pattern Recognition. IEEE, 2020: 9301–9309.
5. THUDI A, DEZA G, CHANDRASEKARAN V, et al. Unrolling sgd: understanding factors influencing machine unlearning[C]//Proceedings of the 2022 IEEE 7th European Symposium on Security and Privacy. IEEE, 2022: 303–319.
6. CHAI C, WANG J, LUO Y, et al. Data management for machine learning: A survey[J]. IEEE Trans. on Knowledge and Data Engineering, 2023, 35(5): 4646–4667.
7. LIU B, LIU Q, STONE P. Continual learning and private unlearning[A]. 2022.
8. CAO Y, YANG J. Towards making systems forget with machine unlearning[C]//Proceedings of the 2015 IEEE Symposium on Security and Privacy. IEEE, 2015: 463–480.

9. WU Y, DOBRIBAN E, DAVIDSON S. Deltagrad: rapid retraining of machine learning models[C]//Proceedings of the 37th International Conference on Machine Learning. PMLR, 2020: 10355–10366.
10. SCHELTER S, GRAFBERGER S, DUNNING T. Hedgecut: maintaining randomised trees for low-latency machine unlearning[C]// Proceedings of the 2021 International Conference on Management of Data. Association for Computing Machinery, 2021: 1545–1557.
11. BOURTOULE L, CHANDRASEKARAN V, CHOQUETTE-CHOO C A, et al. Machine unlearning[C]// Proceedings of the 2021 IEEE Symposium on Security and Privacy. IEEE, 2021: 141–159.
12. GINART A, GUAN M, VALIANT G, et al. Making ai forget you: data deletion in machine learning[C]//Advances in Neural Information Processing Systems. 2019: 3518–3531.
13. FELPS D L, SCHWICKERATH A D, WILLIAMS J D, et al. Class clown: data redaction in machine unlearning at enterprise scale[A]. 2020.
14. FU S, HE F, TAO D. Knowledge removal in sampling-based bayesian inference[A]. 2022.
15. MEHTA R, PAL S, SINGH V, et al. Deep unlearning via randomized conditionally independent hessians[C]//Proceedings of the 2022 IEEE/CVF Conference on Computer Vision and Pattern Recognition. IEEE, 2022: 10422–10431.
16. IZZO Z, SMART M A, CHAUDHURI K, et al. Approximate data deletion from machine learning models[C]// Proceedings of the 24th International Conference on Artificial Intelligence and Statistics. PMLR, 2021: 2008–2016.
17. CHEN Y, XIONG J, XU W, et al. A novel online incremental and decremental learning algorithm based on variable support vector machine[J]. Cluster Computing, 2019, 22: 7435–7445.
18. NEEL S, ROTH A, SHARIFI-MALVAJERDI S. Descent-to-delete: Gradient-based methods for machine unlearning[C]// Algorithmic Learning Theory. 2021: 931–962.
19. HUANG H, MA X, ERFANI S M, et al. Unlearnable examples: making personal data unexploitable[C]//Proceedings of the 9th International Conference on Learning Representations. 2021.
20. ZHANG H, NAKAMURA T, ISOHARA T, et al. A review on machine unlearning[J]. SN Computer Science, 2023, 4 (4): 337.
21. YOON Y, NAM J, YUN H, et al. Few-shot unlearning by model inversion[A]. 2022.
22. FU S, HE F, XU Y, et al. Bayesian inference forgetting[A]. 2021.
23. MARCHANT N G, RUBINSTEIN B I, ALFELD S. Hard to forget: Poisoning attacks on certified machine unlearning[C]// Proceedings of the AAAI Conference on Artificial Intelligence. AAAI, 2022: 7691–7700.
24. YE J, FU Y, SONG J, et al. Learning with recoverable forgetting[C]// Proceedings of the Computer Vision–ECCV 2022, 17th European Conference. Springer, 2022: 87–103.
25. HE Y, MENG G, CHEN K, et al. Deepobliviate: a powerful charm for erasing data residual memory in deep neural networks[A]. 2021.
26. KIM J, WOO S S. Efficient two-stage model retraining for machine unlearning[C]// Proceedings of the IEEE/CVF Conference on Computer Vision and Pattern Recognition. IEEE, 2022: 4361–4369.
27. CHUNDAWAT V S, TARUN A K, MANDAL M, et al. Zero-shot machine unlearning[A]. 2022.
28. NGUYEN Q, OIKAWA R, DIVAKARAN D, et al. Markov chain monte carlo-based machine unlearning: Unlearning what needs to be forgotten[C]// Proceedings of the 2022 ACM on Asia Conference on Computer and Communications Security. Association for Computing Machinery, 2022: 351–363.
29. CHEN C, SUN F, ZHANG M, et al. Recommendation unlearning[C]// Proceedings of the ACM Web Conference 2022. Association for Computing Machinery, 2022: 2768–2777.
30. GOLATKAR A, ACHILLE A, RAVICHANDRAN A, et al. Mixed-privacy forgetting in deep networks[C]// Proceedings of the 2021 IEEE/CVF Conference on Computer Vision and Pattern Recognition. IEEE, 2021: 792–801.
31. PESTE A, ALISTARH D, LAMPERT C H. Ssse: Efficiently erasing samples from trained machine learning models[A]. 2021.

32. GOLATKAR A, ACHILLE A, SOATTO S. Forgetting outside the box: scrubbing deep networks of information accessible from input-output observations[C]// Proceedings of Computer Vision—ECCV 2020. Springer, 2020: 383–398.
33. ZENG Y, WANG T, CHEN S, et al. Learning to refit for convex learning problems[A]. 2021.
34. NGUYEN T, HUYNH T, NGUYEN P, et al. A survey of machine unlearning[A]. 2022.
35. XU J, WU Z, WANG C, et al. Machine unlearning: Solutions and challenges[J]. IEEE Trans. on Emerging Topics in Computational Intelligence, 2024: 1–19.

# Part IV
# Data Ecosystem and Data Governance

Data elements mainly include data collected by internet applications, IoT devices, enterprises, and government agencies. With the growing power of computing capacity and AI algorithms, the larger the volume of data, the richer the knowledge that can be extracted, and thus the greater the value of data elements. This further underscores the need to implement data-sharing mechanisms and enhance standards and protocols for data trading and circulation. However, as data ecosystems evolve, both the methods of data generation and their fundamental characteristics undergo transformation, exerting varying impacts on science, technology, and society, and giving rise to different ethical issues. At present, the most prominent concerns are privacy, monopolization, and fairness. Compared with the current state of data element markets at home and abroad, China is still in the early stages of cultivating such a market and faces numerous problems and challenges.

This chapter aims to provide an overview of the development and governance of data elements. Following the main trajectory of data evolution, data has progressed from numerical scientific data to structured enterprise data and diverse personal data. Its application domains have expanded from the natural sciences to engineering and social fields, driving the emergence of new technologies across various disciplines and bringing unprecedented ethical challenges. For China, improving the data element market is a key component in building a unified, open, and orderly competitive market system, while data transparency is an essential path for future data governance.

# Chapter 10
# Data Market

In the era of big data, data resources have emerged as a new factor of production, alongside traditional elements such as labor, capital, and land, thereby gaining unprecedented status and significance. As core activities within the data element market, data trading and circulation offer vital channels for integrating data resources, dismantling information silos and barriers, and are increasingly becoming key drivers of social, economic, and technological progress both domestically and globally.

For China, developing a data element market is essential to building a unified, open, and well-regulated competitive market system. It also plays a critical role in upholding and improving the socialist basic economic system and in advancing the development of a socialist market economy. Advancing market-oriented reforms in the allocation of data elements—by promoting their autonomous and orderly flow, eliminating institutional and systemic barriers, and enabling allocation through market rules, prices, and competition—will help unlock market dynamism and creativity. This, in turn, supports the implementation of the new development philosophy and facilitates the formation of a data element market characterized by market-determined pricing, efficient and fair allocation, and orderly data flows. Ultimately, such a market will drive qualitative, efficient, and dynamic growth in the digital economy.

## 10.1 Introduction

In the era of the digital economy, big data has become a critical foundational and strategic resource for nations, profoundly shaping global production, circulation, distribution, and consumption patterns, as well as influencing economic systems, social behaviors, and governance capacities. This shift presents new opportunities for countries to enhance their competitive advantage. To fully harness the potential of its vast data resources, unlock the value of data elements, accelerate the digital transformation of traditional industries, and foster a sustainable and robust digital



X. Meng, *Data Privacy and Data Governance*, Big Data Management,
https://doi.org/10.1007/978-981-95-5787-5_10

economy, digital society, and data-driven government, China has successively introduced a series of key policy documents, including:

- **August 2015**—≪ The Outline for Promoting the Development of Big Data≫ emphasized the importance of "innovation-driven development," calling for accelerated deployment and deeper application of big data. It recognized big data as an essential tool for modernizing governance, improving public services, and driving economic and industrial development.
- **October 2019**—≪ The Decision of the CPC Central Committee on Some Major Issues Concerning Upholding and Improving the Socialist System with Chinese Characteristics and Advancing the Modernization of the National Governance System and Governance Capacity≫(hereinafter referred to as the "Decision") highlighted the need to advance digital government by strengthening orderly data sharing and recognizing data as a new type of production factor with strategic significance.
- **March 2020**—≪ The Opinions of the CPC Central Committee and the State Council on Establishing a More Perfect Market-oriented Allocation Mechanism and System for Data≫ (hereinafter referred to as the "Opinions" ) explicitly proposed "accelerating the development of the data element market." It offered guidance in three key areas: promoting open access to government data, enhancing the utility of social data resources, and strengthening data integration and security, all aimed at building a unified, efficient, and standardized data element market.
- **May 2021**—≪ The Report on Data Valorization and Data Element Market Development (2021)≫ introduced a three-step framework for "data valorization": data resourceization, data assetization, and data capitalization. Among these, data assetization-enabling data to generate economic value through circulation and transaction-is identified as the core driver of data element market development, benefiting both data providers and users.

Designating data as a new type of production factor underscores its transformation into a fundamental asset that enterprises must possess to sustain production and business operations. The data element market refers to the marketplace formed through the exchange and circulation of data elements. It encompasses not only the transactional or buyer-seller relationships involved in data valorization, but also the physical and digital platforms where such transactions occur.[1]

Currently, data elements primarily originate from sources such as internet applications, Internet-of-Things (IoT) devices, enterprises, and government agencies. As computing power and artificial intelligence (AI) algorithms continue to advance, larger volumes of data enable the extraction of richer insights, thereby increasing the intrinsic value of data as a production factor. This highlights the critical importance of promoting open data sharing and continually refining standards and mechanisms for data trading and circulation. Sections 10.2 and 10.3 of this chapter will respectively introduce the fundamentals of data trading and data circulation.

[1] ≪Report on Data Valorization and Data Element Market Development (2021)≫.

**Data trading** is a core component of the data element market. The objects of trade extend beyond raw data to include processed datasets and data-derived products such as trained models. The data trading market connects data providers, intermediaries, and buyers, offering a streamlined channel for the integration of data resources and the dismantling of information silos and barriers. Through such markets, fragmented and large-scale data assets are aggregated and exchanged, unlocking their latent economic and social value.

**Data circulation** refers to the process by which data is transferred from suppliers to consumers in accordance with established protocols and regulations. Alongside data trading, data circulation is a critical pillar of China's data element market. In April 2018, the China Academy of Information and Communications Technology (CAICT) released the White Paper on Key Technologies for Data Circulation, the first domestic white paper dedicated to this subject. It identifies four primary challenges to effective data circulation in China: limitations in data resources, issues of data quality, inadequate pricing mechanisms, and regulatory compliance. From a global perspective, promoting lawful, secure, and orderly cross-border data circulation will be a major trend in future international development. Ensuring such circulation proceeds without compromising personal privacy or national security is vital for fostering a sound and sustainable global data exchange ecosystem.

## 10.2 Data Transactions

Data trading serves as a critical mechanism connecting data owners, intermediaries, and buyers, offering a streamlined channel for the integration of data resources and the elimination of information silos and barriers. Data owners typically refer to individuals who generate data-such as users who, often unknowingly, produce large volumes of behavioral data when browsing websites or using applications. Data buyers may include both the original data collectors and third parties who purchase raw data or its derivatives, such as query analytics or machine learning models trained on such data. By facilitating the aggregation and exchange of massive, fragmented datasets, data trading plays a pivotal role in unlocking the latent value of data assets.

With the rapid advancement of machine learning, model-based data product trading has become increasingly mainstream. In the transformation of raw data into data-driven products, a central challenge is how to obtain high-quality data and extract maximum value with minimal data volume. Addressing this challenge hinges on effective data pricing and benefit allocation mechanisms. Accurate pricing not only incentivizes the contribution of high-quality data-thus supporting the development of superior data products-but also ensures fair returns to data providers, fostering a virtuous cycle of continuous data quality improvement.

This section introduces three representative frameworks for data trading: the free-trading framework, the paid-trading framework, and the model-trading framework.

## 10.2.1 Free Transaction Framework

In the era of big data, data has become a form of wealth-an embodiment of productivity, innovation, and competitiveness. On one hand, service providers can employ machine learning algorithms to analyze the behavioral patterns of individuals or groups using the vast amounts of data generated by users, thereby gaining substantial commercial advantages through strategies such as targeted advertising. On the other hand, data sharing between enterprises and governments can enhance service delivery and generate mutual benefits. However, in China, regulatory oversight of data collection remains largely at the policy level. While service providers are required to disclose their data collection practices before users engage with their services, there is a lack of effective technical mechanisms to rectify the current disordered and opaque data-collection landscape.

In the expansive and fragmented mobile application market, the illegal or non-compliant collection and misuse of personal data is particularly widespread. Many service providers offer seemingly "free" services but require users to grant broad data permissions as a condition of use-otherwise, access is denied. Although users are notified that data will be collected, providers typically do not specify what data are collected, when the collection occurs, or how the data will be used.

From the perspective of most users, the collection of their data is viewed as an inconsequential by-product of service usage. To fulfill their needs, users are coerced into consenting to data collection, thus perpetuating a model that is ostensibly free but, in reality, exchanges personal data for services. This unregulated model of data collection presents serious risks to data security and privacy. Once collected, users lose control over their data. If sensitive personal information-either direct or inferred-is accessed, exploited, or sold by untrustworthy entities, users may face significant threats to both property and personal safety.

One approach to mitigating privacy concerns in the free-trading framework is for service providers to adopt privacy-preserving technologies during data collection, such as local differential privacy (LDP) [1]. For instance, Apple Inc. claims to employ LDP in its iOS systems to perform statistical analyses, such as tracking emoji usage frequency. Unlike traditional raw-data collection, LDP enables users to send perturbed versions of their data, thereby offering a degree of privacy protection. However, because the level of privacy protection is solely determined by the service provider, the actual safeguards may be weak-especially when providers prioritize statistical accuracy. In practice, this means providers have little incentive to enforce strong privacy guarantees. For example, according to Apple's publicly available technical report,[2] the privacy parameters implemented are relatively conservative; the perturbations introduced on the user side are often minimal, resulting in reported data that closely resembles the original values.

[2] https://www.apple.com/privacy/docs/Differential_Privacy_Overview.pdf.

### 10.2.2 Paid Transaction Framework

An alternative to the free-trading framework is to treat personal data as a valuable asset owned by the user, thereby transforming user data into a form of compensation and shifting away from the traditional model of implicit data collection. This book refers to this paradigm as the paid-trading framework. A representative model within this framework is the Pay-by-Data (PbD) scheme [2], whose overall architecture is illustrated in Fig. 10.1. The PbD model introduces three core components between the data owner (user) and the data purchaser (application):

1. **Data Collection**: The data collection module enables users to securely store and manage their personal data, with support for both real-time data transmission and retrieval of historical records. This empowers users with greater control over their data assets.
2. **Data Pricing**: Through a dedicated pricing protocol, applications are no longer monetized via traditional payment methods; instead, users "pay" for services with their data. As shown in Fig. 10.1b, under the traditional pay-by-money (PbM) model, users pay a monetary fee to access services, while service providers continue to collect data implicitly throughout usage-gaining both money and data. In contrast, the PbD model formalizes data as the explicit currency of exchange.
3. **Authentication Mechanism**: An authentication mechanism strictly governs application access to user data, ensuring that the scope and volume of data collected adhere precisely to the terms specified in the data-pricing agreement.

In summary, the paid-trading framework offers users clear visibility into which personal data are being collected and how those data will be used. It also enables users to receive compensation for their data contributions, thereby granting them greater autonomy and control over their personal information.

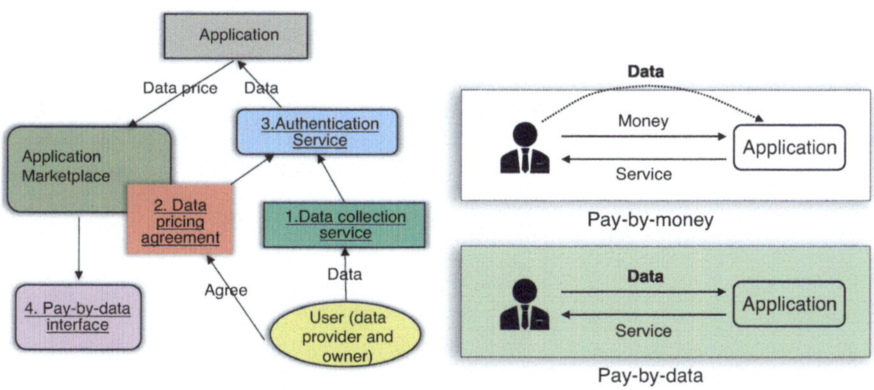


(a) Pay-by-Data Framework (b) From Pay-by-money to Pay-by-data

**Fig. 10.1** Paid transaction framework

### 10.2.3 Model Trading Framework

In both the free-trading and paid-trading frameworks, the traded object is the data itself. However, in the era of artificial intelligence, machine learning models-trained on user data-have also emerged as valuable commodities. These models can be regarded as crucial data elements in their own right, forming the basis of what this book refers to as the model-trading framework. In addition to the data owner and data buyer, this framework introduces a third party: the data intermediary [3]. Data intermediaries typically serve as the bridge between owners and buyers, responsible for transforming raw data into data products, conducting pricing, and managing benefit allocation. A representative example of this framework is Dealer [3], whose data trading workflow is depicted in Fig. 10.2.

In the Dealer model, each data owner provides the intermediary with a value-expectation function, which specifies the minimum compensation required for the use of their data-such as its inclusion in the training set of a machine learning model. After analyzing market demand and surveying available data, the intermediary purchases data from owners, selects optimal subsets based on their expected value, and transforms these into data products, such as trained models. These products are then offered to data buyers. When a buyer selects and purchases a specific model, the intermediary distributes the corresponding revenue among the contributing data owners, in accordance with their value-expectation functions.

Objectively, systematically, and fairly quantifying the value of individual data items-and establishing a reasonable, controllable, and dynamic pricing mechanism for data elements-remains a critical challenge for the model-trading framework. To address this issue, several data valuation methods have been proposed. A commonly used baseline is the leave-one-out (LOO) method, which evaluates the contribution of a data item by measuring the change in model accuracy when the item is removed from the training set. While intuitive and straightforward, the LOO approach has notable

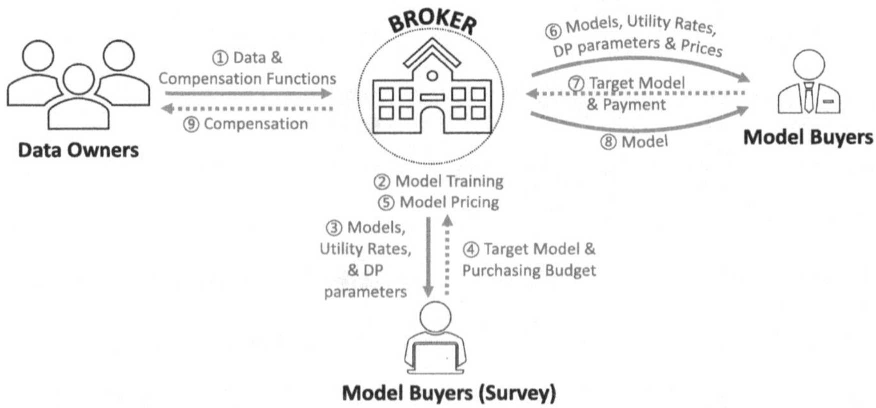


**Fig. 10.2** The framework of dealer, an end-to-end model marketplace with differential privacy

limitations. For example, if the dataset contains a data item p and its duplicate p', the removal of p may not affect the model's performance, thereby underestimating its value. In such cases, LOO fails to capture the true marginal contribution of individual data points.

A more alternative is the Shapley Value [4], a foundational concept in cooperative game theory introduced by Nobel Laureate Lloyd Shapley. The Shapley Value provides a principled way to measure each participant's contribution in a cooperative setting and is the unique solution that satisfies key axioms: symmetry, efficiency, dummy (redundancy), and additivity. Owing to these desirable properties, the Shapley Value has been widely adopted in data trading to evaluate the importance and value of data contributions. Empirical studies demonstrate that it significantly outperforms methods such as LOO, especially in scenarios involving redundancy, interaction effects, or imbalanced data utility.

**Definition 1** (*Shapley Value*) Let $Z = \{z_1, \ldots, z_n\}$ be the dataset, and $\mathcal{U}(\mathcal{S})$ be the utility value of the coalition $\mathcal{S}$ under the utility function $\mathcal{U}$. The Shapley Value $\mathcal{SV}_i$ of data item $z_i$ is defined as:

$$\mathcal{SV}_i = \frac{1}{n} \sum_{\mathcal{S} \in Z - \{z_i\}} \frac{\mathcal{U}(\mathcal{S} \cup \{z_i\}) - \mathcal{U}(\mathcal{S})}{\binom{n-1}{|\mathcal{S}|}}$$

Nevertheless, although the Shapley Value provides a fair assessment of the value of individual data items, its exact computation requires enumerating and evaluating each item's marginal contribution to every possible coalition. As the number of data items increases, the computational cost grows exponentially, making exact calculation infeasible for large-scale training datasets. A common solution is to adopt approximation algorithms, with the Monte Carlo sampling algorithm being the most representative. The core idea is to randomly sample subsets of data items, compute each item's marginal contribution across all permutations within the sample, and, through multiple iterations, obtain an approximate Shapley Value. Based on this approximation, data intermediaries can evaluate the value of each user's data item, incorporate data cost considerations, and select a training dataset that optimally balances overall data value with total cost for model training.

## 10.3 Data Circulation

Like data trading, data circulation is also a vital mechanism for unlocking the latent value of data assets, especially amid the ongoing expansion of the big-data industry. The White Paper on Key Technologies for Data Circulation identifies four primary areas where challenges and obstacles currently hinder effective data circulation:

1. **Data Resources**. Efficient data circulation requires data to be continuous, sourced from multiple origins, and standardized. In practice, however, supply often comes

from a single source that processes data according to specific requirements before providing it to the demand side. This "personalized demand, singular supply" model significantly impedes improvements in circulation efficiency.

2. **Data Quality**. Due to the distinctive characteristics of data resources, quality issues such as missing values represent only a small part of the problem. In most cases, data quality can only be verified post hoc-after the data has been used. Furthermore, data quality varies significantly across sources, quality metrics are inconsistent, and comprehensive evaluation systems remain underdeveloped.
3. **Data Pricing**. As a tradable asset, data must be reasonably priced; however, establishing fair and consistent pricing mechanisms remains a major challenge. A core tension arises from the divergence in pricing logic: suppliers tend to base prices on data processing costs, while demand-side entities prefer to price according to the data's utility or contribution, making it difficult to reach a unified market pricing standard.
4. **Circulation Compliance**. Ensuring that data circulation is legal, compliant, secure, and privacy-preserving poses another urgent challenge. Growing concerns around information security and personal privacy have brought increased scrutiny to circulation practices. Currently, China mainly relies on policy and regulatory frameworks to govern such activities. Although technical solutions-such as secure multi-party computation, blockchain, federated learning, and trusted execution environments-are under active development, none has yet been widely adopted in practice. Beyond technical concerns, several regulatory and operational issues remain unresolved, including the permissible scope of data circulation, the legitimacy of participating entities, security during circulation processes, and the authorization of data usage.

From a global perspective, countries and regions currently adopt differing stances on cross-border data flows. The European Union places a strong emphasis on personal data protection and enforces strict regulations on the export of data beyond its borders. Through comprehensive legislation-most notably the enactment and implementation of the ≪General Data Protection Regulation≫ (GDPR)-the EU has established foundational principles and corresponding enforcement mechanisms for personal data protection. In contrast, the United States primarily relies on industry self-regulation, granting individual sectors the autonomy to set their own standards and constraints, with relatively limited oversight at the legislative and regulatory levels. At present, China adopts a more pragmatic approach, actively promoting the development of cross-border data circulation within the framework of ASEAN cooperation and the Belt and Road Initiative.

While so-called "data isolationism" may offer stronger safeguards for personal privacy, trade secrets, and national security, enabling cross-border data flows does not imply unrestricted or unregulated movement of data. In the long term, provided that the fundamental requirements mentioned above are not violated, fostering lawful, compliant, and orderly cross-border data circulation will become a key direction in international development, for three main reasons:

1. Cross-border data flows are an inevitable requirement of economic globalization. In the context of ongoing global economic integration and trade liberalization, restricting such flows would hinder the operations of multinational enterprises, cross-border e-commerce, global supply chains, and international service outsourcing.
2. Cross-border data flows are an inevitable requirement for national technological innovation. In the era of artificial intelligence, innovation is increasingly driven by data as the core resource, algorithms as the engine, computing power as the foundation, and distributed collaboration as a defining feature. Overemphasizing data localization would obstruct the development of a digital society and hamper progress in technological innovation.
3. Cross-border data flows are an inevitable requirement for building a community with a shared future for mankind. The global outbreak of COVID-19 has highlighted the urgent need for international cooperation in areas such as pharmaceuticals, vaccines, diagnostics, and public health. Facilitating the sharing of scientific research data and relevant information is essential for jointly developing effective responses and achieving mutual benefit and win-win outcomes.

To ensure reasonable and orderly cross-border data circulation, the following considerations must be addressed. First, the protection of personal data privacy must be prioritized. The malicious use or unauthorized sale of personal data can pose serious threats to individuals' privacy, property, and even physical safety. Second, the security of enterprise data must be safeguarded. As fundamental units of the national economy and key players in market activities, enterprises serve as the main market entities. Any leakage, interception, or theft of enterprise data may lead to the infringement of trade secrets and intellectual property rights, and could ultimately undermine the competitiveness of the nation's digital industries. Third, the protection of critical national data infrastructure is essential. Data from sectors such as oil and gas pipelines, energy, transportation, finance, military affairs, biotechnology, healthcare, and fiscal and taxation systems are highly sensitive. If such data were to be leaked or compromised, it could pose significant threats to national security.

## 10.4 Summary

This chapter began by introducing the concepts of data elements and the data-element market, emphasizing the importance of unlocking the latent value of data, advancing the development of big data, actively building a data-element market, and fostering a sustainable and healthy digital society.

It then explored two foundational activities within the data-element market: data trading and data circulation. Based on the nature and characteristics of the traded objects, data-trading frameworks can be categorized into three types: the free-trading framework, the paid-trading framework, and the model-trading framework. The first two frameworks treat data itself as the commodity. In the free-trading framework, services are seemingly provided free of charge, but are in fact exchanged for user data. Since users lack the ability to monitor or trace how their personal data are used, this framework poses significant privacy risks. The paid-trading framework, by contrast, explicitly recognizes user data as a tradable asset. It establishes a pre-defined agreement between users and service providers, thereby preventing the covert collection of user data and ensuring that data are stored and exchanged in a secure and controllable manner. In the model-trading framework, the traded commodity is a machine learning model. Because raw data are not exchanged directly-only data derivatives are transacted-this framework reduces the risk of direct privacy leakage. The primary research challenge in this context becomes the design of objective, systematic, and fair data valuation mechanisms and benefit allocation schemes.

With respect to data circulation, the chapter examined both domestic and cross-border flows. Domestically, the key challenges fall into four categories: data resources, data quality, data pricing, and compliance. For cross-border data circulation, the main challenge lies in enabling orderly and lawful data flows while ensuring the highest standards of personal privacy and national security. At present, China remains in the early stages of developing its data circulation ecosystem, and the path forward is both long and demanding.

## References

1. YE Q, MENG X, ZHU M, et al. A Survey on Local Differential Privacy[J]. Journal of Software, 2018, 29(7).
2. WU C, HU S, Lee C H. et al. Multi-platform data collection for public service with Pay-by-Data[J/OL]. Multimedia Tools and Applications, 2020, 79:33503–33518(2019-08-03)[2022-09-09]. https://doi.org/10.1007/s11042-019-07919-0.
3. LIU J, LOU J, LIU J, et al. Dealer: an end-to-end model marketplace with differential privacy[J]. Proceedings of the VLDB Endowment. New York:ACM: VLDB, 2021, 14(6):957–969.
4. SHAPLE L. STOCHASTIC G[J]. Proceedings of the national academy of sciences, 1953, 39(10):1095–1100.

# Chapter 11
# Data Monopoly

In the era of data-driven machine learning, rapid digitalization across all sectors has triggered an unprecedented explosion in data volume. Massive datasets, processed by algorithms such as machine learning, generate substantial societal value but also give rise to pressing data-ethical challenges. Alongside well-documented privacy concerns, the issue of data monopolization is equally critical. This term refers to the concentration of vast amounts of data in the hands of a small number of dominant "data oligarchs." Research shows that between 2018 and 2020, the top 10% of data collectors amassed 99% of all data. Such concentration erects barriers to competition, undermines consumer welfare, increases risks to information security and personal privacy, and stifles technological innovation. Addressing and regulating data monopolization is therefore both essential and urgent.

This chapter begins by analyzing the current state of data monopolization in China's mobile-application market, drawing on the ≪China Privacy Risk Analysis Report≫ released by the Meng Xiaofeng team [1]. It then examines the causes and consequences of data monopolization. Finally, it outlines three prevailing models of data governance and argues that data transparency is the fundamental remedy-the only sustainable path for the future of data governance.

## 11.1 Introduction

Advances in hardware and software technologies have spurred the rapid deployment and adoption of Internet of Things (IoT) applications, accelerating digital transformation across sectors such as modern agriculture, healthcare, transportation, and commerce. Individuals and organizations now generate vast quantities of data through diverse devices, causing global data volumes to expand at an exponential rate.



X. Meng, *Data Privacy and Data Governance*, Big Data Management,
https://doi.org/10.1007/978-981-95-5787-5_11

As early as 2013, the Internet Data Center (IDC), in its Digital Universe Study, projected that global data volume would grow at an average annual rate of 58%, surpassing 40 ZB by 2020.

Data inherently possess value-one of the defining characteristics of big data [2]. In 2012, the Obama administration's ≪Big Data Research and Development≫ Initiative recognized data as a strategic foundational resource. In 2017, The Economist famously likened data to"the oil of the twenty-first century." In 2020, the Opinions of the CPC Central Committee and the State Council on Establishing a More Perfect Market-oriented Allocation Mechanism and System for Data elevated data to a production factor on par with labor, capital, and technology. According to PwC's Global Top 100 Companies 2018, four of the five largest companies by global market capitalization were data-driven technology giants. The derivative value that data can generate is immense: it enables firms to optimize product and service quality, supports customized and personalized marketing strategies such as targeted advertising, and serves as both the foundation of profitability and a decisive resource for sustaining competitive advantage in data-intensive industries.

As a result, intense competition over data has emerged. Notable disputes include those between SF Express and Cainiao over Fengchao data, between Huawei and Tencent over WeChat data, and between Weibo and Maimai over user information. As industries become increasingly data-centric, the competition for-and concentration of-data intensifies. Today, big data are predominantly concentrated in the hands of platform-based Internet technology companies that operate two-sided markets. This accumulation has created widening disparities in data holdings across firms and institutions, giving rise to the phenomenon of data monopolization.

Does data monopolization truly exist? The term data monopolization first emerged during the 2007 merger review of Google and DoubleClick, yet no universally accepted definition has since been established. In Move Fast and Break Things: How Facebook, Google, and Amazon Cornered Culture and Undermined Democracy, Jonathan Taplin contends that monopolies do exist in the digital era: platforms such as Facebook, Google, and Amazon have secured enormous market share and profitability precisely by controlling vast troves of data.

Traditionally,"monopoly" implies exclusive control, typically identified in industrial contexts by market dominance. Data monopolization, however, constitutes a distinct form of monopoly that can be examined from multiple dimensions-data ownership, control, circulation, information protection, and monetization. Given that neither industry nor academia has yet precisely defined the competitive advantages and market power that data confer on firms, this book focuses on two core aspects: data ownership and data control. From an ownership perspective, data monopolization refers to the concentration of the majority of data in the hands of a small number of companies-so-called data oligarchs. By virtue of their massive datasets, these entities enjoy significant competitive advantages and hold the potential to abuse their dominant market positions. Regulatory and competition authorities worldwide have acknowledged the anticompetitive risks posed by such ownership and control, producing research reports and amending relevant policies. In January 2019, China explicitly incorporated data monopolization into its antitrust enforcement framework for the first time.

To better understand the current state of data monopolization in China, Professor Meng Xiaofeng's team at Renmin University conducted a large-scale quantitative analysis involving 30 million real users and 300,000 mobile applications, publishing the China Mobile User Privacy Risk Index Analysis Report for three consecutive years (2018–2020). The findings are striking: just 10% of data collectors accounted for 99% of all user-permission data, revealing an exceptionally severe degree of concentration. Building on this evidence, this section provides an in-depth analysis of the data-monopolization landscape and examines its underlying causes and harms.

Given the severity of the current situation, effective data governance has become imperative. This section outlines three principal governance models currently in practice: (1) localized governance implemented at the data-source stage; (2) intermediary governance established during data circulation; and (3) comprehensive regulatory frameworks spanning the entire lifecycle of data collection, circulation, and use. Ultimately, however, the root cause of data monopolization-and the ethical challenges it entails-lies in the opacity of data collection, circulation, and utilization. This book therefore contends that data transparency must serve as the central principle and the only sustainable path for the future of data governance.

## 11.2 Status of Data Monopoly

With the problem of data monopolization already emerging, how severe is it? To facilitate research on this issue, this section first clarifies the various stakeholders involved throughout the data lifecycle and defines their respective roles. It then draws on the ≪China Privacy Risk Index Analysis Report≫ released by Professor Meng Xiaofeng's team at Renmin University of China to provide an overview of the current state of data monopolization in China, revealing the severity of the present situation.

### *11.2.1 Definitions and Concepts*

To quantify the extent of data monopolization in the mobile-application market, Professor Meng Xiaofeng's team conducted a permission-based analysis of large-scale data collection from 2018 to 2020, drawing on data from 30 million real users and 300,000 mobile applications. For clarity, the analysis distinguishes four principal actors:

- **Data Producers**: Individuals or organizations that generate data; in the mobile-application context, these are typically end users.

- **Data Collectors**: Individuals or organizations that actively or passively collect data; in the mobile-application context, these are usually app developers.
- **Data Users**: Individuals or organizations that process or utilize data in any form; in the mobile-application context, they may be the data collectors themselves or third parties acquiring data through circulation or sharing.
- **Data Regulators**: Individuals or organizations responsible for ensuring the legality of data collection, circulation, and use; these are typically government agencies or trusted third parties.

*Data oligarchs* often serve simultaneously as data collectors, processors, and users, owning and controlling vast quantities of data. At present, these oligarchs are primarily data-driven technology giants-particularly mobile internet companies.

This analysis focuses on the mobile data-collection context, in which data collectors obtain user information by requesting system permissions through mobile applications. Such permissions may grant access to device system information, network status, GPS location, and personal data such as contact lists. Using a permission-based approach, the study measures the volume of user data obtained via these requested permissions, excluding operational data generated through user interactions with the app's services. The findings reveal an exceptionally severe imbalance: the top 10% of data collectors acquire 99% of all user-permission data-far exceeding the 80/20 distribution pattern commonly observed in social wealth.

## *11.2.2 Overall Situation*

The overall state of data monopolization is assessed based on data-collection patterns observed between 2018 and 2020. To interpret these patterns, data collectors are categorized by the order of magnitude of permissions obtained. Collectors acquiring 100 million or more permissions are designated as "hundred-million-level permission collectors," those acquiring between 10 million and 100 million as "ten-million-level permission collectors," and so forth.

The analysis produces three key findings:

- Based on the 2020 aggregate data-collection landscape, data monopolization is highly pronounced: only 10% of collectors account for 99% of all permissions.
- In 2020, the primary drivers of this monopolization were the top 1% of collectors-classified as "million-level," "ten-million-level," and"hundred-million-level" permission collectors-who collectively captured approximately 93.4% of all permissions.
- A comparison of the 2019 and 2020 landscapes indicates that although the share of permissions held by the top 10% of collectors declined marginally, overall data concentration in the hands of a very small minority has intensified, rendering the monopolization more severe than ever.

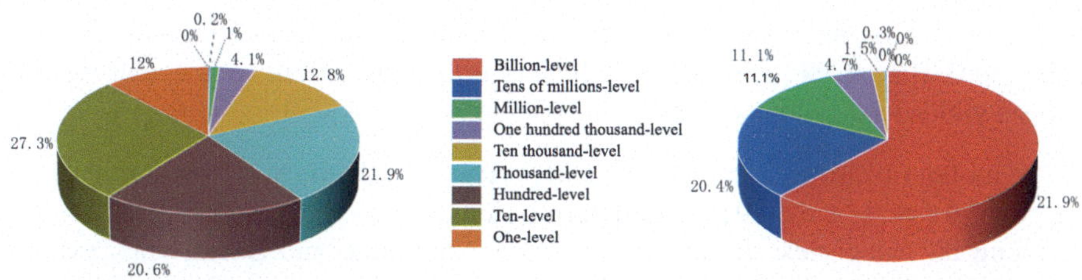


**Distribution of the number of collectors at each permission data acquisition level**

**Distribution of collector permission data at each permission data acquisition level**

**Fig. 11.1** Distribution of the number of permission data collectors and data acquisition in 2020

**Table 11.1** Proportion of data collected by different percentage of permission data collectors

| Proportion of permission data | Percentage of permission data collectors | | | | |
|---|---|---|---|---|---|
| | 0.01% | 0.1% | 1% | 5% | 10% |
| 2018 | 38.44% | 75.48% | 93.81% | 98.57% | 99.42% |
| 2019 | 27.01% | 69.93% | 92.15% | 98.08% | 99.19% |
| 2020 | 46.27% | 73.78% | 92.37% | 97.99% | 99.11% |
| Change | **20.86%** | **3.85%** | **0.002%** | **–0.0009%** | **–0.0008%** |

Specifically, Fig. 11.1 compares the number of collectors at each level with the volume of permissions they obtain. Collectors at the million-, ten-million-, and hundred-million-levels together represent only a small fraction of the total, yet each group commands more than 10% of all permissions, whereas the vast majority of collectors hold less than 3%. Table 11.1 reports the permission-collection statistics from 2018 to 2020, along with the year-over-year changes from 2019 to 2020. For the top 10% of collectors, the change is negative, indicating a slight decline in their share of permissions. By contrast, for the top 1%, the change is markedly positive, demonstrating that this small cohort of data oligarchs has further increased its share-intensifying the overall degree of monopolization.

### *11.2.3 Detailed Analysis*

Building on the overall data-collection landscape, this section examines patterns of data collection across different app categories. Professor Meng Xiaofeng's team surveyed category classifications used on Google Play and major Chinese third-party app stores, segmenting the market into twenty categories: Security, Lifestyle, Social, Office, Finance, Shopping, Education, Kids, Travel & Transportation, Photography, Video, Tools, Communication, News, Medical, Music, Games, Entertainment, Reading, and Sports. Using this taxonomy, the team analyzed the data-collection behavior of the top 0.01%, 0.1%, 1%, 5%, and 10% of collectors within each category. The analysis yields two main conclusions:

- Data monopolization is severe in all categories: in each, the top 10% of collectors account for no less than 91% of all permissions.
- Among all categories, Tools, Audio-Video, Shopping, and Social apps exhibit the highest levels of data monopolization, whereas Lifestyle, Communication, and Sports apps show comparatively lower-though still substantial-concentration relative to the overall landscape.

The situation is depicted in Fig. 11.2. In the Tools, Audio-Video, Shopping, and Social categories, the top 0.1% of collectors amass roughly 80% of all permissions, the top 1% collect about 95%, and the top 5% already reach approximately 99%-whereas, in the overall landscape, the top 10% are required to achieve the same proportion. By contrast, in the comparatively less concentrated Lifestyle, Communication, and Sports categories, the top 1% of collectors still obtain around 75% of permissions-lower than the corresponding overall ratio, yet still striking.

In addition, this section presents a comparative analysis of the five largest collectors to further illustrate the monopolistic landscape. To protect privacy, their identities are anonymized and only aggregate statistics are reported. Among them, the largest collector accounts for 13.19% of all permissions, the smallest for 2.11%, and together they control nearly 32% of the total. In other words, these five entities alone capture roughly one-third of all user data. Three operate apps across more than 18 categories,

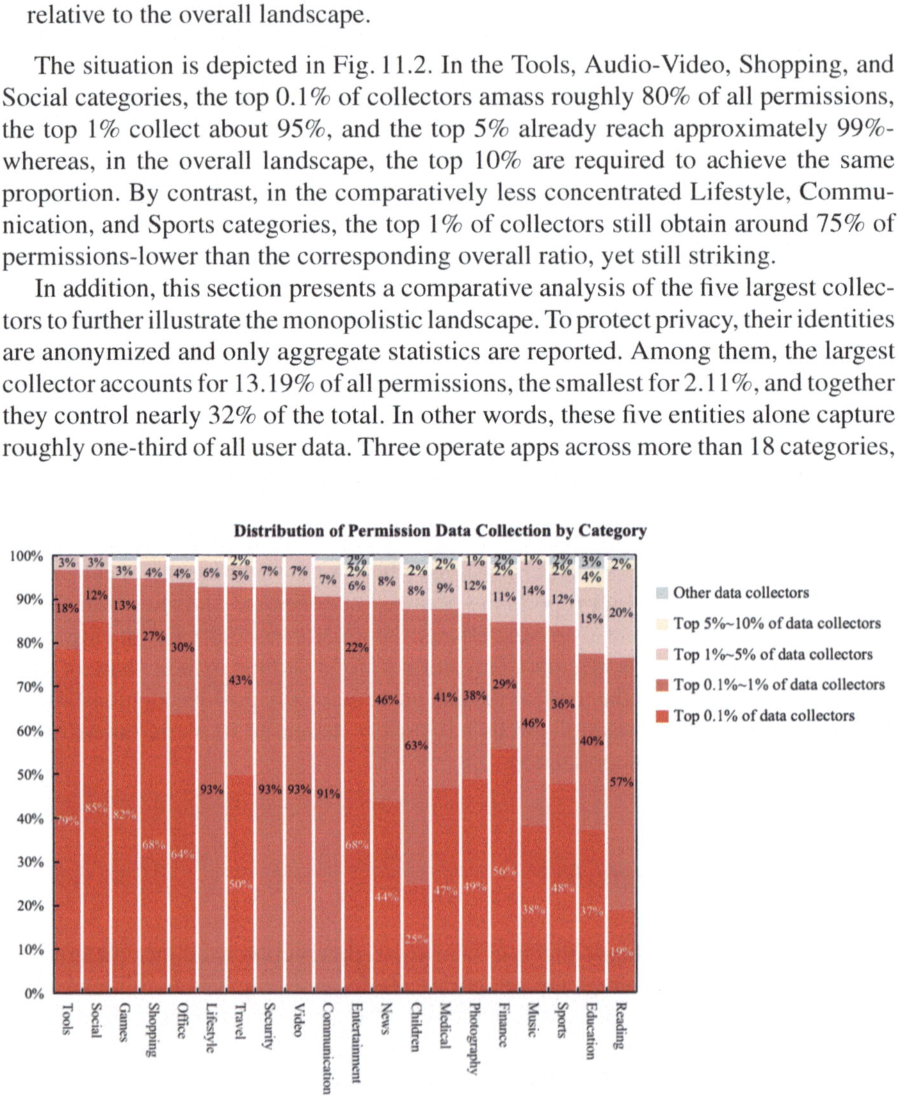


**Fig. 11.2** Distribution of permission data collection by category in 2020

while the remaining two cover about 12 categories, indicating that most of these data oligarchs pursue cross-domain business models. Notably, the apps developed by all five have exceptionally large user bases.

## 11.3 Causes and Harms of Data Monopoly

Given the severity of data monopolization, identifying its root causes is essential. Building on the preceding findings, this section analyzes both the drivers and the harms of data monopolization.

### *11.3.1 Causes of Monopoly*

This analysis argues that the emergence of data monopolization is closely linked to: (i) the intrinsic characteristics of data, (ii) the business models of data collectors, and (iii) the network effects of the AI era. Professor Meng Xiaofeng's team further examined correlations between each collector's total volume of acquired permissions and four factors-the number of developed apps, usage volume, requested permissions, and domains covered-providing empirical support for these arguments. Specifically, the causes of data monopolization can be summarized as follows.

First, data tend to aggregate naturally and are difficult to establish as property, making monopolization easier. In the era of big data, massive datasets are generated continuously at low marginal cost through mobile devices, sensor networks, and other channels. However, individual data points have low value density; their true worth emerges only after mining or applying machine-learning techniques to identify patterns. Such techniques are inherently data-driven: accuracy and utility improve as training-set size increases, creating a natural tendency for data to concentrate. Furthermore, data differ from tangible resources (e.g., oil, minerals) and from intellectual property (e.g., patents, copyrighted works) in that ownership is difficult to define and enforce. Under current legal frameworks, where data ownership remains unsettled, the legitimacy of collection cannot be effectively safeguarded-facilitating monopolization.

Second, the oligarchs' business models-multi-product, cross-domain, high-user-base-are pivotal to monopolisation. "Data oligarchs" (here equated with the top 0.1% of collectors) expand through business diversification, capital operations, and mergers & acquisitions, yielding portfolios that span many products and sectors and attract or retain vast user bases, thereby enabling massive data ingestion. Professor Meng's team shows that, in the mobile-app market, the more apps a collector develops, the higher their usage, and the broader their sectoral reach, the larger the permission dataset they accrue, increasing the likelihood of becoming an oligarch. Notably, the top 0.1% of collectors exceed all others by several multiples along these three dimensions.

Third, network effects in the AI era accelerate monopolisation. AI technologies are data-driven and exhibit strong network effects: as more users adopt an AI-powered product, more user data feed the model, improving its performance, increasing its value, and attracting still more users. Today's data oligarchs are large technology firms that benefit from such feedback loops. Leveraging their vast datasets, they continuously refine products and services, retaining existing users and attracting new ones. Smaller collectors, constrained in product and service enhancement, gradually lose users under competitive pressure. A snowball effect ensues, intensifying data monopolisation.

### *11.3.2 Harms of Monopoly*

The current data-monopoly landscape is severe: data oligarchs reap substantial benefits while posing significant risks to free-market competition. For data collectors, amassing large datasets through lawful means is not in itself illegal; however, exploiting monopolistic advantages to abuse market dominance, restrict competition, or harm consumer interests constitutes a violation of the law. A notable example is the 2017 ruling by the German antitrust authority, which found that Facebook had abused its dominant position by compelling users to accept unreasonable data-use terms.

In summary, data monopolization gives rise to four major risks: First, Barriers to free-market competition [3]. Horizontally, small or start-up firms with limited data reserves are excluded from-or severely hindered in-competing effectively with data oligarchs. Vertically, oligarchs dominate upstream and downstream markets, enabling them to dictate product offerings and pricing. Second, Consumer welfare losses [4]. Reduced competition diminishes consumer choice and bargaining power, leading to lower service quality and the emergence of exploitative practices such as price discrimination and consumer deception. The Wei Zexi incident, triggered by Baidu's paid medical search rankings, is a prominent example. Third, Information-security and personal-privacy risks. Privacy protection-an important non-price competitive factor-receives diminished attention when competition is weak. Italy's 2018 finding that Facebook had illegally shared data with third parties exemplifies this risk. Moreover, the vast quantities of data collected, processed, and stored increase the likelihood of security breaches, as illustrated by the 2018 leak of approximately 50 million users' data via Google+ APIs. Fourth, Suppressed industry-level technological innovation. Data concentration results in resource under-utilization: data-rich oligarchs lack incentives to innovate, while data-poor firms are unable to sustain R&D. Consequently, the overall innovative capacity of the industry declines.

## 11.4 Data Monopoly Governance Paradigm

Confronted with the severe reality of data monopolization, it is essential to curb monopolistic tendencies while fostering secure and equitable data sharing and circulation. Building on the causes and harms identified above, effective data governance must supervise both the sources of data collection and the flows of data-at local and global levels alike. Guided by the principle of "widening the source while regulating the flow," governance should, on one hand, standardize the collection, circulation, and use of data to promote the rational allocation of data resources; on the other hand, it should actively develop privacy-preserving data-sharing mechanisms to encourage broader circulation. Existing governance models can be broadly classified into three types: the local model, the intermediary model, and the global model. This section examines each in turn and argues that data transparency should be the defining principle for the future governance pathway.

### *11.4.1 Partial Paradigm*

The local model applies privacy-preserving techniques to data at its source before circulation, thereby reducing, to some extent, the value of large-scale data collection (Fig. 11.3). Common techniques include perturbation-based anonymization, differential privacy, and cryptography-based secure multi-party computation. Stronger privacy guarantees typically come at the cost of reduced data accuracy and increased computational overhead. As a result, collectors must balance privacy protection against data utility, which in turn constrains the current low-cost data-collection monopoly. Under this model, data oligarchs still retain control over most datasets; monopolization is alleviated but not eliminated, and the trade-off between data governance and industrial output must be carefully managed.

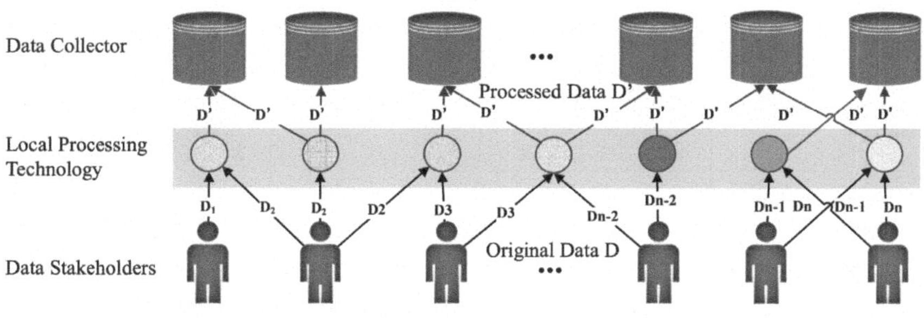


**Fig. 11.3** Local model of data monopoly governance

### 11.4.2 Mediator Paradigm

The intermediary model introduces a third-party platform into the data-circulation process, facilitating data flow and promoting sharing (Fig. 11.4). At present, such platforms fall into three main archetypes: data exchanges, data-crowdsourcing platforms, and data-sharing platforms, each suited to different scenarios. Since the 2015 release of the ≪Action Outline for Promoting Big-Data Development≫, numerous data exchanges have been established nationwide. Government-led exchanges, such as the Guizhou Big-Data Exchange, Shanghai Data Exchange Center, and Yangtze River Big-Data Exchange, focus on packaged-data transactions. Privately operated exchanges, including Juhe Data, JD Wanxiang, and Datatang, primarily provide data through APIs. Data-crowdsourcing platforms offer enterprises and individuals paid channels for supplying and downloading data, with current examples including Baidu Crowdsourcing, NetEase Youdao Crowdsourcing, and Ant Crowdsourcing. Data-sharing platforms adopt either direct or indirect sharing mechanisms. Direct-sharing platforms, governed by infrastructure rules, enable the circulation of asymmetric information among public agencies and facilitate reasonable data sharing among enterprises. A notable example is the "data trust" pilot jointly launched by the UK's AI Lab and the Open Data Institute, which promotes inter-organizational data sharing. Indirect-sharing platforms do not exchange raw data; instead, they share locally trained model parameters, allowing multiple participants to collaboratively train more powerful machine-learning models. This approach aligns with current data-driven technology trends while meeting privacy requirements. Representative cases include WeBank's federated-learning initiative and Huawei's Network AI Engine (NAIE) federated-learning platform. Overall, third-party intermediary initiatives are diverse, but the volumes of data traded or shared remain modest and require further development.

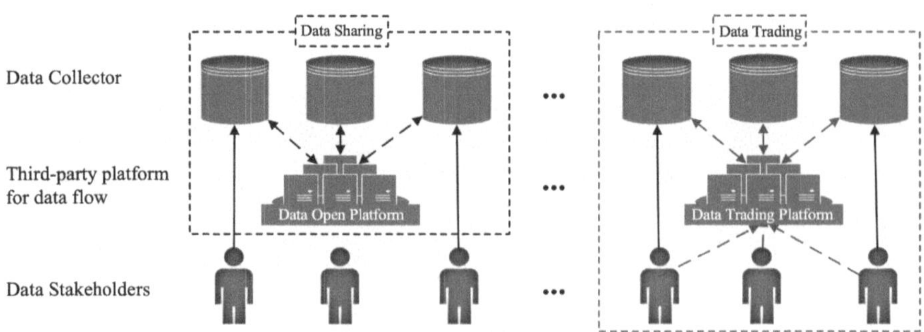


**Fig. 11.4** Intermediary model of data monopoly governance

### 11.4.3 Global Paradigm

The global model governs the entire lifecycle of data-generation, circulation, and use-aiming to weaken the dominance of data oligopolies while enhancing the authority of data generators (i.e., users) and data regulators (Fig. 11.5). This model has two primary variants: centralized and decentralized. In the centralized variant, a unified data-regulation platform manages data in a centralized manner. A representative example is Tim Cook's proposal that the U.S. Federal Trade Commission establish a "data clearinghouse" to supervise data flows and safeguard users' control over their personal information. The decentralized variant leverages technologies such as blockchain and smart contracts to record every stage of data collection, circulation, sharing, use, and settlement. This creates a verifiable, traceable, and auditable framework for data sharing and oversight. Numerous governmental and academic institutions are actively researching this approach. Compared with the local and intermediary models, the global model entails higher implementation costs. At present, it remains under development, with no fully mature large-scale applications yet deployed.

The data governance models discussed above position governments and IT enterprises as the principal actors, offering partial or comprehensive solutions to issues of data monopoly, blockage, and non-interoperability, with an emphasis on achieving balanced and monitorable allocation of data assets. However, the challenge of data monopoly is not merely a matter of uneven distribution; it is also a core ethical concern in the era of artificial intelligence. The persistence-and intensification-of data monopoly exacerbates other ethical issues, including data privacy and data discrimination [5]. As previous studies have noted, a "barrier lake" of big data has already formed, data monopoly is growing increasingly severe, and related problems such as privacy infringement are emerging in rapid succession [6]. At its root, these problems arise from a lack of transparency in the processes of data collection, circulation, sharing, usage, and decision-making. This paper argues that data transparency is the fundamental solution and the essential pathway for future data governance. Once

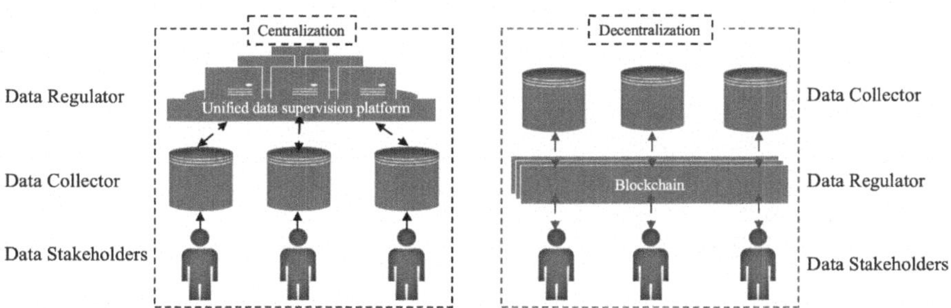


**Fig. 11.5** Global model of data monopoly governance

data become transparent to users or regulators across their entire lifecycle, the overall flow of data can be clearly and accurately understood, enabling improved data sharing while detecting and constraining monopolistic behavior. The concept and implementation of data transparency will be discussed in detail in Chap. 13.

## 11.5 Summary

President Xi Jinping has emphasized that the present moment marks a critical stage for implementing the national big-data strategy and accelerating the construction of a digital China. However, the severe problem of data monopoly has become a significant obstacle to the growth of technology enterprises and the advancement of a digital society. Without adequate big-data support and secure, equitable data sharing among enterprises, the full value of big data cannot be realized. On April 6, 2020, the Central Committee of the Communist Party of China and the State Council issued the ≪Opinions on Building a More Perfect Mechanism and System for the Market-oriented Allocation of Factors≫, proposing to accelerate the cultivation of the data element market, promote the open sharing of government data, enhance the value of social data resources, and strengthen the integration and security protection of data resources. These directives make resolving data-monopoly issues-and evaluating and supervising the rational allocation and use of data-more urgent than ever. At the same time, they impose higher demands on the methods of data sharing and circulation, as well as on data quality. Treating data as a production factor must be embedded within a robust data-governance framework, one that carefully balances the rights, responsibilities, and interests of all stakeholders throughout the data lifecycle. In the future, data governance must proceed along two parallel tracks: on one hand, improving existing governance models and making full use of current tools; on the other, actively developing a transparent governance framework to address data-ethics challenges rooted in data monopoly. Such an approach will help build a healthy and orderly Chinese big-data ecosystem and promote the rational, standardized development of the big-data industry.

## References

1. MENG X, ZHU M, LIU J. Research on Data Monopoly and Its Governance Modes[J]. Journal of Information Security Research, 2019, 5(48): 31–39.
2. MAYER-SCHÖNBERGER V, CUKIER K. Big data: A revolution that will transform how we live, work, and think[M]. New York: Houghton Mifflin Harcourt, 2013.
3. ZHENG X. Research on the legal nature of data from the perspective of data nature (in Chinese) [C]//. Financial Innovation Law Review (2018 Issue 1.Total Issue 4), 2018: 118–131.

4. NIU X. Antitrust laws and regulations on data monopoly (in Chinese)[J]. Economic Law Series, 2018(02): 370–394.
5. MENG X, WANG L. Data privacy,monopoly and fairness for AI[J]. Big Data Research, 2020, 6(1): 35–46.
6. MENG X, ZHU M, LIU J. Quantitative Research on Privacy Risk of Large Scale Mobile Users[J]. Journal of Information Security Research, 2019, 5(09): 778–788.

# Chapter 12
# Data Fairness

## 12.1 Introduction

In the era of big data, data-driven algorithms permeate nearly every aspect of daily life. A typical day illustrates this ubiquity: upon waking, we check the news on our phones, guided by recommendation algorithms that have learned our preferences; at lunch, we choose a restaurant suggested by an algorithm; when traveling, we let an algorithm plan our route; even weighty decisions-such as employee hiring and judicial sentencing-are now shaped by algorithmic outputs.

Amid this growing reliance, concerns over fairness have steadily emerged. For instance, South Korea's AI chatbot "Lee Luda" made discriminatory remarks about women, sexual minorities, and people with disabilities, and was forced offline less than twenty days after its release. Word embeddings trained on Google News texts [1] revealed gender bias, analogizing "man" to "doctor" and "woman" to "nurse." More critically, fairness issues in high-stakes domains can jeopardize fundamental rights and even lives. In the United States, the COMPAS sentencing system was found to disproportionately label Black defendants as high-risk for recidivism compared with White defendants. In the United Kingdom, the Babylon medical-diagnosis app faced accusations of gender bias: when given a 60-year-old female smoker with sudden chest pain and nausea, it suggested a panic attack or inflammation; the same symptoms in a 60-year-old male smoker produced a heart-attack diagnosis and an urgent emergency-care recommendation. Artificial intelligence was once envisioned as a force to benefit all of humanity, yet these examples offer a sobering reality: ensuring fairness in AI remains a complex and protracted challenge.

This chapter begins by defining the concept of fairness, then examines methods for measuring fairness across four application scenarios, aiming to provide readers with both reflection and practical insight.



X. Meng, *Data Privacy and Data Governance*, Big Data Management,
https://doi.org/10.1007/978-981-95-5787-5_12

## 12.2 Understanding Fairness

Before exploring solutions to fairness problems, it is essential to first clarify what fairness means. Academic discussions of fairness span decades and disciplines. This section outlines representative perspectives from psychology, philosophy, and computer science.

- **Psychology**: In 1965, psychologist Adams proposed *equity theory* [2], focusing on fairness in salary allocation and framing it as a subjective perception arising from social and historical comparisons. Social comparison occurs when an employee compares the ratio of personal pay to input with that of another employee; historical comparison occurs when an employee compares the ratio of current pay to input with that of a previous period. Fairness is perceived only when these ratios are equal. A key limitation of equity theory is that "input" is inherently difficult to measure. In practice, input is often assessed through performance appraisals, yet any appraisal method is partly reasonable and partly flawed.
- **Philosophy**: In *A Theory of Justice* [3], Rawls introduces the thought experiment of the *veil of ignorance*, which removes individuals' current social roles and statuses, returning them to a hypothetical original position of equality in which no one knows what role they will eventually occupy in society. Rawls argues that, under such conditions, people would collectively establish fair social rules to protect the disadvantaged. While thought-provoking, the "veil of ignorance" has been critiqued for several assumptions and ambiguities: (i) it presumes universal risk aversion, which may not hold; (ii) it leaves the concept of "disadvantaged group" undefined, making it unclear whether disadvantage stems from innate factors or lack of effort; and (iii) its egalitarian orientation may weaken incentives for productivity.
- **Computer Science**: Pitoura [4] emphasizes the distinction between fairness and equality, noting that equal treatment does not necessarily imply fairness. The U.S. case *Griggs v. Duke Power Co.* illustrates this point. In the 1950s, Duke Power required a high-school diploma for employment in its higher-paying departments. While the requirement appeared equal for all applicants, in the social context of the time, 34% of white applicants had graduated from high school compared to only 18% of Black applicants. In effect, the policy disproportionately disadvantaged Black applicants. The court ruled that the requirement was akin to Aesop's fable of offering milk in identical containers to both the fox and the stork-formally equal but substantively inequitable.

It is evident that fairness is understood differently across disciplines, and while these perspectives offer valuable conceptual guidance, they provide no concrete means of resolving fairness issues. Consequently, scholars in technical fields have sought to translate this inherently subjective notion into an objectively computable problem.

## 12.3 Classic Methods

Using concrete application scenarios, this section introduces fairness calculation methods in four contexts: cake cutting, price discrimination, algorithmic bias, and data bias.

### *12.3.1 Cake Cutting Problem*

The cake-cutting problem [5, 6] is a classic example of fair division. Let the cake be represented by the interval [0, 1], and let the set of participants be $N = 1, \ldots, n$. Each participant $p$ has an unknown valuation function $V_p$ over the cake. A division procedure allocates to each participant $p$ a piece $C_p$. The question is: under what conditions can the division be considered "fair"? Mathematicians have proposed two widely recognized criteria:

**Definition 27** (*Proportionality*) $\forall p \in N, ; V_p(C_p) \geq \frac{1}{n}$, i.e., each participant believes that the piece received is worth at least $\frac{1}{n}$ of the whole cake.

**Definition 28** (*Envy-freeness*) $\forall p, k \in N, ; V_p(C_p) \geq V_p(C_k)$, i.e., each participant believes that the piece received is at least as valuable as any other participant's piece.

When $n = 2$, the "I cut, you choose" method is a simple proportional division and can also be proven to satisfy envy-freeness. Suppose two individuals, A and B, are to divide the cake:

1. A cuts the cake into two pieces.
2. B chooses one piece.
3. A takes the remaining piece.

If A were to cut the cake into one large and one small piece, B would choose the larger one. To avoid this disadvantage, A will divide the cake into two pieces that are equal in A's own valuation. As a result, $V_A(C_A) = V_A(C_B)$ and $V_B(C_B) \geq V_B(C_A)$, satisfying the envy-freeness criterion.

When $n > 2$, a proportional division can be achieved recursively using the "I cut, you choose" principle. The first $n - 1$ participants recursively apply the division procedure; the $n$-th participant then asks each of the first $n - 1$ participants to divide their own share into $n$ parts, selecting one part from each. This method can be proven to satisfy proportionality, but it does not guarantee envy-freeness.

For example, when $n = 3$, A and B first use "I cut, you choose" to divide the cake into two pieces. Each then divides their piece into three parts, and C selects one part from A and one part from B. If A and B collude to allocate the entire cake to A, C would receive only $\frac{1}{3}$ of the cake while A would receive $\frac{2}{3}$, violating envy-freeness.

Although the cake-cutting problem has a long history, achieving both proportional and envy-free division remains challenging. Constructing envy-free allocations for more than two participants is particularly difficult; to date, only the three-person case has a relatively complete solution. Selfridge and Conway [5] independently proposed such an algorithm, which proceeds as follows:

(1) A divides the cake into three pieces, $X_1$, $X_2$, $X_3$, each of which A values equally; that is, $V_A(X_1) = V_A(X_2) = V_A(X_3) = \frac{1}{3}$.
(2) B selects the piece B values most and trims it. For example, if $V_B(X_1) > V_B(X_2) \geq V_B(X_3)$, B cuts off a portion $X'$ from $X_1$ such that $V_B(X_1 \setminus X') = V_B(X_2)$.
(3) The remaining three pieces-$X_1 \setminus X'$, $X_2$, and $X_3$ in this example-are chosen in the order C, B, A. If the trimmed piece ($X_1 \setminus X'$) is not taken by C, B must take it. Let the person among B and C who takes the trimmed piece be $T$, and let the other be $\overline{T}$.
(4) $\overline{T}$ divides the trimmed-off portion ($X'$ in this example) into three parts that $\overline{T}$ values equally.
(5) These three parts are chosen in the order $T$, A, $\overline{T}$.

### *12.3.2 Price Discrimination Problem*

Price discrimination refers to a seller offering the same product to different consumers at different prices. In the era of big data, some e-commerce platforms and service websites analyze and process users'data to covertly set higher reservation or purchase prices for certain existing customers in the same transaction scenario-a practice known as "big-data killing the familiar". This issue has increasingly drawn public concern, and regulators have introduced multiple legislative measures. In August 2020, the Ministry of Culture and Tourism issued the ≪Interim Provisions on the Administration of Online Travel Business Services≫, explicitly prohibiting online travel operators from abusing big-data analytics or other technical means to set unfair trading conditions based on tourists' consumption records or travel preferences, thereby infringing upon their lawful rights and interests. On August 20, 2021, ≪China's Personal Information Protection Law≫ was promulgated, with Article 24 specifically regulating ≪big-data killing the familiar≫; it requires that personal information processors using personal information for automated decision-making ensure the transparency of the decision-making process and the fairness and impartiality of results, and must not impose unreasonable differential treatment on individuals with respect to transaction prices or other trading conditions.

Addressing the issue of price discrimination, Cohen et al. [7] studied the impact of imposing fairness constraints on total social welfare. They assumed that the seller's objective is to set separate prices for each consumer group to maximize profit, and on this basis proposed four definitions of fairness constraints: price fairness, demand fairness, consumer-surplus fairness, and no-purchase-valuation fairness.

Suppose a seller offers a single product to two consumer groups, labeled group 0 and group 1. The unit cost of the product is $c$. For $i = 0, 1$, group $i$ has population size $d_i$, and the seller sets price $p_i$. Consumers in group $i$ value the product at $V_i \sim F_i(\cdot)$; hence the fraction of group $i$ that purchases the product is $\overline{F_i}(p_i)$. Consumer surplus is defined as the difference between a consumer's valuation and the actual purchase price, so the consumer surplus for group $i$ is $S_i(p_i) = E[(V_i - p_i)^+]$. The seller's profit from group $i$ is $R_i(p_i) = d_i(p_i - c)\overline{F_i}(p_i)$. In the absence of fairness constraints, the seller's objective is profit maximization, i.e., $p_i^* = \arg\max R_i(p_i)$.

Price fairness requires that the prices charged to each consumer group be similar, i.e., $p_i$ are similar; demand fairness requires that the purchase proportions for each group be similar, i.e., $\overline{F_i}(p_i)$ are similar; consumer-surplus fairness requires that the average surplus in each group be similar, i.e., $S_i(p_i)$ are similar; and no-purchase-valuation fairness requires that the average valuation among consumers who do not purchase be similar across groups, i.e., $N_i(p_i) = E[V_i \mid V_i < p_i]$ are similar. Cohen et al. [7] introduce a parameter $\alpha$ to control the strictness of the fairness constraints. Their experiments show that, under a moderate degree of price fairness, total social welfare increases as the constraint tightens; however, when the constraint becomes overly strict, total social welfare decreases. Under no-purchase-valuation fairness, total social welfare rises as the constraint tightens, but demand from one group may disappear entirely.

### *12.3.3 Algorithmic Bias Problem*

The algorithmic bias problem refers to biases that arise during the training of machine learning models. Such issues are typically addressed by incorporating fairness constraints into the model's training objective function or by employing adversarial training. For example, Li et al. [8], in a federated learning setting, define fairness as the variance of model accuracy across different devices and optimize an objective function subject to fairness constraints during training.

Fairness constraints are commonly classified into two broad categories: individual fairness and group fairness. Individual fairness requires that any two similar individuals receive similar treatment from the algorithm, which typically necessitates a task-relevant distance metric to quantify similarity between pairs of individuals. Group fairness requires that the algorithm's output not be influenced by attributes irrelevant to the task; attributes such as gender, religion, and race-known as protected attributes-should not affect outcomes. Under group fairness, the population is partitioned according to protected attributes, and all groups should be treated similarly by the algorithm.

In classification tasks, common definitions of group fairness can be broadly categorized into three types: base rate fairness, accuracy-based fairness, and calibration-based fairness.

**Definition 29** (*Base rate fairness*)

$$P[\hat{Y} \mid A = 0] = P[\hat{Y} \mid A = 1]$$

where $\hat{Y}$ is the prediction of a binary classifier and $A$ is a protected attribute. This definition requires that the probability of being predicted as positive is the same across groups with different values of $A$. Base rate fairness is also known as *demographic parity*.

**Definition 30** (*Accuracy-based fairness*)

$$P[\hat{Y} \mid Y = 1, A = 0] = P[\hat{Y} \mid Y = 1, A = 1]$$

where $\hat{Y}$ is the prediction of a binary classifier, $Y$ is the true label, and $A$ is a protected attribute. This definition requires that the true positive rate be equal across groups, and is also known as *equal opportunity*.

**Definition 31** (*Calibration-based fairness*)

$$P[Y = 1 \mid S = p, A = 0] = P[Y = 1 \mid S = p, A = 1]$$

where $S$ is the predicted probability of belonging to a given class, $Y$ is the true label, and $A$ is a protected attribute. This definition requires that, for any predicted probability $p$, the actual probability of being positive is the same across groups.

Moreover, Kusner et al. [9] proposed the notion of counter factual fairness based on causal inference techniques. They argue that an algorithm is fair if the distribution of its predictions remains unchanged when the protected attribute is hypothetically altered, while all other factors that are not causally dependent on the protected attribute are held constant.

**Definition 32** (*Counter factual fairness*)

$$P[\hat{Y}_{A \leftarrow a}(U) = y \mid X = x, A = a] = P[\hat{Y}_{A \leftarrow a'}(U) = y \mid X = x, A = a]$$

where $\hat{Y}$ denotes the classifier, $A$ is the protected attribute, and $X$ represents the remaining attributes. The triplet $(U, V, F)$ forms a causal model, where $U$ is the set of exogenous variables not determined by any variable in the observable set $V$; $V$ is the set of endogenous variables, with $V \equiv A \cup X$; and $F$ is the set of structural equations expressing the value of each endogenous variable as a function of $U$ and the other variables in $V$.

All the above fairness definitions are formulated for a single protected attribute, such as determining whether an algorithm discriminates against women. For intersecting protected attributes-such as assessing whether an algorithm discriminates against Black women-Foulds et al. [10] drew on the concept of differential privacy to introduce *differential fairness*. This approach uses a fairness cost parameter $\epsilon$ to bound the difference in the algorithm's output probabilities across different groups.

**Definition 33** (*$\epsilon$-differential fairness*)

$$e^{-\epsilon} \le \frac{P_{M,\theta}[M(x) = y \mid s_i, \theta]}{P_{M,\theta}[M(x) = y \mid s_j, \theta]} \le e^{\epsilon}$$

where $M$ is the classification algorithm, $x \sim \theta$ denotes user data, and $s_i, s_j$ represent different protected attributes. Under this definition, regardless of how protected attributes are combined, the algorithm's output probabilities must remain within a multiplicative factor of $e^{\epsilon}$ across groups.

In tasks such as recommender systems and natural language processing, definitions of fairness vary widely. At present, there is no unified definition of fairness for machine learning algorithms, and existing definitions often conflict with one another, making it impossible to satisfy them all simultaneously.

### *12.3.4 Data Bias Problem*

Because machine learning algorithms are highly dependent on training data, any biases present in the data are likely to be inherited by downstream tasks, giving rise to the *data bias problem*. Consequently, some researchers focus on removing bias from the training data itself. For example, in 2019, International Business Machines Corporation (IBM) released the *Diversity in Faces* (DiF) facial-recognition dataset [11], which provides a balanced and diverse set of human-face images to reduce bias in facial-recognition systems. Amini et al. [12] employed a variational autoencoder to learn the latent structure of a dataset and then reweighted data points during training according to the learned latent distribution.

Current approaches to mitigating data bias focus primarily on balancing dataset classes, with common techniques including *data resampling* and *data augmentation*.

Data resampling can be divided into *under-sampling* and *over-sampling*. Under-sampling reduces the number of samples in the majority class; for example, random under-sampling removes majority-class samples at random. Over-sampling increases the number of samples in the minority class; for example, random over-sampling duplicates minority-class samples at random. Both methods have drawbacks: random under-sampling may discard important samples containing implicit information, while random over-sampling can lead to model overfitting. Building on random over-sampling, Chawla et al. [13] proposed the *Synthetic Minority Over-sampling Technique* (SMOTE), which synthesizes new samples similar to those in the minority class. Specifically, for each minority-class sample, SMOTE uses the $k$-nearest neighbor algorithm to find $k$ neighbors, randomly selects $N$ of these neighbors, and performs random linear interpolation to generate new synthetic samples.

Data augmentation is a widely used data-preprocessing technique in computer vision. By applying geometric transformations (e.g., flipping, rotating, cropping, scaling) and color transformations (e.g., adding noise, blurring, erasure, filling) to images, it effectively increases both the volume and the diversity of image data. Similarly, in the field of natural language processing, text-augmentation techniques expand textual data through methods such as back-translation, random word replacement, or substitution of non-core words.

Furthermore, based on the sources of data bias, Mehrabi et al. [14] present a detailed taxonomy of bias within the closed loop of user interaction, data, and algorithms, with the aim of encouraging future researchers to examine the interactions among different types of bias and to develop targeted mitigation strategies for each.

## 12.4 Summary

As Nicholas Carr, former executive editor of the ≪Harvard Business Review≫, observed, when we rely entirely on computers to understand the world, our own intelligence gradually degenerates into artificial intelligence. The problem of data fairness in the age of AI serves as yet another warning: AI algorithms are not inherently objective or impartial; they can also embody the biases of human society. This challenge is both technical and social in nature. It is hoped that, with broad engagement from all sectors of society, scholars in both the technical and social domains will work together to devise effective solutions.

## References


1. BOLUKBASI T, CHANG K W, ZOU J Y, et al. Man is to computer programmer as woman is to homemaker? debiasing word embeddings[J]. Advances in neural information processing systems, 2016, 29: 4349–4357.
2. ADAMS J S. Inequity in social exchange[J]. Advances in experimental social psychology, 1965, 2: 267–299.
3. RAWLS J. A theory of justice: Revised edition[M]. Cambridge: Harvard university press, 1999.
4. PITOURA E. Social-minded measures of data quality: fairness, diversity, and lack of bias[J]. Journal of Data and Information Quality (JDIQ), 2020, 12(3): 1–8.
5. BRAMS S J, BRAMS S J, TAYLOR A D. Fair Division: From cake-cutting to dispute resolution[M]. Cambridge: Cambridge University Press, 1996.
6. ROBERTSON J, WEBB W. Cake-cutting algorithms: Be fair if you can[M]. Boca Raton: CRC Press, 1998.
7. COHEN M C, ELMACHTOUB A N, LEI X. Price Discrimination with Fairness Constraints[C]//Proceedings of the 2021 ACM Conference on Fairness, Accountability, and Transparency. New York, NY: ACM, 2021: 2–2.
8. LI T, SANJABI M, BEIRAMI A, et al. Fair resource allocation in federated learning[EB/OL]. (2019-05-25)[2022-08-01]. https://arxiv.org/pdf/1905.10497.pdf.
9. KUSNER M, LOFTUS J, RUSSELL C, et al. Counterfactual fairness[C]//Proceedings of the 31st International Conference on Neural Information Processing Systems. [S.l.]: Neural Information Processing Systems Foundation, Inc., 2017: 4069–4079.
10. FOULDS J R, ISLAM R, KEYA K N, et al. An intersectional definition of fairness[C]//Proceedings of IEEE 36th International Conference on Data Engineering (ICDE). Piscataway, NJ: IEEE, 2020: 1918–1921.

11. MERLER M, RATHA N, FERIS R S, et al. Diversity in faces[EB/OL]. (2019-01-29)[2022-08-01]. https://arxiv.org/pdf/1901.10436.pdf
12. AMINI A, SOLEIMANY A P, SCHWARTING W, et al. Uncovering and mitigating algorithmic bias through learned latent structure[C]//Proceedings of the 2019 AAAI/ACM Conference on AI, Ethics, and Society. New York, NY: ACM, 2019: 289–295.
13. CHAWLA N V, BOWYER K W, HALL L O, et al. SMOTE: synthetic minority over-sampling technique[J]. Journal of artificial intelligence research, 2002, 16: 321–357.
14. MEHRABI N, MORSTATTER F, SAXENA N, et al. A survey on bias and fairness in machine learning[J]. ACM Computing Surveys (CSUR), 2021, 54(6): 1–35.

# Chapter 13
# Data Transparency

Previous chapters have examined the main technical approaches to privacy protection as well as key issues in the data ecosystem, including data circulation, data monopolies, and data fairness. At the root of these problems lies the opacity of data. Enhancing the reasonable and appropriate transparency of data acquisition, sharing, and usage not only facilitates the resolution of these issues but also serves as the final safeguard when they arise. For example, in cases of privacy leakage or data misuse, data transparency enables regulators to quantitatively assess the status of data collection, thereby providing technical support for addressing problems such as privacy breaches and monopolistic practices. When such issues occur, transparency in data acquisition and sharing allows regulators to determine who misused the data, where the misuse occurred, and under what circumstances—making traceability and accountability possible.

This section begins by defining the concept of data transparency and examining its intrinsic connections to privacy protection, data monopolies, and decision interpretability. It then introduces a data-transparency framework and explains how to technically implement several key stages within it, including transparency in data acquisition, sharing, cloud storage, and decision-making. Particular emphasis is placed on leveraging blockchain technology to enable transparency in data acquisition and sharing, thereby establishing a foundation for tracing and holding parties accountable in cases of data-privacy violations or monopolistic practices.

## 13.1 Introduction

At present, vast amounts of data are continuously collected by various entities, with acquisition and sharing processes relying solely on the credit endorsement of third parties. Such endorsement merely informs users of what data are collected, how they



X. Meng, *Data Privacy and Data Governance*, Big Data Management,
https://doi.org/10.1007/978-981-95-5787-5_13

are shared, and how they will be used. However, because the processes of data acquisition, sharing, and usage remain externally invisible, these commitments cannot be independently verified, resulting in a lack of transparency. Incidents of enterprises leaking users' private data occur with alarming frequency. While existing privacy-preserving techniques—such as differential privacy—provide certain safeguards, they remain insufficient to fully address the privacy-leakage risks inherent in large-scale data collection. Given the rapidly evolving and highly complex nature of data-related issues, no single privacy-preserving method can cover every possible risk.

Data transparency seeks to record relevant information during data acquisition, sharing, and usage, thereby enhancing the visibility of the value-realization process in the big-data environment. When combined with policy compliance, violation detection, and privacy auditing, it can serve as a secondary safeguard—providing traceability and accountability when privacy-preserving techniques fall short—and can also support data evaluation, regulation, and the mitigation of data monopolies [1]. Such measures are essential to building a healthy and orderly data ecosystem [2]. In particular, improving transparency in data acquisition and sharing can supply evidence for addressing privacy leakage, data abuse, and monopolistic practices, while enhancing transparency in data-driven decisions can help ensure their accuracy and fairness.

Currently, data transparency is pursued through two primary approaches: legal regulations and technical measures. Legal regulations impose transparency requirements across the entire data life cycle, serving both as a deterrent and as a basis for ex-post enforcement. Technical measures, by contrast, emphasize ex-ante prevention and provide evidentiary support for ex-post actions, drawing on established traceability and accountability mechanisms and increasingly leveraging emerging technologies such as blockchain.

## 13.2 Transparency Framework

Data transparency was first proposed in 2017 by Professor Elisa of Purdue University, USA, who defined it as the ability of data subjects to access information related to themselves. She recommended achieving this goal through data-transparency policies, logging systems, and algorithmic transparency. The research on data transparency presented in this book builds on this lineage, aiming to ensure transparency throughout the entire big-data life cycle. Moreover, it situates data-transparency research within the broader big-data ecosystem, offering a clearer taxonomy, deeper exploration, and a systematic explanation of the intrinsic relationships among data transparency, data-privacy protection, data-driven decision-making, and data monopolies.

Industry has likewise demonstrated an urgent demand for transparency in realizing big-data value. In a 2019 *Time* magazine commentary, Apple CEO Tim Cook called for a new framework to enhance corporate transparency in handling user data and proposed the establishment of a data clearinghouse, requiring all data intermediaries to register so that users could track the data bundles being sold. Similarly, Gartner's 2020 report on strategic technology trends identified "transparency and traceability" as one of the ten key strategic technology trends. Today, data transparency is recognized as an essential safeguard for unlocking big-data value and as a novel perspective for strengthening data-privacy protection and data governance.

Importantly, data transparency must address the needs of all stakeholders across the big-data life cycle, acknowledging that each has distinct transparency requirements.

**Definition 34** (*Data Transparency*) Data transparency refers to the ability of every participating entity, during the process of realizing big-data value, to access all data information that pertains to itself.

Here, data information includes raw data, derived data, and decision data. The participating entities consist of five roles: data contributors, data collectors, data consumers, data processors, and data supervisors. Specifically, data contributors are individuals or institutions that generate data; data collectors are individuals or institutions—such as service providers and researchers—that collect data; data consumers are individuals or institutions that use data in any form; data processors are individuals or institutions that, with authorization, process data on behalf of data consumers; and data supervisors are institutions—primarily government agencies and trusted third-party organizations—that supervise data sharing and circulation throughout the entire data life cycle. These roles may overlap; for example, when a data collector also uses and has the capability to process the data, it simultaneously acts as a data processor and a data consumer.

Data-transparency research should address the transparency needs of all participating entities. Drawing on the big-data life cycle and the specific transparency requirements of each stakeholder, we categorize data transparency into five components: data-acquisition transparency, data-sharing transparency, cloud-storage-service transparency, data-decision transparency, and legal-regulation transparency. The *data-transparency framework* and the corresponding information contained in each component are illustrated in Fig. 13.1.

**1. Data-Acquisition Transparency**

Data-acquisition transparency refers to recording detailed information about what data are collected, in what form, and for what purpose. This ensures that data contributors, data collectors, and data supervisors can all access the relevant records. At present, acquisition transparency is primarily achieved through transparency-enhanced tools, data-usage agreements, and auditable access-control mechanisms.

**2. Data-Sharing Transparency**

Based on the manner of data sharing, data-sharing transparency can be categorized into *traceability-accountable data sharing* and *verifiable statistical analysis and machine learning*. In scenarios where raw data are accessed or circulated, traceability-accountable data sharing records the flow of data so that data contributors and data

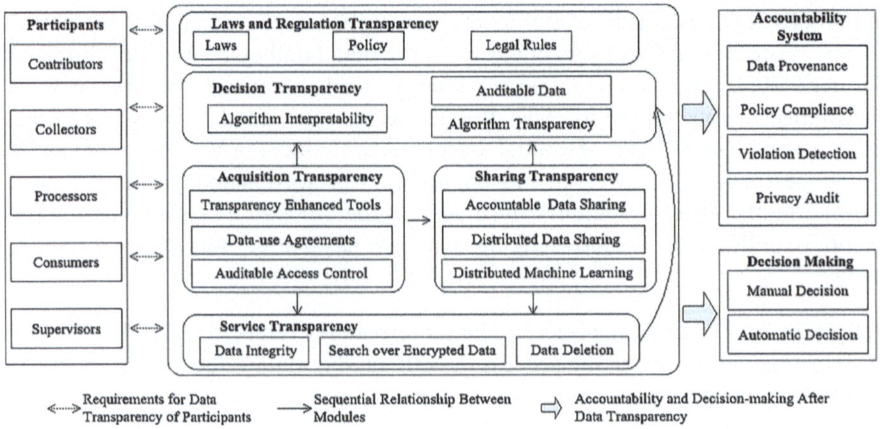


**Fig. 13.1** Data transparency framework

supervisors can trace and hold parties accountable for sharing activities and privacy leaks, while data processors and data consumers can use these records to demonstrate lawful use. When transmission costs, legal restrictions, or other constraints prevent disclosure of raw data, sharing can instead be conducted via distributed-dataset-sharing techniques or distributed machine learning without revealing the original data. In such cases, the encrypted data and parameters provided by data providers (including data contributors and data collectors) must be recorded so that data consumers can verify the sharing process.

**3. Cloud-Storage-Service Transparency**
With the growing adoption of cloud-storage services by enterprises and individuals, an increasing volume of data is stored on cloud servers for ease of access and management. However, traditional cloud-data-security and privacy-preservation techniques—such as data-integrity verification, verifiable searchable encryption, and deterministic data deletion—often rely on trusted third parties, and their implementation processes are opaque. Cloud-storage-service transparency seeks to eliminate this opacity by making storage operations verifiable and accountable.

**4. Data-Decision Transparency**
Because data underpin decision-making, data consumers must be able to audit and trace decision-related data. Achieving data-decision transparency also requires support from algorithmic interpretability and algorithmic transparency. Algorithmic interpretability primarily concerns the interpretability of machine-learning models—i.e., providing reasonable explanations of the decision-making principles underlying specific algorithms and assessing whether they exhibit unfairness. Algorithmic transparency involves appropriately disclosing information about the decision-making algorithms themselves.

**5. Legal-Regulation Transparency**

Legal regulations are a crucial means of promoting data transparency beyond the technical domain. Governments and organizations worldwide have enacted laws and regulations that establish informed consent as a fundamental requirement for the acquisition, sharing, use, and storage of personal data. Informed consent requires that, when collecting personal data, data collectors fully inform data subjects about how their data will be collected, processed, and utilized, and obtain explicit consent. For instance, the EU's ≪General Data Protection Regulation≫ (GDPR) enshrines transparency as a fundamental right of data subjects.

Implementing the five components of data transparency described above enables the information required by each participating entity to be recorded as traceability data. Specifically, realizing data-acquisition transparency and data-sharing transparency ensures that information on how data are obtained and circulated is documented. Consequently, when incidents such as privacy leakage or data misuse occur, data supervisors can use these records to trace the events and hold non-compliant parties accountable. Realizing cloud-storage-service transparency increases the trustworthiness of cloud-storage services. Realizing data-decision transparency allows data consumers to audit decision data, thereby enhancing the credibility of big-data-driven decisions. Finally, transparency requirements stipulated in legal regulations provide legal safeguards for implementing data transparency.

The realization of data transparency relies, on the one hand, on comprehensive and rigorous legal support. Legal regulations serve as a deterrent and provide a basis for ex-post sanctions. Fulfilling the transparency requirements set out in such regulations rests on the foundations of legal constraints, third-party credit endorsements, and moral self-discipline. On the other hand, the technical implementation of data transparency equips participating entities with the means to obtain information relevant to themselves. It enables ex-ante prevention and provides evidence for ex-post actions. Overall, legal and technical approaches are mutually supportive and complementary.

This section focuses on achieving data transparency and traceability accountability through technical means. Traditional accountability systems typically record how users' data are managed, who has accessed them, and when the data were modified or misused. Because every workflow pathway may require accountability, traditional technical methods generally emphasize accountability across all stages of the workflow—for instance, unauthorized access to security systems or unauthorized retrieval of secure data. However, big-data acquisition takes diverse forms, and its sharing and circulation are highly complex, while traditional accountability systems are mostly designed for small-scale datasets and struggle to cope with the variability, complexity, and often low quality of big data. Moreover, most traditional traceability and accountability techniques are centralized and lack transparency, causing their implementation to depend heavily on trusted third parties. In summary, technically achieving data transparency and traceability accountability has become an urgent challenge to address.

## 13.3 Transparency Techniques

Blockchain technology, with its inherent characteristics of openness, transparency, immutability, and decentralization, is naturally well-suited for traceability and accountability. As such, it has become a key pathway for realizing data transparency. In the context of data-acquisition transparency and data-sharing transparency, blockchain can act as a trusted *ledger* that records detailed information on data acquisition and sharing. For data-cloud-storage-service transparency and data-decision transparency, blockchain's decentralized architecture enables secure verification, data management, and quality assurance. These data-transparency requirements align closely with the core features of blockchain.

At present, blockchain plays an increasingly important role in enhancing transparency across the entire data life cycle—including acquisition, sharing, storage, and decision-making—thereby providing strong technical support for traceability and accountability. This section examines blockchain applications in three key areas: data-acquisition and data-sharing transparency, data-cloud-storage transparency, and data-decision transparency.

### *13.3.1 Transparency in Data Acquisition and Sharing*

Data-acquisition and data-sharing transparency covers traceability-accountable data acquisition and sharing, verifiable distributed dataset sharing, and verifiable distributed machine learning, as outlined in Sect. 12.3. This subsection focuses on how blockchain enables traceability-accountable data acquisition and sharing by recording the flow of data during these processes, thereby providing technical support for privacy-preserving traceability and accountability as well as for addressing data monopolies.

In traditional data-acquisition and data-sharing processes, data collectors draft data-usage agreements to inform users about the collection, sharing, and intended uses of their data. Users—acting as data contributors—retain rights of informed consent and control only within the constraints of applicable laws and the assurances of third-party credit endorsements. However, because the processes of data acquisition and sharing are externally invisible, compliance with such agreements cannot be independently verified. A 2014 Pew Research Center report on privacy in the United States revealed that 91% of respondents believed they had lost control over how their personal data were collected and used, while 61% expressed frustration over not understanding how their information was being utilized. Similarly, the 2016 ≪Chinese Netizen Rights Protection Survey Report≫ found that 84% of respondents had experienced the adverse consequences of personal-privacy leakage. The lack of transparency in data acquisition and sharing has thus exacerbated the severity of privacy breaches.

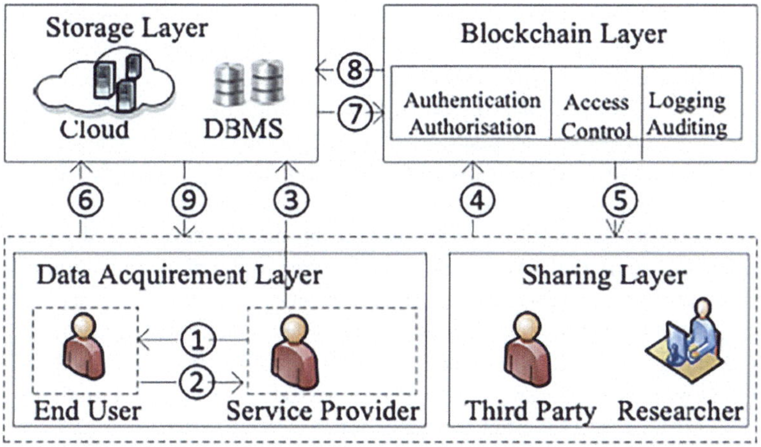


**Fig. 13.2** Transparency in data acquisition and sharing

Integrating blockchain into data-acquisition and data-sharing workflows allows relevant information to be immutably recorded on a decentralized, open, and tamper-resistant ledger, thereby ensuring stronger accountability. Existing research has explored blockchain-based mechanisms to enhance transparency in the acquisition and circulation of privacy-sensitive data in domains such as mobile applications, healthcare, and the Internet of Things [3]. In particular, blockchain-based permission management and access control can transparently log details of data acquisition and sharing, thereby improving both transparency and user controllability throughout the entire process.

When a service provider requests data from a user, the blockchain-based framework for data acquisition and sharing can be organized into four layers: the *data-acquisition layer*, *data-storage layer*, *data-sharing layer*, and *blockchain layer*, as illustrated in Fig. 13.2.

In the data-acquisition layer, data contributors retain the right to know the content, form, and purpose of data collection. Current research integrates access-control technologies to achieve transparency in data-collection permissions (Steps 1–3 in Fig. 13.2). At the same time, users themselves manage these permissions, ensuring that both the content and form of data collection remain transparent and under user control [3].

In the data-storage layer, once acquired, the data are stored either by the service provider or by a third-party storage organization. Due to blockchain's inherent storage limitations, the prevailing approach stores only metadata on-chain while keeping the actual data off-chain. Off-chain storage can leverage traditional database management systems, cloud storage, or distributed storage systems. To preserve data confidentiality, encryption techniques are typically applied to the data.

In the data-sharing layer, whenever a sharing request occurs, the requester must first submit an access request (Steps 4–5 in Fig. 13.2). Users deploy their data-sharing policies onto the blockchain as smart contracts, tailored to their own preferences. However, because blockchain inherently provides transparency, the sharing layer must also mitigate privacy risks associated with exposing the sharing relationship itself. The identities of both sharing parties are recorded on-chain, and this information could be obtained by an attacker. Such attackers may conduct linkage attacks by correlating the recorded identities with external datasets. For example, in a medical scenario, if a patient grants a physician access to their medical data, the physician's identity is recorded on the blockchain, thereby implicitly revealing the physician-patient relationship. An attacker could cross-reference the physician's identity with other datasets to infer sensitive patient information.

In the blockchain layer, a decentralized access-control process is executed (Steps 6–9 in Fig. 13.2), ensuring that every data-access event is immutably recorded on the blockchain as a transaction. Blockchain-based access-control methods can be broadly categorized into two types: transaction-based and smart-contract-based.

The transaction-based approach manages access-control policies or permissions directly through blockchain transactions. Many such methods leverage the security of Bitcoin, using the `OP_RETURN` opcode to store policies or permissions on the Bitcoin blockchain. Because Bitcoin Script is not well-suited for implementing complex business logic, it is often combined with the Discretionary Access Control (DAC) model. Practical deployments must also account for scalability, computational, and storage constraints. For example, in IoT data-sharing scenarios, a virtual-chain layer can be added above the blockchain to improve scalability [4]; for devices with limited computational and storage capacity, an edge-device layer can be introduced beneath the blockchain, where edge devices perform authentication, transaction creation, data collection, and data transmission to the storage layer [5].

The smart-contract-based approach encodes access-control policies as smart contracts, which are then automatically executed on the blockchain. Current research explores integrating this approach with traditional access-control models such as Discretionary Access Control (DAC) and Attribute-Based Access Control (ABAC), thereby combining the flexibility of smart contracts with established access-control paradigms.

- The DAC model grants permissions based on user identity; when integrated with smart contracts, it enables transparent permission judgments for users with different identities. Some implementations employ Ethereum smart contracts; however, as policy scale increases, Ethereum's execution costs rise and its permission management becomes less flexible [6]. Moreover, Ethereum's scalability must be evaluated against real-world requirements. To reduce contract-execution costs and meet scalability demands, several studies adopt consortium blockchains combined with cloud storage, enabling data sharing in domains with high privacy requirements such as healthcare and social networks [7]. For specific scenarios, consensus protocols can also be customized to application needs to improve scalability. For example, in IoT applications, transparent data sharing among stakeholders on edge devices can be achieved by designing consensus mechanisms, transaction types, and block structures suited to the computation and storage capacities of those devices.

- The ABAC model represents entities and constraints using attributes, establishing relationships between attributes and permissions according to the access requester's authorization conditions. Integrating blockchain with ABAC enables fine-grained sharing while supporting both identity-privacy protection and transparency. Current research predominantly combines consortium blockchains with ABAC. Because ABAC does not cause policies to grow exponentially with the number of users, it has been widely adopted; however, a balance must be struck between the granularity of accountability and the level of privacy protection required.

Through the four layers described above, information on data acquisition and the identities of data-sharing parties are recorded on the blockchain. Leveraging blockchain's openness, immutability, and decentralization, this design achieves transparency in both data acquisition and sharing circulation. Once such information is recorded, data supervisors and data owners can perform traceability and accountability by relying on the recorded policy-compliance and violation-detection data.

At present, research on data transparency and traceability accountability remains in its early stages, with many issues yet to be resolved. First, users lack effective control during data acquisition: they must either accept the data-collection agreement drafted by the data collector and surrender all requested data, or refuse and forgo the service. A core challenge in implementing data-acquisition transparency is how to return control to users, enabling them to determine the content, purpose, and form of their data while still receiving services based solely on the data they agree to share. Second, service providers act as both data collectors and service deliverers, yet whether they comply with the data-usage agreement when sharing data is often opaque. Traceability accountability presupposes complete traceability records; however, ensuring that every data-acquisition and data-sharing event is recorded remains difficult. In addition to technical measures, support from policies, laws, and regulations is indispensable. Moreover, when blockchain is employed to achieve data transparency, factors such as scalability, interoperability across multiple blockchains, and privacy protection within the blockchain itself all influence the feasibility of implementation.

### 13.3.2 Transparency in Cloud Data Storage

An increasing number of data owners (DO) are storing their data in the cloud to benefit from the storage services offered by cloud service providers (CSP). Because complete trust between DO and CSP cannot be assumed, technologies such as data-integrity verification, searchable encryption, and deterministic data deletion are essential for securing cloud-stored data and safeguarding privacy. Existing methods typically assume that CSP is semi-trusted and DO is honest and trustworthy, introducing a trusted third-party auditor (TPA) to assist DO in performing verification. However, these assumptions are restrictive in real-world deployments, and most current approaches still lack transparency. In practice, TPA may make errors or collude, and DO may also act maliciously. Therefore, the interactions among CSP, TPA, and DO must be rendered more transparent and trustworthy.

By leveraging blockchain, cloud-storage-service transparency can be achieved without dependence on a trusted third party. Furthermore, blockchain can also ensure cloud-storage-service fairness without requiring such a party.

**1. Data Integrity Verification**

Data-integrity verification methods primarily include Provable Data Possession (PDP) and Proof of Retrievability (POR). PDP enables efficient verification of whether the cloud correctly stores the data, while POR not only detects data loss or corruption but also supports recovery. Traditional schemes typically rely on a TPA to perform verification, with the DO trusting the result returned by the TPA. However, this verification process lacks transparency. Although some studies attempt to mitigate TPA untrustworthiness and verification opacity through DO re-audit, multi-TPA verification, or trusted hardware, these approaches still introduce additional trusted parties.

Integrating blockchain with traditional integrity-verification methods can enhance transparency and trustworthiness, and can be implemented in either decentralized or centralized modes. In the decentralized mode, the TPA is replaced by the blockchain network. For example, [8] combines PDP with Ethereum for integrity verification, though it does not address the reduction of GAS costs. Similarly, [9] employs PDP on Ethereum to achieve integrity verification and ensures third-party-independent service fairness. In the centralized mode, a TPA still performs verification, but the challenge information is recorded on the blockchain for subsequent re-audit. For instance, [10] utilizes the nonce field in blocks to construct integrity-verification challenges, enabling the DO to re-audit the TPA's results. This method supports batch processing and improves verification efficiency, but requires the DO to possess sufficient computational capability for re-audit.

**2. Searchable Encryption**

Searchable-encryption schemes can be classified by functionality into single-keyword search, conjunctive-keyword search, and complex logical-structure search; and by cryptographic construction into Symmetric Searchable Encryption (SSE) and Asymmetric Searchable Encryption (ASE). Most existing integrity-verification methods for searchable-encryption results assume a trusted TPA to perform public verification, which introduces trust dependencies and limits transparency.

Integrating blockchain with traditional searchable-encryption methods can enhance both transparency and trustworthiness, and can be realized in two modes: decentralized search and centralized search. In the decentralized mode, blockchain-network nodes execute smart contracts to perform the search in place of the CSP. The consensus process ensures the correctness of search results, removing the need for the DO to perform result verification [11]. In the centralized mode, the CSP still executes the search but, alongside returning the results to the DO, records the corresponding verification information on the blockchain. Beyond traditional centralized cloud storage, blockchain integration also supports integrity verification of keyword-search results in decentralized cloud-storage systems such as Storj and Filecoin [12].

**3. Deterministic Data Deletion**

Deterministic data-deletion techniques can be broadly categorized into overwriting-based deletion and cryptography-based deletion. In a typical process, the DO issues a deletion request, the CSP executes the deletion, and then returns a single-bit response—"success" or "failure." However, such a response provides no assurance that the data have actually been deleted, leaving the process opaque. Existing approaches attempt to achieve verifiable deterministic deletion through assumptions such as user access to storage media, the hourglass model, or by employing trusted hardware and trusted third parties, yet these methods still offer limited transparency [13].

Integrating blockchain into deterministic data-deletion schemes can enhance transparency and accountability. In this approach, the CSP continues to perform the physical deletion, but—adhering to the trust-but-verify principle—both the DO's deletion request and the CSP's deletion proof are recorded on the blockchain. This enables public verification, increases transparency, and mitigates the risk of malicious behavior by either the DO or the CSP. For instance, the method in [14] employs an overwriting strategy, assumes accountability between the DO and the CSP has been established via identity authentication, and incorporates a time server to generate timestamps for deletion proofs.

### *13.3.3 Transparency in Data Decision-Making*

In the data-decision process modeled by "data-information-knowledge-wisdom," raw data are first collected, then processed into valuable information for decision-making; inductive and deductive reasoning transforms this information into knowledge, which is subsequently discussed and applied to reach a final decision. However, in the big-data environment, this model faces significant challenges. Tampered data and single points of failure in data-quality management can undermine the reliability of decision data; likewise, biased training data, flawed algorithm design, and algorithmic errors can compromise the reliability of decision algorithms. Accordingly, data-decision transparency must achieve three objectives: ensuring the auditability of decision data, enabling the explainability of algorithms, and guaranteeing algorithmic transparency.

Blockchain, as a decentralized distributed database, can enhance the auditability of decision data. By building on acquisition transparency, sharing transparency, and cloud-storage-service transparency, blockchain enables data provenance tracking, thereby supporting decision-data audits by data consumers. In addition, its decentralized storage model allows data consumers to verify whether data have been tampered with and trace their origins—capabilities that are particularly valuable in domains with high data-integrity requirements such as finance and insurance [15], healthcare [16], and supply chains [17]. The practical adoption of blockchain for decision-data management depends critically on its scalability, security, and privacy. Given blockchain's inherent storage limitations, the prevailing approach stores metadata on-chain and the actual data off-chain, performing query analysis over these trusted datasets. However, most existing blockchain query systems provide only basic queries for blocks, transactions, and accounts, lacking support for advanced operations. Real-world applications demand more complex functionalities—such as range queries, Top-$k$ queries, query-integrity verification, encrypted queries, and fine-grained online query provenance [18].

Heterogeneous formats and standards across multi-source data also degrade data quality, thereby impacting the reliability of data-driven decisions. Traditional data-quality management and control methods typically rely on a trusted third party, which introduces a lack of transparency, single points of failure, and high consumption of time and resources. By leveraging smart contracts to enforce uniform data formats and compliance rules, data-quality control can be made more transparent and verifiable [19].

## 13.4 Summary

Ensuring that data are used correctly, appropriately, and in a standardized manner has become a fundamental and urgent issue in the big-data ecosystem. Establishing a robust data-transparency governance system is both an effective pathway and an essential measure. Data transparency seeks to enhance visibility across the entire value-realization process of big data, thereby providing technical foundations for implementing traceability and accountability. However, the high velocity, variety, and complexity of big data greatly increase the difficulty of developing effective traceability and accountability mechanisms. Tracking data that have undergone transformations across platforms and domains remains particularly challenging. Although data transparency can facilitate traceability and accountability, it may itself involve sensitive metadata and inadvertently expose information during accountability processes. Furthermore, as an inherently interdisciplinary problem, data transparency places data acquisition, sharing, and circulation under a new governance paradigm. Ensuring that users possess sufficient legal and regulatory literacy to understand and respond to these changes is an open challenge that calls for joint efforts from the academic community, industry, policymakers, and society at large.

## References


1. MENG X, LIU L. Blockchain and Data Governance[J]. China Science Fund, 2020, 34(1): 12–17.
2. MENG X, LIU L.Transparency Based on Blockchain: Issues and Challenges[J]. Journal of Computer Research and Development, 2021, 58(2): 237–252.
3. ZYSKIND G, NATHAN O, PENTLAND A. Decentralizing Privacy: Using Blockchain to Protect Personal Data[C]//Proceedings of the IEEE Security and Privacy Workshops. San Jose: IEEE Computer Society, 2015: 180–184.
4. ALI M, NELSON J, SHEA R, ET AL. Blockstack: A Global Naming and Storage System Secured by Blockchains[C]// Proceedings of the USENIX Annual Technical Conference. Denver:USENIX, 2016: 181–94.
5. OUADDAH A, ELKALAM A A, OUAHMAN A A. FairAccess: a new Blockchain-based access control framework for the Internet of Things[J]. Security and Communication Networks, 2016, 9(18): 5943–5964.
6. AZARIA A , EKBLAW A , VIEIRA T , et al. MedRec: Using Blockchain for Medical Data Access and Permission Management[C]//Proceedings of 2nd International Conference on Open and Big Data. Vienna:IEEE Computer Society, 2016: 25–30.
7. TRUONG NB, SUN K, LEE GM, et al.GDPR-Compliant Personal Data Management: A Blockchain-Based Solution[J]. IEEE Transactions on Information Forensics and Security, 2020, 15: 1746–1761.
8. HAO K, XIN J, WANG Z, et al. Decentralized Data Integrity Verification Model in Untrusted Environment[C]//Proceedings of the Second International Joint Conference APWeb-WAIM. Macau:Springer, 2018: 410–424.
9. ZHANG Y, DENG R H, LIU X, et al. Blockchain based Efficient and Robust Fair Payment for Outsourcing Services in Cloud Computing[J]. INFORMATION SCIENCES, 2018, 462: 262–277.
10. XUE J, CHUNXIANG X U, ZHAO J, et al. Identity-based public auditing for cloud storage systems against malicious auditors via blockchain[J]. Science China(Information Sciences), 2019, 62(3): 32101–32104.
11. HU S, CAI C, QIAN W, et al. Searching an Encrypted Cloud Meets Blockchain: A Decentralized, Reliable and Fair Realization[C]//Proceedings of International Conference on Computer Communications. Honolulu:IEEE Computer Society, 2018: 792–800.
12. CAI C, YUAN X, CONG W. Towards trustworthy and private keyword search in encrypted decentralized storage[C]//Proceedings of IEEE International Conference on Communications. France,IEEE Computer Society, 2017: 1–7.
13. HAO F, CLARKE D, ZORZO A F. Deleting Secret Data with Public Verifiability[J]. IEEE Transactions on Dependable & Secure Computing, 2016, 13(6): 617–629.
14. XUE L, YU Y, LI Y, et al. Efficient attribute-based encryption with attribute revocation for assured data deletion[J]. Information sciences, 2018, 640–650.
15. HOANG T V, LENIN M, MUKESH K M, et al. Blockchain-based Data Management and Analytics for Micro-insurance Applications[C]//Proceedings of the 2017 ACM on Conference on Information and Knowledge Management, Singapore:ACM, 2017: 2539–2542.
16. TSAI J. Transform Blockchain into Distributed Parallel Computing Architecture for Precision Medicine[C]//Proceedings of IEEE International Conference on Distributed Computing Systems. Vienna:IEEE Computer Society, 2018: 1290–1299.
17. XU X, LU Q, LIU Y, et al. Designing blockchain-based applications a case study for imported product traceability[J]. Future Generation Computer Systems, 2019, 92(3): 399–406.
18. XU C, ZHANG C, XU J. vChain: Enabling Verifiable Boolean Range Queries over Blockchain Databases[C]//Proceedings of the 2019 International Conference on Management of Data. The Netherlands:ACM, 2018: 141–158.
19. WU C, ZHOU L, XIE C, et al. Data Quality Transaction on Different Distributed Ledger Technologies[C]//Proceedings of the International Conference on Big Scientific Data Management. Beijing:Springer, 2018: 301–318.

The manufacturer's authorised representative in the EU is Springer
Nature Customer Service Centre GmbH, Europaplatz 3, 69115 Heidelberg,
Germany. If you have any concerns regarding our products, please
contact ProductSafety@springernature.com

Printed and bound by CPI Group (UK) Ltd, Croydon, CR0 4YY
21/09/2026
02219990-0004